香港國際詩歌之夜 2019

INTERNATIONAL POETRY NIGHTS IN HONG KONG

《沉默與言説》

封面影像：北島
封面設計：麥安

國際統一書號（ISBN）：978-988-237-120-0

出版：香港中文大學出版社
香港 新界 沙田．香港中文大學
傳真：+852 2603 7355
電郵：cup@cuhk.edu.hk
網址：www.chineseupress.com

Speech and Slience

Cover Image: Bei Dao
Cover Design: Ann Mak

ISBN: 978-988-237-120-0

Published by The Chinese University of Hong Kong Press
The Chinese University of Hong Kong
Sha Tin, N.T., Hong Kong
Fax: +852 2603 7355
Email: cup@cuhk.edu.hk
Website: www.chineseupress.com

Printed in Hong Kong

沉　默　與　言　說

香港國際詩歌之夜十週年

International Poetry Nights in Hong Kong – 10th Anniversary Celebration

SPEECH AND SILENCE

主辦單位	**Organizer**
香港詩歌節基金會	Hong Kong Poetry Festival Foundation
編輯	**Editors**
宋子江	Chris Song
柯夏智	Lucas Klein
陳嘉恩	Shelby K. Y. Chan
王淩	Ling Wang

塔明・阿爾巴霍迪 巴勒斯坦	**Tamim AL-BARGHOUTI** Palestine
安娜・露易莎・阿瑪拉爾 葡萄牙	**Ana Luísa AMARAL** Portugal
馬克西姆・阿梅林 俄羅斯	**Maxim AMELIN** Russia
雷納托・桑多瓦爾・巴希加盧波 秘魯	**Renato Sandoval BACIGALUPO** Peru
簡・博文 美國	**Jen BERVIN** United States
阿巴斯・貝東 黎巴嫩	**Abbas BEYDOUN** Lebanon
米若什・別德日茨基 波蘭	**Miłosz BIEDRZYCKI** Poland
安娜・布蘭迪亞娜 羅馬尼亞	**Ana BLANDIANA** Romania
鍾國強 香港	**Derek CHUNG** Hong Kong
路易絲・杜普蕾 加拿大	**Louise DUPRÉ** Canada
弗羅斯特・甘德 美國	**Forrest GANDER** United States
黃有源 南韓	**HWANG Yu-Won** South Korea
毛子 中國大陸	**MAOZI** Mainland China
馬圖拉 愛沙尼亞	**MATHURA** Estonia
塞爾希奧・萊蒙迪 阿根廷	**Sergio RAIMONDI** Argentina
安娜・里斯托維奇 塞爾維亞	**Ana RISTOVIĆ** Serbia
薩奇達南丹 印度	**K. SATCHIDANANDAN** India
馬丁・索羅楚克 斯洛伐克	**Martin SOLOTRUK** Slovakia
阿列斯・斯特格 斯洛文尼亞	**Aleš ŠTEGER** Slovenia
瑪麗亞・斯捷潘諾娃 俄羅斯	**Maria STEPANOVA** Russia
托絲・克里斯蒂娜 匈牙利	**TÓTH Krisztina** Hungary
苡若瑪・恩梅彬憂 尼日利亞	**Ijeoma UMEBINYUO** Nigeria
安納斯塔西斯・威斯托尼迪斯 希臘	**Anastassis VISTONITIS** Greece
揚・瓦格納 德國	**Jan WAGNER** Germany
恩尼斯特・維茨納 德國	**Ernest WICHNER** Germany
楊佳嫻 台灣	**YANG Chia-Hsien** Taiwan
四元康祐 日本	**YOTSUMOTO Yasuhiro** Japan
余幼幼 中國大陸	**YU Youyou** Mainland China
遠岸 中國大陸	**YUAN An** Mainland China
鄭小瓊 中國大陸	**ZHENG Xiaoqiong** Mainland China
周雲蓬 中國大陸	**ZHOU Yunpeng** Mainland China

沉默與言說——
香港國際詩歌之夜 2019 代序

維特根斯坦指出：「對不可言說的東西，必須保持沉默。」這是他《邏輯哲學論》的主題。1914 年第一次世界大戰爆發後，維特根斯坦和特拉克爾同在東部戰線打仗，但從未謀面。他收到特拉克爾的明信片，希望能見上一面，而特拉克爾近於崩潰，住在克拉克夫的軍醫院。1914 年 11 月 6 日，維特根斯坦趕到那家醫院時，特拉克爾三天前服用過量的可卡因死去。

哲學家和詩人就這樣永遠錯過了，就像他們各自使用不同的語言系統一樣：維特根斯坦旨在把可說的東西弄清楚，而特拉克爾則是把不可說的東西表現出來。或許換句話來說，在哲學止步的地方正是詩歌的開端。

在某種意義上，沉默與言說也是詩歌的主題，它恰恰正是邏輯以外的無邊的開闊地。正如晉代文學家陸機所言：「課虛無以責有，叩寂寞而求音」（引自《文賦》），可謂一語中的。

如果可能的話，為了借助詩歌來闡釋詩歌，我想選保爾．策蘭的一首短詩，更進一步切入主題：

〈用一把可變的鑰匙〉

用一把可變的鑰匙
打開那房子
無言的雪在其中飄動。

你選擇什麼鑰匙
往往取決於從你的眼睛
或嘴或耳朵噴出的血。

你改變鑰匙，你改變詞語
和雪花一起自由漂流。
什麼雪球會聚攏詞語
取決於回絕你的風。

這是一首很重要的詩，甚至可以説，它是打開策蘭詩歌的「鑰匙」。這首詩有兩組中心意象：詞和雪。第二段的第一句「你改變鑰匙，你改變詞語」，已經暗示鑰匙就是詞。而第一段第三句提到「無言的雪」，即雪代表不可言説的。詞與雪，有著可言説與不可言説的區別。而詩歌寫作的困境，正是要用可言説的詞，表達不可言説的雪：「用一把可變的鑰匙 / 打開那房子 / 無言的雪在其中飄動。」鑰匙是可變的，你是否能找到打開不可言説的房子的鑰匙，取決於詩人的經歷：「你選擇什麼鑰匙 / 往往取決於從你的眼睛 / 或嘴或耳朵噴出的血。」第二段可以理解為寫作狀態：「你改變鑰匙，你改變詞語 / 和雪花一起自由漂流」，在這裡詞與雪花匯合，是對不可言説的言説的可能。「什麼雪球會聚攏詞語 / 取決於回絕你的風」，在這裡，風代表著苦難與創傷，也就是説，只有與命運處於抗拒狀態的寫作，才是可能的。

這是 2019 年第六屆香港國際詩歌之夜的主題。

從 2009 年創辦首屆香港國際詩歌之夜迄今正好十週年了，成為國際詩歌相輔相成的高峰。特別強調的是，這屆詩歌盛會共邀請三十位國際詩人和華語詩人，除了香港作為主場，也包括中國的十座城市。我們曾説過，如果全球化是「大陸」，那麼詩歌就是「島嶼」。在全球化的新版圖的背後，構成文明、宗教、意識形態以及權力與金錢等一系列的抗衡與衝突；而象徵島嶼的詩歌，成為人類精神家園的保證。

北島
2019 年 5 月 17 日

Speech and Silence—
International Poetry Nights in Hong Kong 2019

"That of which we cannot speak," Ludwig Wittgenstein wrote, concluding his *Tractatus Logico-Philosophicus*, "we must pass over in silence." In 1914, at the outbreak of the First World War, both Wittgenstein and Austrian poet Georg Trakl were both stationed at the Eastern Front—but they never met. Wittgenstein received a postcard from Trakl, and they had hoped to meet, but Trakl was suffering from depression, staying in the military hospital in Kraków. By the time Wittgenstein made it to the hospital, on November 6, 1914, he arrived to discover that Trakl had died three days earlier, of a cocaine overdose.

Philosophers and poets are always missing each other just like this, and the systems of language they work in are often at odds: while Wittgenstein was trying to work out what could be said, Trakl was trying to express the inexpressible. Or to put that another way, poetry starts where philosophy ends.

To a certain degree, speech and silence are the fundamental subjects of poetry, the vast expanses beyond logic. As Lu Ji wrote in his fourth century *Rhymeprose on Literature*, writing "demands presence by divining absence, knocking on silence in search of sound."

Or, if we might explicate poetry with the help of a poem, I think Paul Celan can bring us further into our theme. In Pierre Joris's translation:

WITH A VARIABLE KEY

With a variable key
you unlock the house, in it
drifts the snow of the unsaid.
Depending on the blood that gushes
from your eye or mouth or ear,
your key varies.

Varies your key so varies your word
that's allowed to drift with the flakes.
Depending on the wind that pushes you away,
the snow cakes around the word.

This is an important poem—it may even legitimately be called the "key" to Celan's poetry. Two central images are at work here, words and snow. The first line of the second stanza, "Varies your key so varies your word," gives the implication that the key is the word. The third line of the first stanza, on the other hand, mentions "the snow of the unsaid," where snow represents the unspeakable. Words and snow, then, distinguish the said from the unsayable, and the task of writing poetry is precisely to make the words we speak express the snow of what we cannot: "With a variable key / you unlock the house, in it / drifts the snow of the unsaid." The key may change, but whether it will open up the house of the unsayable comes down to the skill of the poet: "Depending on the blood that gushes / from your eye or mouth or ear, / your key varies." The second stanza presents the conditions for writing: "Varies your key so varies your word / that's allowed to drift with the flakes." Word here merges with snowflake, presenting the possibility of saying the unsayable. "Depending on the wind that pushes you away, / the snow cakes around the word": if what the wind represents is suffering and trauma, then the only possibility is to write in a state of resistance.

This, then, is the theme of International Poetry Nights in Hong Kong 2019.

It has been ten years since 2009, when we held our first International Poetry Nights in Hong Kong, to mark the pinnacle of international poetry. This year we are hosting thirty poets from around the world, and in addition to our main arena in Hong Kong, we are also holding events in ten cities in mainland China. As we have said, if globalization is our "continent," then poetry is our "island." This brave new world may be defined by contentions and conflicts between civilizations, religions, ideologies, as well as power and money, but the island symbolized by poetry represents the promise of a spiritual homeland for all humanity.

Bei Dao
May 17, 2019

(Translated from Chinese by Lucas Klein)

目錄 Contents

香港國際詩歌之夜 2019
INTERNATIONAL POETRY NIGHTS IN HONG KONG

塔明・阿爾巴霍迪（巴勒斯坦）的詩歌在阿拉伯語世界通過新舊媒體得到廣泛傳播和誦讀。他多次在體育館和露天劇場舉辦詩歌朗誦會，入場觀眾數以千計。2004 年，他獲得波士頓大學政治學博士學位。2007 年，他的詩作〈在耶路撒冷〉成為當地家喻戶曉的作品，他因此獲巴勒斯坦報紙譽為「耶路撒冷詩人」。在2011 年1 月埃及革命期間，網路截斷，地區電視遭禁播，他用視頻錄製的詩作〈在望〉每隔兩個小時就投射到開羅解放廣場。阿爾巴霍迪1977 年生於埃及開羅，著有七本通俗及古典阿拉伯語詩集，以及兩本關於阿拉伯世界政治和歷史的學術類書籍。

Tamim Al-Barghouti (Palestine) is a poet widely read throughout the Arab world through new and old media. His poetry readings are attended by thousands in stadiums and amphitheaters. He received his Ph.D. in Political Science from Boston University in 2004. Since 2007, Tamim's work "Fil Quds" became a household poem in Jerusalem. Palestinian newspapers dubbed him "The Poet of Jerusalem." During the Egyptian uprising of January 2011, a television recording of Tamim's lyrical poem "Hanet" was projected in Cairo's Tahrir Square every couple of hours on makeshift screens, despite the ban on the internet and regional news channels. Born in Cairo in 1977, Tamim published seven poetry collections in both colloquial and classical Arabic and two academic books on Arab politics and history.

塔明・阿爾巴霍迪

TAMIM AL-BARGHOUTI

中文翻譯：唐珺

English translation by Tamim Al-Barghouti, Radwa Ashour, and Ahdaf Soueif

في العالم العربي تعيش (بالعامية المصرية)

في العالم العربي تعيش
كما قط ساكن تحت عربية
عينيه ما تشوفش م الدنيا دي حاجة الا الجزم
في العالم العربي تعيش
كما بهلوان السيرك تحتك بهلوان دايس عليه
وفوق دماغك بهلوان دايس عليك
والكل واقف محترم
في العالم العربي تعيش،
مباراة بقى لها ألف عام
لعيبة تجري يمين شمال
والكورة طول الوقت في إدين الحكم
في العالم العربي، تقول للبنت حبيتك
وتبقى البنت بتحبك، وبتموت فيك
تناولك بالألم
في العالم العربي تعيش
تشتم في طعم المية والطعمية والقهوة وروادها وفى مراتك وأولادها وحر وزحمة
الأتوبيس
وفي اللي بيعمله إبليس، وفي التفليس
ولو سألوك تقول الحمد الله ربنا يديمها نعم

في العالم العربي تعيش، كما دمعة في عيون الكريم المحنة تطردها يرجعها الكرم
في العالم العربي تعيش تلميذ في حوش المدرسة من غير فطار عينه على الشارع
وبيحيي العلم
في العالم العربي تعيش، بتبص في الساعة وخايف نشرة الأخبار تفوت
علشان تشوف ع الشاشة ناس
في العالم العربي
تموت

你活在阿拉伯世界

你活在阿拉伯世界，
就像住在汽車底盤下的貓，
鞋底是雙眼唯一看到的世界。

你活在阿拉伯世界，
像個馬戲團的小丑，
你踩在一個小丑的頭上，
另一個小丑踩在你的頭上，
所有人畢恭畢敬直直挺立。

你活在阿拉伯世界，
就像加入一場踢了上千年的球賽，
球員們左突右進，
球卻始終被裁判拿在手中。

在阿拉伯世界，
你對一個女孩説愛她，
若她也愛你愛到痴狂，
會搧你一個耳光。

你活在阿拉伯世界，
咒罵水的味道、炸豆丸子的味道、咖啡館和裡面的顧客，
咒罵老婆、孩子、公交車的悶熱和擁擠，
咒罵魔鬼伊布里斯的行徑，咒罵破產。
可當你被問起這一切，你會説：
「讚頌全歸真主，願福澤長存。」

你活在阿拉伯世界，像有尊嚴的人眼中的淚水，
苦難把你趕走，尊嚴又拽你回來。
你活在阿拉伯世界，像清晨校園裡的小學生，
一邊向國旗敬禮，一邊瞧著校外的街。
你活在阿拉伯世界，盯著時間，生怕錯過新聞，
為了看到屏幕裡阿拉伯世界的人們
死去。

In the Arab World, Live

In the Arab world, live
Like a cat that lives under a car
Shoes are all you see of life

In the Arab world, live
Like a circus clown
A clown stands on your head
You stand on the next clown's
Everyone stands with utmost respect
Serious and very well dressed

In the Arab world, live
Through a football match
That has been going on for a thousand years
Players dash here and there
And the ball always remains
In the hands of the referee

In the Arab world, live
To tell a girl you love her
And, if she loves you back,
she'll slap you in the face!

In the Arab world, live
To curse the taste of water, falafel,
The coffee-shop and its customers
Your wife and her children
The crowd and the heat in the bus
The tricks of Satan
Being broke
And when you're asked about all that
You say:
"We thank God
May He keep showering us with His blessings"

In the Arab world, live
Like a school boy
Who has to salute the flag in the school yard every morning
While longing for the street outside

In the Arab world, live
Like a hesitant tear in the eyes of the dignified
Pain exiles you
Dignity holds you back

In the Arab world live
Watching the time
Lest you miss the news on TV

Only to see
How people
In the Arab world, die.

(Translated by Tamim Al-Barghouti)

في القدس

مَرَرْنا عَلى دارِ الحبيب فرَدَّنا
عَنِ الدارِ قانونُ الأعادي وسورُها
فَقُلْتُ لنفسي رُبما هيَ نِعْمَةٌ
فماذا تَرَى في القدسِ حينَ تَزُورُها
تَرَى كُلَّ ما لا تستطيعُ احتِمالَهُ
إذا ما بَدَتْ من جَانِبِ الدَّرْبِ دورُها
وما كلُّ نفسٍ حينَ تَلْقَى حَبِيبَها   تُسَرُّ ولا كُلُّ الغِيابِ يُضِيرُها
فإن سرَّها قبلَ الفِراقِ لِقاؤُه   فليسَ بمأمونٍ عليها سرُورُها
متى تُبْصِرِ القدسَ العتيقةَ مَرَّةً
فسوفَ تراها العَيْنُ حَيْثُ تُدِيرُها

في القدسِ، بائعُ خضرةٍ من جورجيا برمٌ بزوجته يفكرُ في
قضاءِ إجازةٍ أو في في طلاءِ البيتْ
في أحكامها في القدس، توراةٌ وكهلٌ جاءَ من مَنْهاتِنَ العُليا يُفَقَّهُ فتيةَ البُولُونِ
في القدسِ شرطيٌ من الأحباشِ يُغْلِقُ شَارِعاً في السوقِ،
رشَّاشٌ على مستوطنٍ لم يبلغِ العشرينَ،
ىقُبَّعة تُحَيِّي حائطَ المبكَى
وسياحٌ من الإفرنجِ شُقْرٌ لا يَرَوْنَ القدسَ إطلاقاً
تَراهُم يأخذونَ لبعضهم صُوَرَاً
مَعَ امْرَأَةٍ تبيعُ الفِجْلَ في الساحاتِ طُولَ اليَومْ
في القدسِ دَبَّ الجندُ مُنْتَعِلِينَ فوقَ الغَيمْ

والقدس تعرف نفسها، فاسأل هناك الخلق يدْلُلْكَ الجميعُ
فكلُّ شيئ في المدينة
ذو لسانٍ، حين تَسأَلُهُ، يُبينْ

في القدس يزدادُ الهلالُ تقوساً مثلَ الجنينْ
حَدْباً على أشباهه فوقَ القبابِ
تَطَوَّرَتْ ما بَيْنَهم عَبْرَ السنينَ عِلاقةُ الأَبِ بالبَنينْ

في القدس أبنيةٌ حجارتُها اقتباساتٌ من الإنجيلِ والقرآنْ
في القدس تعريفُ الجمالِ مُثَمَّنُ الأضلاعِ أزرقُ،
فَوْقَهُ، يا دامَ عِزُّكَ، قُبَّةٌ ذَهَبِيَّةٌ،
تبدو برأيي، مثل مرآة محدبة ترى وجه السماء مُلَخَّصَاً فيها
تُدَلِّلُها وَتُدْنيها
تُوَزِّعُها كَأَكْياسِ المعُونَةِ في الحِصَارِ لمستَحِقِّيها
إذا ما أُمَّةٌ من بعدِ خُطْبَةِ جُمْعَةٍ مَدَّتْ بِأَيْدِيها
وفي القدس السماءُ تَفَرَّقَتْ في الناسِ تحمينا ونحميها
ونحملُها على أكتافِنا حَمْلاً إذا جَارَت على أقمارِها الأزمانْ

في القدس أعمدةُ الرُّخام الداكناتُ
كأنَّ تعريقَ الرُّخامِ دخانْ
ونوافذُ تعلو المساجدَ والكنائس،
أَمْسَكَتْ بيدِ الصُّباحِ تُرِيهِ كيفَ النقشُ بالألوانِ،

في القدسِ صَلَّينا على الأَسْفَلْتْ
في القدسِ مَن في القدسِ إلا أنْتْ

وَتَلَفَّتَ التاريخُ لي مُتَبَسِّماً
أَظَنَنْتَ حقاً أنَّ عينَك سوفَ تخطئهم، وتبصرُ غيرَهم
ها هُم أمامَكَ، مَتْنُ نصٍّ أنتَ حاشيةٌ عليهِ وَهَامشٌ
أَحَسبتَ أنَّ زيارةً سَتُزيحُ عن وجهِ المدينةِ يا بُنَيَّ
حجابَ واقِعِها السميكَ لكي ترى فيها هَواكْ
في القدسِ كلُّ فتى سواكْ
وهي الغزالةُ في المدى، حَكَمَ الزمانُ بِبَيْنِها
ما زِلتَ تَرْكُضُ إثْرَهَا مُذْ وَدَّعَتْكَ بِعَيْنِها
رفقاً بِنَفسكَ ساعةً إني أراكَ وَهَنْتْ
في القدسِ من في القدسِ إلا أَنْتْ

يا كاتبَ التاريخِ مَهْلاً،
فالمدينةُ دهرُها دهرانِ
دهر أجنبيٌّ مطمئنٌ لا يغيرُ خطوَه وكأَنَّه يمشي خلالَ النومْ
وهناك دهرٌ، كامنٌ متلثمٌ يمشي بلا صوتٍ حِذار القومْ

في القدس لو صافحتَ شيخاً أو لمستَ بنايةً
لَوَجَدْتَ منقوشاً على كَفَّيكَ نَصَّ قصيدَةٍ
يابْنَ الكرامِ أو اثْنَتَيْنْ

في القدس،رغمَ تتابعِ النَّكَباتِ، ريحُ براءةٍ في الجوِّ، ريحُ طُفُولَةٍ،
فَتَرى الحمامَ يَطِيرُ يُعلِنُ دَوْلَةً في الريحِ بَيْنَ رَصَاصَتَيْنْ

ترابُها في القدس تنتظمُ القبورُ، كأنهنَّ سطورُ تاريخِ المدينةِ والكتابُ
الكل مرُّوا من هُنا
فالقدسُ تقبلُ من أتاها كافراً أو مؤمنا
أُمرر بها واقرأ شواهدَها بكلِّ لغاتِ أهلِ الأرضِ
فيها الزنجُ والإفرنجُ والقِفْجَاقُ والصِّقْلابُ والبُشْنَاقُ
والنساكُ، والتاتارُ والأتراكُ، أهلُ الله والهلاك، والفقراءُ والملاك، والفجارُ
فيها كلُّ من وطِئَ الثَّرى
يا كاتب التاريخِ ماذا جَدَّ فاستثنيتنا
أرأيتها ضاقت علينا وحدنا!
يا شيخُ فلتُعِدِ الكتابةَ والقراءةَ مرةً أخرى، أراك لَحَنْتْ

نائياً عن بابها العين تُغْمِضُ، ثمَّ تنظرُ، سائقُ السيارةِ الصفراءِ، مالَ بنا شَمالاً
والقدس صارت خلفنا
والعينُ تبصرُها بمرآةِ اليمينِ،

وَهْوَ يقول: "لا بل هكذا"،
فَتَقُولُ: "لا بل هكذا"،
حتى إذا طال الخلافُ تقاسما
فالصبحُ حُرٌّ خارجَ العَتَبَاتِ لَكِنْ
إن أرادَ دخولَها
فَعَلَيهِ أن يَرْضَى بحُكْمِ نوافذِ الرَّحمنْ

في القدس مدرسةٌ لمملوكٍ أتى مما وراءَ النهرِ،
باعوهُ بسوقِ نِخَاسَةٍ في إصفهانَ
اليُسْرَى، لتاجرٍ من أهلِ بغدادٍ أتى حلباً فخافَ أميرُها من زُرْقَةٍ في عَيْنِهِ
المغولِ وصاحبَ السلطانْ فأعطاهُ لقافلةٍ أتت مصراً، فأصبحَ بعدَ بضعِ سنينَ غَلاَّبَ

الزيتْ في القدس رائحةٌ تُلَخِّصُ بابلاً والهندَ في دكانِ عطارٍ بخانِ
والله رائحةٌ لها لغةٌ سَتَفْهَمُها إذا أصْغَيتْ
وتقولُ لي إذ يطلقونَ قنابل الغاز المسيِّلِ للدموعِ عَلَيَّ:
"لا تحفل بهم"
وتفوحُ من بعدِ انحسارِ الغازِ، وَهْيَ تقولُ لي: "أرأيتْ!"

في القدس يرتاحُ التناقضُ، والعجائبُ ليسَ ينكرُها العِبادُ،
كأنها قِطَعُ القِمَاشِ يُقَلِّبُونَ قَدِيمها وَجَدِيدَها،
والمعجزاتُ هناكَ تُلْمَسُ باليَدَيْنْ

在耶路撒冷

我們途經愛人的家，
卻被敵人的法律和高牆阻擋。
我自言自語這或是一種恩典，
當你來到耶路撒冷，會看到什麼？
你會見到一切忍無可忍之事，
當路旁顯現愛人的家。
見面不一定令人喜悅，
別離不一定是傷害。
若相見的喜悅以別離告終，
這番喜悅便並不牢靠。
你只需見過一次古老的耶路撒冷，
從此無論你在何處，滿眼皆是她。

在耶路撒冷，來自格魯吉亞的蔬果商對妻子心生厭倦，
想著休個短假或給家刷一刷漆。
在耶路撒冷，一本《托拉》和一個來自上曼哈頓的中年男人，
他在給一群波蘭少年講解律法。
在耶路撒冷，一個埃塞俄比亞裔警察封鎖市場的街道，
一把機關槍掛在未滿二十的定居者肩頭，
一頂禮帽向哭牆致敬。
金髮的法蘭克人全然無視聖城，
你看見他們互相拍照，
站在一個從早到晚在廣場上賣蘿蔔的婦女旁。
在耶路撒冷，穿軍靴的士兵們行進在雲端。
在耶路撒冷，我們在瀝青上祈禱。

تَغَيَّرَتْ ألوانُها في الشمسِ، مِنْ قبلِ الغيابْ
إذ فاجَأَتْني بسمةٌ لم أدْرِ كيفَ تَسَلَّلَتْ للوَجْهِ
قالت لي وقد أَمْعَنْتُ ما أَمْعنْتْ
يا أيها الباكي وراءَ السورِ، أحمقُ أَنْتْ؟
أَجُنِنْتْ؟
لا تبكِ عينُكَ أيها المنسيُّ من متنِ الكتابْ
لا تبكِ عينُكَ أيها العَرَبيُّ واعلمْ أَنَّهُ
في القدسِ من في القدَسِ لكنْ
لا أَرَى في القدسِ إلا أَنْتْ

在耶路撒冷，總有人在耶路撒冷，除了你。

歷史扭頭衝我笑：
你真以為你的眼睛可以錯過這些人，
可以看得見其他人？
他們就在你眼前，他們是正文，
而你，不過是個腳註或空行。
我的孩子，你以為一次旅行
足以揭開城市面龐上厚重的現實面紗，
你便能看見你想看的一切？

在耶路撒冷，所有少年都在耶路撒冷，除了你。

她是空間中的羚羊，時間在她的領地裡統治。
她看著你，向你告別，可你仍在她身後奔跑追尋。
善待自己吧，我看見你愈發萎靡不振。

在耶路撒冷，總有人在耶路撒冷，除了你。

歷史之書啊，且慢！
這座城市有兩條時間線：
一條是外國的、安心的、踩著不變的步伐，就像在睡夢中行進。
還有一條，是隱匿的、遮掩的，杳無聲息地前行，警示著眾人。

耶路撒冷熟知自己，
你可以問那裡的人，所有人會告訴你：
聖城裡的所有事物，都有舌頭，
只需你發問，它必將闡明。

在耶路撒冷，新月蜷曲得像胎兒，
月的下方彎卷著一個個相似的穹頂，
歲月的流逝裡它們變得像父親與兒子。

在耶路撒冷，一些建築的石頭引用自《聖經》和《古蘭經》。
在耶路撒冷，美的定義是八邊形和藍色。
在其上方，願主保佑你，是一個金色穹頂。
在我看來，穹頂像一方凸面鏡，
眼看著天空的面貌壓縮其間，把玩它、拉近它，
又分散它，像圍困中給亟需者的救援品。
整個民族，在主麻日的佈道後，伸出手去拿。
在耶路撒冷，天空分割給人們，
它保護我們，我們保護它，
一旦時間沒有善待它的衛星，
我們把天空扛在肩頭。

在耶路撒冷，黑灰的大理石柱，
就像濃煙滲透進它的紋理之中。
清真寺和教堂裡高聳的窗，
拽住清晨，教它如何用色彩雕刻。
清晨說：「不，得像這樣。」

玻璃窗說：「不，得像這樣。」
直至分歧久而久之成為包容共享。
清晨可以在門檻外自由繪畫，
若想進入，
它必須遵從主的玻璃窗。

在耶路撒冷，有座由某位奴隸所建的學校，
他來自河的彼端，
在伊斯法罕的奴隸市場被賣給一個前往阿勒頗的巴格達商人，
阿勒頗王子懼怕奴隸左眼裡的藍色，
將他贈與一個前往埃及的商隊。
多年後，奴隸打敗了蒙古人，成為素丹君王。

在耶路撒冷，在宰特汗市場的香料店裡，
有一種集結了巴比倫與印度的香氣。
真的，這香氣有自己的語言，只要你聆聽，定能聽懂。
當他們把催淚彈朝我扔來，它對我說：「不要理會他們。」
待瓦斯彈消散，香氣重新瀰漫，對我說：「你瞧是不是？」

在耶路撒冷，矛盾休養生息，
奇跡之於朝拜者並不陌生，
它像一張時新時舊的布塊。
在這裡，奇跡可被雙手感知。

在耶路撒冷，如果你與一位老者握了手，
或觸摸了一座房屋，
你會發現，我的朋友，你的掌心將刻上一首詩歌，
或是兩首。

在耶路撒冷，儘管災難連連，
但空氣裡，飄散著無辜的風，
童年的風，
你看見鴿子在風中飛翔，
在兩枚子彈間宣佈一個國家的誕生。

在耶路撒冷，墳墓整齊排列，
它們像城市史的一行行字句，而經書是城的土壤。
所有人從這裡經過，
耶路撒冷迎接所有的叛教者或信徒。
請來到這裡，讀一讀用所有民族語言寫就的墓碑。
這裡有黑種人、法蘭克人、欽察人、斯拉夫人、波斯尼亞人、
韃靼人、土耳其人、神的子民、毀滅的子民、
窮人與富人、縱慾者與禁慾者，
這裡是所有腳踩這土地的人。
歷史之書啊，發生了什麼，以致你把我們排除在外？
你是否看見它唯獨容不下我們？
長者啊，請重新書寫、重新朗讀吧，
我看見你出了錯。

眼睛閉上，遂又睜開，
黃車司機帶我們向北而去，遠離她的城門。
耶路撒冷在我們身後，
眼睛從右視鏡看著她，
她的色彩在陽光下變換，逐漸消失。
正當我潸然淚下，突然一抹微笑莫名溜上臉龐，
它對我說：
高牆下痛哭的人哪，你是傻子嗎？
你瘋了嗎？
被經典遺忘的人啊，你不要哭泣，
阿拉伯人啊，不要哭泣。要知道，
在耶路撒冷，總有人在耶路撒冷，
但是，我在耶路撒冷，只看見你。

In Jerusalem

We passed by the home of the beloved
But were turned back by the enemy's law and the enemy's wall

I said to myself
Perhaps it's a blessing
What will you see in Jerusalem when you visit?

You'll see everything you cannot bear
When her houses start appearing at the side of the road

On meeting her beloved, not every soul rejoices
Nor does every absence harm

If the joy of meeting ends in parting
How dangerous then is that very joy

For once your eyes have seen Jerusalem
You'll see only her, wherever you look

In Jerusalem
A greengrocer from Georgia, bored with his wife
Thinks of going on holiday or painting his house
In Jerusalem
A Torah—

And a middle-aged man from Upper Manhattan
Arrives to teach young Polish men how to read it
In Jerusalem
A policeman from Ethiopia seals off a street in the market
A machine gun hangs from the shoulder of a teenage settler
A hat bows to the Wailing Wall

Blond tourists who don't see Jerusalem at all
Take photos of each other
Beside a woman who sells mint on the streets every day
In Jerusalem there are walls of basil
In Jerusalem there are barricades of concrete

In Jerusalem, jackboot soldiers march on clouds
In Jerusalem, we pray on the asphalt

In Jerusalem there's whoever's in Jerusalem
Except for you

And History turned to me, smiling:
"Did you really think your eye
Could miss all these

And see
... the others?

Here they are before you
They are the text
While you're a footnote or a margin
You thought, my son, a visit could draw from the face of the city
The thick veil of her present
So that you might see there what you wish?

Everyone is in Jerusalem
Except for you

And she is the deer in the distance
You've raced in pursuit of her
Since she offered her farewell glance
Go gentle on yourself—I see you fading

In Jerusalem there's whoever's in Jerusalem
Except for you

But History, wait—
For the city has two timelines
One, foreign, complacent, steady-paced
As though sleepwalking
Another that lies in wait
Masked, cautious, silent
And Jerusalem knows herself

Ask the people there, everyone will tell you
Everything in the city has a tongue which, when you ask, will speak;

In Jerusalem the crescent moon curls tight as a fetus
Curving over its likenesses on the domes;
Through the years they've become like a father and his sons

In Jerusalem there are buildings whose stones are quoted from Bible and
Quran

In Jerusalem beauty is octagonal and blue
Supporting, gentle listener, a golden dome,
That looks like, I think, a convex mirror
Containing the sky, playing with it, pulling it close
Distributing the sky, like aid in a siege
To the deserving
As the people, after the Friday sermon
Reach their hands to receive it

In Jerusalem, the sky gives herself out to the people,
She protects us
We protect her
For we would carry her on our shoulders
If times were to be hard
on her moons

In Jerusalem, dark marble columns rise
As though their veins were smoke
Windows, high in church and mosque,
Hold morning's hand, showing him how to paint with color
He says, "like this"
The windows say, no—
Like that—
Until they compromise
Morning is free to paint outside the threshold, but
To enter through God's Windows
he must abide by their rules

In Jerusalem there's a school built by a Mamluke
Who came from beyond the river,
Was sold at a slave market in Isfahan
To a merchant from Baghdad, who traveled to Aleppo
Gave the Mamluke to Aleppo's prince
Fearing the blueness in the Mamluke's left eye—
The Prince passed him along to a caravan heading for Egypt
Where soon, he became Conqueror of the Moghuls
and Sovereign Sultan

In Jerusalem there's a scent
That summarizes Babel and India in an herbalist's shop
At Khan Al-Zayt!
I swear, a scent with a language you'll understand

If you listen;
It says to me—
When they pitch their gas canisters at me
“Ignore them”
And when the gas has gone
That perfume fills the air again, and says
“You see?”

In Jerusalem contradictions take their rest
And miracles are not strange
People touch them like bits of fabric old and new
Miracles here are handled, put to use

In Jerusalem if you shake hands with an old man
Or touch a building
You’ll find etched on your palm a poem, my friend
Or two

In Jerusalem, despite the many disasters
An air of innocence
A breeze of childhood
A pigeon flying aloft
Declares independence in the wind between two bullets

In Jerusalem, rows of graves are lines of the city’s history
Her dust the book
Everyone has passed through
For Jerusalem welcomes the faithful and the faithless
Walk through
Read her tombstones in every nation’s language
Here lie the Africans and the Franks
The Kipceks and the Slavs and the Bosniaks
The Tartars and the Turks
The people of God and of Destruction
The poor and the rich
The debauched and the ascetic
Here lies everyone who’s ever trod the earth
Scribe of History, why have you excluded us?

Has the city
Suddenly become
Too small?

Old man, re-write and think again
I see you’re in error

The eye closes, then looks once more

The driver of the yellow car turns north, away from the gates
And now Jerusalem is behind us
I see her in the right rear-view mirror
Her colors change in the sun and disappear

Well into tears
A smile surprises me

And says:
"Oh you who weep behind the wall, are you a fool?
Have you lost your mind?!

Let your eye not weep, you who've been dropped from the text
Let your eye not weep, young Arab, and know
That in Jerusalem there's whoever's in Jerusalem
But, in Jerusalem
I see no-one, except for you"

(Translated by Radwa Ashour and Ahdaf Soueif)

安娜．露易莎．阿瑪拉爾（葡萄牙），著有超過三十本詩集、一本話劇劇本、一本長篇小說以及數本兒童讀物。其作品已經獲翻譯成廿多種語言在世界各地出版，包括巴西、哥倫比亞、法國、德國、意大利、墨西哥、荷蘭、西班牙、瑞典、英國、美國和委內瑞拉。她贏得多個國家與國際獎項和名銜，曾獲巴黎和波爾圖等城市頒發文學獎章、Premio Correntes d'Escritas 文學獎、Giuseppe Acerbi 詩歌獎、葡文作家協會大獎、筆會虛構類書籍獎、羅馬基金會國際文學獎，以及Jacinto PradoCoelho 散文獎。阿瑪拉爾現於波爾圖大學任教，主要從事女性主義研究及酷兒研究。

Ana Luísa Amaral (Portugal) has published over thirty books of poetry, a play, a novel, essays, and several books for children. Her works are translated into over twenty languages (Chinese included) and published in several countries, such as Brazil, Colombia, France, Germany, Italy, Mexico, the Netherlands, Spain, Sweden, United Kingdom, the United States, and Venezuela. She was awarded national and international prizes and distinctions, among which the Medal for Services to Literature from the cities of Paris and Porto, the Correntes d'Escritas / Casino da Póvoa Prize, the Giuseppe Acerbi Prize for Poetry, the Great Prize of the Portuguese Association of Writers, the Prize PEN for Fiction, the Fondazione Roma International Prize, as well as the Prize of Essay Jacinto Prado Coelho. Amaral teaches at the University of Porto and her academic research fields are Feminist and Queer Studies.

安娜·露易莎·阿瑪拉爾

ANA LUÍSA AMARAL

中文翻譯：姚風

English translation by Margaret Jull Costa

Testamento

Vou partir de avião
e o medo das alturas misturado comigo
faz-me tomar calmantes
e ter sonhos confusos

Se eu morrer
quero que a minha filha não se esqueça de mim
que alguém lhe cante mesmo com voz desafinada
e que lhe ofereçam fantasia
mais que um horário certo
ou uma cama bem feita

Dêem-lhe amor e ver
dentro das coisas
sonhar com sóis azuis e céus brilhantes
em vez de lhe ensinarem contas de somar
e a descascar batatas

Preparem a minha filha
para a vida
se eu morrer de avião
e ficar despegada do meu corpo
e for átomo livre lá no céu

Que se lembre de mim
a minha filha
e mais tarde que diga à sua filha
que eu voei lá no céu
e fui contentamento deslumbrado
ao ver na sua casa as contas de somar erradas
e as batatas no saco esquecidas
e íntegras

遺囑

我的飛機即將起飛
我有畏高症
不得不服用鎮定劑
並且噩夢連連

如果我死了
我希望女兒永遠記住我
希望有人為她唱歌，即使唱得走調
有人幫助她幻想
而不是只給她準時的時間表
或者一張舒適的床

請給她愛以及
觀察事物本質的能力
叫她幻想藍太陽和明媚的天空
而不只是教她如何加減乘除
如何去削土豆皮

請教會我的女兒
面對生活
倘若我遭遇空難
身體分離
化為原子在天空自由飄浮

請我的女兒不要忘記我
希望我的女兒
之後告訴她的女兒
我曾在天空飛行
而且心感安慰，因為高興地看到
我的女兒算錯了家裡的賬目
而且把全部的土豆
都忘在了袋子裡

Testament

I'm about to fly off somewhere
and my fear of heights plus myself
finds me resorting to tranquillisers
and having confused dreams

If I should die
I want my daughter always to remember me
for someone to sing to her even if they can't hold a tune
to offer her pure dreams
rather than a fixed timetable
or a well-made bed

To give her love and the ability
to look inside things
to dream of blue suns and brilliant skies
instead of teaching her how to add up
and how to peel potatoes

To prepare my daughter
for life
if I should die on a plane
and be separated from my body
and become a free-floating atom in the sky

Let my daughter
remember me
and later on say to her own daughter
that I flew off into the sky
and was all dazzle and contentment
to see that in her house none of the sums added up
and the potatoes were still in their sack forgotten
entire

Título por haver

No meu poema ficaste
de pernas para
o ar
(mas também eu
já estive tantas vezes)

Por entre versos vejo-te as mãos
no chão
do meu poema
e os pés tocando o título
(a haver quando eu
quiser)

Enquanto o meu desejo assim serás:
incómodo estatuto:
preciso de escrever-te
do avesso
para te amar em excesso

題目待定

在我的詩中
你
四腳朝天
（但我很多次
也曾經這樣）

在詩句之間
我看見你用手
撐在
我詩歌的地面
腳觸及到標題
（我願意的話
才會起標題）

你叫我產生這樣的願望：
在這不舒服的姿勢中
我要倒轉著
寫你
為的是愛你無窮盡。

Title to Be Decided

In my poem you were
all topsy
turvy
(but then I've often
been the same)

I can see you between the lines
performing a handstand
on the floor of my poem
your feet touching the title
(to be decided when I
so choose)

You'll stay there as long as I wish:
in that awkward position:
I need to write you
upside down
to offer you my love
unbounded

Perguntas

A vizinha do prédio ao lado
que perdeu o filho num acidente,
sempre que passa por mim de manhã,
cumprimenta-me, sorrindo,
dizendo-me "bom dia"

E eu tenho dias em que penso
o que faz ela para olhar o sol,
depois de acordar no seu quarto,
de abrir a janela para esta rua estreita,
e saudar-me e sorrir-me

Julgo que tem fé,
porque a vejo por vezes saindo da igreja
que fica ao lado do jardim
que nos é comum

Deve ser isso o que a mantém,
a faz vestir-se todos os dias, tomar o cesto das compras,
escolher legumes naquela mercearia:
os minúsculos gestos de que a vida é feita
quando a guerra é ausente

Mas que guerra por dentro sentirá ela,
nesse exacto momento em que abre os olhos
e pensa o filho ali,

no cemitério por detrás da igreja,
ao lado do jardim,
nunca mais lhe podendo dizer
"bom dia, mãe"?

問題

旁邊住宅樓裡的女鄰居
兒子死於車禍
她每天早上見到我
都會面帶微笑
問候我：「早安！」

有時候，我想知道
她每天在臥室醒來
打開朝向狹窄街道的窗子
是什麼讓她望望太陽
然後微笑著問候我

我想她一定是個信徒
因為我有時看見她從教堂出來
教堂就在公園旁邊
是我們共有的教堂

或許這就是讓她活下去的原因
叫她每天穿好衣服，拿起菜籃子
去菜市場買菜：
沒有發動戰爭的時候
是這些微小的細節構成了我們生活

但是，每當她睜開睡眼
想到他的兒子
就葬在教堂後面的墓地

花園的旁邊
但他再也不會對她説
「媽，早安！」，此刻
她的內心又會經受怎麼的戰爭？

Questions

Whenever the next-door neighbour
who lost her son in an accident
passes me in the morning,
she greets me with a smile
and says "Good morning"

And there are days when I wonder
how she can bear even to look at the sun,
when she wakes in her bedroom,
when she opens the window onto this narrow street,
when she greets me with a smile

I think she must be a believer,
because I sometimes see her leaving the church
next to the park
we share in common

That's probably what keeps her going,
what helps her get dressed each day, pick up her shopping basket,
buy vegetables from the local shop:
the tiny gestures that make up our lives
when there's no war being waged

But what must be the war raging inside her,
when she opens her eyes
and thinks of her son there,

in the cemetery behind the church,
beside the park,
the son who will never again say to her:
"Morning, Mum"?

Nú: Estudo em comoção

Em que meditas tu
quando olhas para mim dessa maneira,
deitada no sofá
diagonal ao espaço onde me sento,
fingindo eu não te olhar?

Em que pensa o teu corpo
elástico, alongado,
pronto a vir ter comigo
se eu pedir?

As orelhas contidas em recanto,
as patas recuadas,
o que atravessa agora o branco dos teus olhos:
lua em quarto-crescente,
um prado claro?

E quando dormes, como noutras horas,
que sonhos te viajam:
a mãe, a caça, a mão macia, o salto
muito perfeito
e alto, muito esguio?

Onde: a noite sem frio
que nos abrigará
um dia

e que há-de ser
(só pode ser)

igual?

裸體：激情研究

你躺在沙發上
與我坐的地方形成
對角線
你這樣凝視著我，而佯裝不看你
此時你在想些什麼？

如果我呼喚你
你富有彈性而修長的身體
會跑向我
此刻你的身體會想些什麼？

耳朵隱縮
毛茸茸的爪子收斂
正在穿過你眼白的是：
一輪新月
還是青青的草地？

當你睡去，正如在其他時候，
你在經歷怎樣的夢：
母親，狩獵，一隻柔軟的手，抑或一個完美的
跳躍
很有高度，而且瀟灑的跳躍？

地點：有一天
不冷的夜晚
會庇護我們

它必須
（只能這樣）
與其他的夜晚

一樣嗎？

Nude: A Study in Poignancy

What are you thinking about
when you look at me like that,
as you lie on the sofa,
diagonal to the place I sit,
with me pretending not to look at you?

What is your body thinking about,
your long, elastic body,
ready to come to me
if I call?

Ears slightly pricked,
paws furled,
what can you see now in the whites of your eyes:
a crescent moon,
a pale meadow?

And when you sleep, at other times,
what dreams travel through you:
your mother, a mouse, a soft hand, a leap
so perfect
and high, so lithe?

Where: the uncold night
that will one day
shelter us

and that will
(as it must)
be the same for both?

Quarto-crescente

Porque vejamos: uma lua destas
já nem lua é. A lua quer-se grande,
leitosa, apontável às crianças:
olha o homem da lua, os olhos, a

vassoura. Mas uma lua destas
desfazendo-se em sombras, um ar
de quem passou o dia em claro
já nem lua é. Que não exija então

o impossível, que não se finja
a sério a pedir versos e algum olhar:
o poeta não usa telescópio,
nem se vai acordar uma criança
por gomos de luar.

新月

因為我們看到，這樣的月亮
已經不算是月亮，月亮應該很大，
呈奶白色：可指著它對孩子們說：
看，月亮人，他的眼睛，

他的掃帚。但像這樣的月亮
碎成斑影，神情
像一個失眠的人，
根本不是月亮。那就別要求

不可能的事。不要佯裝認真，
向詩人索要詩句與見解：
詩人不使用望遠鏡，
也不會為一縷月光
去叫醒一個孩子。

Crescent Moon

Because you see, a moon like this
isn't even a moon. The moon should be big,
milky-white, worth pointing out to children:
Look at the man in the moon, his eyes, his

broom. But a moon like this,
dissolving into shadows, with the air
of someone who hasn't slept all day,
isn't a moon at all. So don't ask for the

impossible, don't pretend seriously
to demand poems and insights:
the poet doesn't use a telescope
and isn't going to wake up a child
for the sake of a sliver of light.

馬克西姆·阿梅林（俄羅斯），詩人，隨筆作家、翻譯家、詩歌研究者與出版人，著有四本詩集及一部收錄詩歌、論文、隨筆的合集。畢業於庫爾斯克商學院，曾於軍隊服役，在莫斯科高爾基文學院學習。譯有古希臘與拉丁詩歌（品達、卡圖盧斯和《普里阿普斯之書》）及當代格魯吉亞、意大利、烏克蘭詩人的作品。他選編了十八至二十世紀俄國詩人的作品集及當代俄羅斯和格魯吉亞詩歌選集，並加上註釋。他是《當代俄羅斯各民族詩選》的發起人和編者，該詩選被譯為五十七種語言。阿梅林是俄羅斯筆會及「文學翻譯大師」協會會員，身兼「人文聯合出版社」（OGI）總編輯。

Maxim Amelin (Russia) is a poet, scholar of poetry, essayist, translator and publisher. He graduated from the Commercial College in Kursk, served in the Soviet Army and studied at the Gorky Literary Institute in Moscow. He has published four books of poetry and a collection of poems, articles and essays. He has translated Greek and Latin classics (Pindar, Catullus, and Carmina Priapea) and contemporary Georgian, Italian and Ukrainian poets. Amelin edited and annotated editions of Russian poets from the eighteenth to the twentieth centuries, as well as numerous poetry anthologies of Russian and Georgian poetry. He was the initiator and curator of the *Anthology of Contemporary Poetry of the Peoples of Russia* in 57 languages. Amelin is a member of the Russian PEN-Club and the Guild of Literary Translators. He serves as editor-in-chief of OGI Publishing House.

馬克西姆·阿梅林

MAXIM AMELIN

中文翻譯：徐曼琳

English translation by Derek Mong and Anne O. Fisher

«Поспешим»

Поспешим
стол небогатый украсить
помидорами алыми,
петрушкой кучерявой и укропом,

чесноком,
перцем душистым и луком,
огурцами в пупырышках
и дольками арбузными. — Пусть масло,

как янтарь
солнца под оком, возблещет
ослепительно. — Черного
пора нарезать хлеба, белой соли,

не скупясь,
выставить целую склянку. —
Виноградного полная
бутыль не помешает. — Коль приятно

утолять
голод и жажду со вкусом! —
Наступающей осени
на милость не сдадимся, не сдадимся

ни за что. —
Всесотворившему Богу
озорные любовники
угрюмых ненавистников любезней.

「快來裝點這樸素的桌子」

快來
裝點這樸素的桌子，
用鮮紅的番茄，
用茴香和捲曲的西芹，

用蒜，
用芳香的花椒和洋蔥，
用長著小毛刺的黃瓜
和一塊塊西瓜。—— 讓黃油，

如琥珀般
的太陽在眼前，閃現
耀眼的光芒。—— 是時候了
切幾塊黑色的麵包，再撒滿白色的鹽，

千萬別吝嗇，
請拿出整整一瓶兒。——
滿瓶的葡萄酒
也不會礙事兒。—— 多麼愉快

如果能
消饑解渴，又能咀嚼品味！
那將至的秋天
無論如何我們絕不向你祈求，絕不祈求

你的恩典。——
創造萬物的上帝啊
淘氣的情人
比陰鬱的懷疑者更得你寵愛。

"Let's hurry"

Let's hurry
to grace this meager table
with red tomatoes
and stacks of melon wedges,

with onions
and dill, with parsley and peppers,
with garlic and goose-pimpled
cucumbers. Let the oil,

resplendent
as sunlit amber, glimmer.
It's time to slice
black bread, to strew salt

lavishly.
Let's offer bottles full
of wine and tipple
till they're gone. How pleasant

to placate
our palates and sup with taste!
We won't give up,
we won't give in to autumn,

not a bit.
For God, the Creator of All,
likes naughty lovers
far more than dreary doubters.

«Мне хотелось бы собственный дом иметь»

Мне хотелось бы собственный дом иметь
на побережье мертвом живого моря,
где над волнами небесная стонет медь,
ибо Нот и Борей, меж собою споря,
задевают воздушные колокола,
где то жар, то хлад, никогда — тепла.

Слабым зеницам закат золотой полезней,
розовый, бирюзовый, и Млечный путь,
предостерегающий от болезней,
разум смиряя, чуткий же мой ничуть
не ужаснется рокотом слух созвучий
бездны, многоглаголивой и певучей.

Сыздетства каждый отзыв ее знаком
мне, носителю редкому двух наречий,
горним, слегка коверкая, языком
то, что немощен выразить человечий,
нараспев говорящему, слов состав
вывернув наизнанку и распластав.

Что же мне остается? — невнятна долу
трудная речь и мой в пустоту звучал
глас, искажаясь, — полуспасаться, полу-
жить, обитателям смежных служа начал,
птице текучей или летучей рыбе,
в собственном доме у времени на отшибе.

「我想有一所自己的房子」

我想有一所自己的房子
在充滿生機的大海死氣沉沉的海濱，
海浪之上青銅色的天空在歎息，
因為諾托斯和玻瑞阿斯相互爭鬥，
觸動了空中的風鈴，
那裡時而酷暑，時而嚴寒，從未有過——溫暖。

金黃色、玫瑰色和青綠色的晚霞，
對脆弱的瞳孔十分有益，還有銀河
給我庇護，讓我遠離疾病，
讓我神志安寧，我敏銳的聽覺
一點也不害怕大海深處的轟鳴，
它雖然濤聲喧嘩但卻和諧動聽。

從童年時起它的每一聲迴響我都熟悉，
我是少有的通曉兩種語言的人，
人類翻遍詞典盡情鋪展的
詞彙都無法表達的旨趣，
天國的語言，稍加改變，
就能用歌唱的聲調，將其呈現。

那我還剩下什麼？——在大地上
這艱深的語言模糊不清，我的聲音在空谷中
響起，雖已失去本意，——一半自救，一半
活著，為那些有相似天性的居民，
為遊弋的鳥兒或者飛翔的魚兒，
在自己的房子裡孤獨地與時間為鄰。

"I wish I owned my own home"

I wish I owned my own home
on the dead sands of a living sea,
where Notus and Boreas squabble and wrestle,
bumping the air's bells till the brassy sky
chimes high above the wave's moan—
where I shiver or fever but never feel warm.

My palsied pupils bask in the sun's gold
(its roses, its turquoise); the Milky Way
shields me from disease. All my mental tremors
are calmed. Meanwhile I'm not dismayed—
despite my soft eardrums—by the sea's garrulous
music, this polyphonous, singing abyss.

I find each sound or susurrus familiar,
for I'm that rare native-speaker of two dialects;
I've yanked base words by their root, turned them
inside out, then spread them flat
and spoken—with small alterations—what makes
human speech balk. I know vertiginous talk.

But what's left for me now that difficult speech
is inaudible in the vale? Now that I twist and prattle
in the wilderness? Might I sometimes live,
might I save myself, serving both sides
of that audience—the flying fish, the swimming flock—
in my own home, beyond time's boondocks.

«По утрам, восстав как из гроба»

По утрам, восстав как из гроба,
продираю глаза с трудом,
и расплывчато глядя в оба,
сам не зная, куда ведом,

в мысленной барахтаюсь каше,
полудрему и полуявь
разграничить силюсь, но чаши
весовые — то влевь, то вправь —

ни на миг не могут на месте
удержаться, — сквозь сновидень
глас трубы, запеченной в тесте,
внятно слышу, на Судный день

пробуждение — мню — похоже,
выбирая одно из двух —
онеметь, иль воскликнуть: «Боже!
мой Тебе утреннюет дух»[1]

1 Всё стихотворение представляет собой джазовую импровизацию на тему двух стихов из «Евгению. Жизнь Званская» (1808) Гавриила Державина:
Восстав от сна, взвожу на небо скромный взор,
Мой утренниюет дух правителю вселенной…

「每天清晨， 我在棺木中醒來」

每天清晨，我在棺木中醒來，
費力地睜開惺忪的雙眼，
竭力想看清模糊的世界，
連自己也不知道，該去向何方，

我在思想的稀粥裡掙扎，
哪一半是迷茫，哪一半是清醒
我試圖弄清，可是秤上的
粥碗 —— 時而向左，時而向右傾 ——

一刻也無法在一個點上
站穩，—— 穿過夢境
號角的聲音，和著麵烘烤，
它清醒可聽，惟願

我能甦醒 —— 就像最後的審判，
二者必選其一 ——
要麼噤口不語，要麼大聲呼喊：「主啊！
早禱時為你獻上我的心靈。」

"Rising at morning from my graveside"

Rising at morning from my graveside,
I rub these eyelids till they're lucid,
and then, squinting windward,
I set off—unsure where I'm directed—

only to stumble through my thought's thicket.
Daily I strive to divide my half-dreams
from this half-light, but the cupped scales
dip—first to waking, then to fictions—

and won't hold still a whole second.
But through dream's doughy incubation
a trumpet, also baked in pastry, cries—
I clearly hear it, calling me to awaken.

I imagine it's the call to Judgment,
leaving me to choose between one of two
options: go numb or exclaim "My God!
I rouse my spirit to greet You."

Исповедь переписчика

Я — переписчик, обитель святую лет
не покидавший тридцать иль сорок,
знаю немного: книга мертва, если нет
в ней ни описок, ни оговорок;
суть на полях расположена и меж строк,
в буквицах явлена, в титлах скрыта;
время нещадно написанного песок
хрупкий сквозь крупное сеет сито.

Я — переписчик, одежда моя проста,
златом не блещет и перламутром
утварь, полати — для сна, для молитв — уста, —
ночь скоротать — и за дело утром:
в книге любой до конца от начала есть
то ощущение смертной битвы,
зря не одну изведёшь без коего десть,
и не помогут тебе молитвы.

Я — переписчик, смиренное ремесло
дарит возможность продлиться в мире:
медленно книги ветшают, — своих число
помню до точности: три Псалтири,
двадцать Апостолов, девять Палей, семь Пчёл,
пять Шестодневов, и каждый штучен, —
всё бы я мной переписанное прочёл,
если бы грамоте был обучен.

抄寫員的自白

我是一名抄寫員，從未離開過聖母，
　我在她的身邊已經三十或四十載，
我懂得不多：書籍將沒有生命，如果
　裡面既無筆誤，也無偶爾的失言；
時間用篩子無情地
　篩出了寫下的易碎的沙粒；
文章的本質就在字裡行間，
　在節略符中隱藏，在花體首字母中顯現。

我是一名抄寫員，我的衣衫很簡單，
　傢俱既沒有珠母的光澤，更不會金光閃閃
床板——用來睡覺，嘴巴——用來祈禱，
　夜晚消磨時光——清晨任勞任怨：
任何一本書中從開頭到結尾
　都感覺在拼死會戰，
白白地浪費了一刀紙
　我的祈禱卻不能幫助你。

我是一名抄寫員，這個手藝沒什麼光鮮
　它在世間讓光陰延長：
書籍慢慢衰老朽邁，——它們的數量
　我不會忘記：三部詩篇、
二十部使徒行傳、九部帕里亞書、七部蜜蜂圖鑒
　五部創世紀，每部的報酬都是計件，——
如果我通曉文墨，
　我就會通讀自己抄寫的書卷。

The Scribe's Confession

I am a scribe. I haven't left my cloister
　in lo some thirty or forty years,
but this much I know: a book's dead if no
　errata or proviso appears,
for its essence begins where the text ends,
　clear in its illumination, obscured in its title.
Time sieves the sand of what's written
　through the wire mesh of a riddle.

I am a scribe. My clothing is simple;
　my instruments don't dazzle with gold
or mother-of-pearl. I've a plank-bed to sleep on,
　lips for praying; I work while morning unfolds.
In any book you'll find a battle
　waged—from first line to *finis*—to the death,
without which no quire's completed.
　And prayers? Oh no, save your breath.

I am a scribe. My humble craft
　is my short life's lasting balm.
Books decay slowly. I remember precisely
　how many I've done: three Psalms,
twenty Apostols, and nine Palaea Historicas,
　five Hexamerons, and seven Bees.
I'd pore through all I've copied out, imbibe
　the wisdom in words, if only I could read.

«Насыщение, а не вкус»

Насыщение, а не вкус,
о котором водит Француз
неустанно четыре века
языком по полости рта! —
Вся премудрость его пуста
для голодного человека!

Мельтешения скудных блюд
не приемлет привычный люд
к изобилию щей да каши;
нет урчания в животе —
можно думать о красоте:
насыщение — счастье наше!

Преуспеет в словесном тот
ремесле, кто туго набьёт
отощавшему снедью пузо, —
чем богата, всё из печи
с пылу с жару на стол мечи,
да поболе, русская Муза!

「要豐盛，而非品味」

要豐盛，而非品味，
那是法國人講究的東西，
他們用口腔中的舌頭
專注於此已四個世紀！——
所有的絕頂聰明都毫無意義，
對饑餓的人尤其如此！

人們不會接受貧瘠的飯食，
無論它看上去多麼華麗，
我們已習慣豐盛的湯和粥；
重要的是肚子不再咕嚕抗議——
可以想想審美：
可是吃飽，才是我們的福氣！

誰能用吃食
讓瘦弱的人填滿肚子
他就能在詞彙的手藝中取勝，——
俄羅斯的繆斯啊，你越富有，
剛出爐的飯菜就越豐盛，
擺上桌的刀叉就越鋒利！

"Satiety prevails, not taste"

Satiety prevails, not taste,
despite the Frenchman's discerning mouth.
At least four centuries he's spent
loving taste, urbane, and proud.
Still, his subtleties prove paltry
to any man who's hungry.

The normal folk just don't prefer
small plates arrayed until they're dizzy
in lieu of lots of soup and porridge.
It's easier to stomach beauty
when your stomach fills your vest:
satiety is our happiness!

The one who stuffs these folks with pap,
fills 'em up and staves off hunger,
will soon excel in verbal craft.
So empty your fridge, unload your larder,
cook up the contents however you choose—
just don't be stingy, Russian muse!

雷納托．桑多瓦爾．巴希加盧波（秘魯），著有十本詩集，其作品獲翻譯成七國語言，包括丹麥語、英語、芬蘭語、法語、德語、意大利語及葡語。曾主持Nidode Cuervos（Crows' Nest）出版社，主編國際文學雜誌*Evohé*和*Fórnix*。曾任利馬國際詩歌節主席及秘魯文化部編輯資助委員會主席。巴希加盧波於2016年獲Copé Bronze國家詩歌獎。他在秘魯宗鐸天主教大學取得西班牙語文學及語言學碩士學位，繼而在芬蘭赫爾辛基大學獲得羅曼語系文獻學博士學位，曾於秘魯宗鐸天主教大學和里卡多帕爾馬大學任教。

Renato Sandoval Bacigalupo (Peru) has published ten collections of poetry which has been translated into Danish, English, French, Finnish, German, Italian, and Portuguese. He runs the Nido de Cuervos (Crows' Nest) Publishing House as well as international literary magazines *Evohé* and *Fórnix*. He has been the director of the International Poetry Festival in Lima (FIPLIMA) and the director of the Editorial Fund of the Ministry of Culture of Peru. In 2016, he won the Copé Bronze National Prize for Poetry. He studied Hispanic Literatures and Linguistics (Master of Arts) at the Pontifical Catholic University of Peru and completed his doctoral studies in Romanic Philology at the University of Helsinki, Finland. Sandoval has taught at the Pontifical Catholic University of Peru and Ricardo Palma University.

雷納托 · 桑多瓦爾 · 巴希加盧波

RENATO SANDOVAL BACIGALUPO

中文翻譯：趙振江

English translation by Roxana Peramás

Para Tao Yuanming

La música me oye, me arruga,
me deshoja, solo crujidos
y un temblor enjuto rezuman
de mis dientes. Esa flauta
mutilada, la sirena
de las horas anunciando
lo que no saben o ya no entienden,
termitas al vapor y la nota aupada
en la ventana. Una palabra, todas
las palabras, alguna,
ninguna, nada de mí
oye la música
cuando aún respiro.

致陶淵明

音樂將我傾聽，將我弄皺，
使我凋零，只有撕裂聲
和一個消瘦的顫抖
滲出我的牙縫。那支
被切斷的笛子，報時的汽笛
在宣告無人知道
抑或無人理解的事情，
白蟻上了蒸汽，音符上了
窗櫺。一個詞語，所有
詞語，某一個詞語，
無任何詞語，與我毫無干係
只要我還在呼吸
音樂就在傾聽。

For Tao Yuanming

Music hears me, wrinkles me,
strips me, only creaks
and a lean tremor exude
out of my teeth. That mutilated
flute, the mermaid
of the hours announcing
what it is unknown or no longer understood,
steamed termites and the lifted note
in the window. One word, all
the words, some,
none, nothing of me
hears the music
when I still breathe.

Para Po Chu'i

Asciendo a la montaña
de sueño
y me asfixia el sudor de sus piedras.
Aún la plaza dormida en la ladera
es el vértigo de noche tras noche
repudiando la aurora.
Un sinsonte reparte perjurios,
una voz de sombras
corona mis sienes.

致白居易

我攀登
夢中的山
令我窒息的是石頭的汗。
廣場還安睡在山坡上
是夜復一夜的眩暈
在擯棄曙光。
一隻模仿鳥在分發偽誓言，
一個陰影的聲音
為我的雙鬢戴上王冠。

For Po Chu'i

I ascend the mountain
of dream
and the sweat of its stones stifles me.
The square still asleep on the hillside
is the night after night vertigo
repudiating the dawn.
A mockingbird deals perjuries,
a voice of shadows
crowns my temples.

Para Wang Wei

Arde el sol sin piedad
pero el viento es de otoño
en la ribera del hastío. Solo las calles
ensanchan el grito
en perfecto estado de desvelo. Las ventanas
encierran un deseo que de a gotas
se cuela por las ranuras de las puertas
esmirriadas. Nada turba la siesta
de los necios en este día comercial
y sin provecho, apenas
si el bancario que relame sus legañas
o el rocío que aún persiste
en los geranios.

致王維

在厭倦的岸上
秋風送爽
無情似火的驕陽。
只有街道在不眠完美的狀態
使喊叫越演越狂。
窗戶關注從細小的門縫
滲進的一絲慾望。
什麼也不能打攪蠢人們的午睡
在這無利可圖的商貿之日
銀行家艱難地舔著自己的眼屎
或露珠依然
滴在天竺葵上。

For Wang Wei

The sun burns mercilessly
but the wind is autumn breeze
on the shore of boredom. Only the streets
widen the scream
in perfect insomnia. The
windows
enclose a desire that bit by bit
sneaks through the slots of the
scraggy
doors. Nothing disturbs the nap
of the fools in this barren
and business day, hardly
the bank man smacks its rheum
or
the dew that still persists
in the geraniums.

Para Meng Haoran

Él ama su sed
y las fronteras nunca están demasiado lejos
acaso palidecen
bajo el metro que no cesa
y se teme y se supera
y se instalá una y otra vez
en la maraña
de otros nombres y de esos sueños
que anunciaran su caída.
Piano afuera
ese de su entonces a otro tiempo
que si fue
fue para ir y
venir y fustigar el lomo
de la aurora
que hoy tirita
siempre aquí
entre las zarzas
del viento, entonces
como fue.

致孟浩然

熱愛自己的渴望
邊界從未在遠方
難道它們蒼白暗淡
人們在不停的韻律下
恐懼並自我改善
一次又一次
扎根在其他的名字
和那些宣告
自己跌倒的紛亂。
外面平靜
從那時到別的時間
倘若是
為了往返
並鞭打
黎明的脊背
今天
黎明
總在這裡
如往常一般
在黑莓叢中抖顫。

For Meng Haoran

He loves his thirst
and the borders are never too
far
perhaps they pale
under the meter that doesn't cease
and he fears and exceeds himself
and installs again and again
in the tangle
of other names and of those dreams
that will announce his fall.
Piano outside
that of his days to another time
if he went
he went to go and
come and whip the back
of the dawn
that today shivers
always here
among the brambles
of the wind, then
as it was.

Del Taoísmo al Teísmo

El té se asombra ante quien lo bebe,
su sabor lejano en dos ansias se desliza,
no hay labio que lo eleve entre los helechos
ni peonía tan opaca o sumisa.
El sol es un sueño retorcido en el remanso.

從道教到有神論

茶在飲者面前驚奇，
其遙遠的味道化作兩種焦慮，
沒有嘴唇能使它在蕨類中升起
就連如此憂鬱或順從的牡丹也不用提。
太陽是河灣中一個夢被扭曲。

1 原文Del Taoísmo al Teísmo是一個文字遊戲：el té是茶，el teísmo是有神論或一神論。

From Taoism to Teaism

Tea is amazed at whom drinks it,
its distant taste slips in two anxieties,
there is no lip that raises it among the ferns
nor peony so dull or submissive.
The sun is a wicked dream in haven.

簡・博文（美國），詩人和視覺藝術家，著有十本著作，包括她合編的《華麗無物：狄金森與維爾納詩歌信箋》（Christine Burgin / New Directions）、《網》（UDP），以及長詩《絲詩》（Nightboat Books）。《絲詩》既是一本書，又是用液態絲綢製造而成的植入式生物傳感器，後者是博文跟塔夫茲大學絲綢研究所共同製作。博文的詩歌藝術作品曾在三十多個國際展覽中展出，她所獲獎項與獎助學金多不勝數，包括當代藝術基金、羅申伯格駐團藝術家、亞洲文化協會基金及創意資本。

Jen Bervin (United States) is a poet and visual artist. Her publications include ten books, including *Gorgeous Nothings: Emily Dickinson's Envelope Poems with Marta Werner* (Christine Burgin / New Directions), *Nets* (UDP), and *Silk Poems* (Nightboat Books)—a long-form poem presented both as a book and as an implantable biosensor made from liquefied silk developed in collaboration with Tufts University's Silk Lab. Bervin's work has been exhibited internationally and can be found in more than thirty international collections. She has earned numerous awards, fellowships, and grants including the Foundation for Contemporary Art, Rauschenberg Residency, Asian Cultural Council, and Creative Capital.

簡 · 博文

JEN BERVIN

中文翻譯：陳嘉恩

Silk Poems (Excerpts)

IFWEMATE
WEAREALL

CALLED
QUEENS

絲詩（節選）

如果我們交配
我們全都

稱為
皇后

ANEW
MOTHER

DOESNOTHING
HALFWAY

一位新手
媽媽

做事不會
只做一半

SHESWELLS
FLUFFYBELLIED

GREATWITHEGGS
THREETOFIVEHUNDRED

THESIZEOF
SESAMESEEDS

她腫起來
肚皮呼呼脹

充滿卵子
三到五百顆

每顆
芝蔴般大

THEYSPILLFORTH
INTWOBATCHES

AFEWHOURS
RESTBETWEEN

STICKYANDGOLDEN
THEYLODGE

ALLOVERTHE
COCOON

它們湧出
分為兩批

數個小時
棲息於

黏乎乎和金燦燦的地方
它們寄居於

卵囊的四周

HEALTHYEGGS
TURNFROM

YOLKGOLD
TOBLUISH

BLACK
INTENDAYS

健康的卵子由

蛋黃般金黃轉為藍藍

黑黑過程不過十天

INACOOL
DRY

PLACE
THEEGGS

CANGO
DORMANT

UPTO
TENMONTHS

在又冷又乾

的地方卵子

可以休眠

長達十個月

TOBEREVIVED
INAPOUCHWARMED

BETWEENTHE
BREASTSOFAWOMAN

ORLETSBEHONEST
AHEATEDROOM

等待復活
在一個女人的胸脯

之間
溫熱著

不妨老實説
那是個暖房

INIDEAL
CONDITIONS

THEEGGS
STARTINCUBATING

WHENTHEBUDS
ONTHEMULBERRY

ARETWO
CENTIMETERSLONG

在理想的
情況

當桑椹的
蓓蕾

有兩
釐米長

這些卵子
開始孵化

SOITBEGINS
FIRSTINSTAR

MYOWNEGG
TREMBLES

所以它開始於
第一齡期

我自己的卵子
顫抖

STICKYSOFT
IEATAHOLE

THROUGH
ASMALLSPOT

ONITSSURFACE
THROUGHA

MICROPYLE
ON

ONE
END

黏黏軟軟的
我吃出一個小洞

在它表面
通過一個

一丁點的地方
通過一個

卵孔
在

一
邊

IEMERGE
INMYFULLGLORY

UNIVOLTINE
WONDER

SILKWORM
OFTHEYEAR

我出現了
朝氣勃勃

一年一代
年度

非凡的
絲蠶

INAGLITCHOF
NOMENCLATURE

IAMCALLEDAN
ANT

一時
命名錯誤

我給喚作
螞蟻

RESPLENDENT
INFINEBROWNFUZZ

AWRIGGLINGBIT
ANEIGHTH

OFAN
INCHLONG

棕色絨毛纖纖
燦燦生輝

扭來扭去的小東西
八分

之一
吋長

AGLEAMINGBLACK
FACETHEMOON

WOULDLICKIFITCOULD
ILOOKGOOD

亮晶晶的黑
面向月亮

它會舔如果可以的話
我看起來不錯

SOMETHING
DELICIOUS

HITSMYMOUTH
INSTINCTIVELYIOPEN

MULBERRYLEAF
NECTARFLOODSIT

有些東西
美味得很

碰到我的嘴
出於本能我張開

桑葉的
甘露淹沒了它

ISAVOR
GOSLOW

IFEELIAM
CERTAINLYLOVED

我細嚐
慢慢來

我覺得我
當然是被愛的

SURROUNDEDBY
HUNDREDSOFSIBLINGS

NEWBORNSEATING
NEWBORNLEAVES

包圍著我
數以百計的兄弟姐妹

新生兒吃著
新生葉

THECUT
EDGES

THE
TENDERPORTIONS

SOFTSUCCULENT
BETWEENTHEVEINS

切口
邊緣

那些
幼嫩的部分

柔軟豐潤
在葉脈之間

CATERPILLARS
MUSTBEFED

LEAVESOF
THEIROWNAGE

WRITES
WILLIAMSTALLENGE

IN 1609
REMUNERATED

BYTHEENGLISHCROWN
TODOSO

毛毛蟲
必須餵以

跟牠們同齡
的葉子

威廉斯托倫治
於1609年

寫道
因而

獲酬
英國克朗

FUNNYTO
READTHIS

4609YEARS
AFTER

OURFIRST
NARROWFABRICS

WEREBURIEDIN
ZHEJIANGCHINA

有趣的是
讀到這些

4609 年
後

我們首批
織長綢緞

埋葬於
中國浙江

阿巴斯・貝東（黎巴嫩），詩人、小說家與記者，曾就讀於貝魯特黎巴嫩大學及巴黎索邦大學。他曾從事當地的左翼政治運動，年輕時因而身陷囹圄。自從成為全職作家以來，貝東著有多本詩集，作品被翻譯成各種主要的歐洲語言。他從1997年開始擔任貝魯特報紙*As-Safir*的文化版編輯。2017年，他的著作《純真的秋天》獲謝赫・扎耶德圖書大獎。

Abbas Beydoun (Lebanon) is a poet, novelist, and journalist. He studied at the Lebanese University in Beirut and the Sorbonne in Paris. He was involved in left-wing politics and spent time in jail as a young man. Since becoming a full-time writer, he has published numerous volumes of poetry. His works have been translated into all the major European languages. Since 1997, Beydoun has been cultural editor of the Beiruti newspaper *As-Safir*. In 2017, his book *Khareef al Bara'a* (The Autumn of Innocence) won the Sheik Zayed Book Award.

阿巴斯·貝東

ABBAS BEYDOUN

中文翻譯：韓譽

English translation by Khaled Mattawa

الصمت والدم

رأس مصفّف
وزهرية خالية من الورد
لم يعد في ماء القنّينة
المتروكة مفتوحةً من أمس
سوى قليل من الحياة
القماش الأسود
لا ينقشر عن كتفيها
والصمت أكثر من الدم
في هذا العنق

لم أقل شيئاً
دعيني من تقليم أصابعك
نسيت قليلاً من الصابون من خلف الأذن
لكنك بالتأكيد
لم تنسي تحت ثيابك
خيطاً واحداً

沉默與血

梳過的頭
與無花的花瓶
在從昨天就被打開、棄置的
小玻璃瓶的水裡
只剩下些許生命
黑布
脫不開她的雙肩
在這條脖頸裡
沉默比血更多

我沒有說什麼
別再在我這裡剪指甲了
我忘了耳後的一點肥皂沫
但你，一定
沒有忘記你衣服下的
一根線頭

Silence and Blood

Hair brushed and combed,
and a vase without flowers.
Little life remains
in the bottle of water left open
since yesterday.
The fabric is black
and is never peeled off her shoulders.
There is more silence than blood
in this throat.

I didn't say anything.
Leave me out of your nail clipping.
I forgot a bit of soap behind the ears.
But surely
you didn't forget to tidy up
a single thread
of your clothes.

جرح الزجاج

أنتظر في أصغر الحجرات
على أصغر الأسرّة
لست عقلة الإصبع
ولا صبي العجينة
لكنني أفكّر بذلك الجرح
في زجاج نظّارات جدتي
وطالما نسيت نظري
في قاعهما البلّوري
يختفي الجرحُ من أمامها
حين تنظر فيهما
لكنه يعذّب بصرها من وراء المشهد
ضعيفاً متلاشياً
كأنه يرقص في خيال عينيها
كانت تترك نظرها أحياناً
ينام في داخله
وأنا أتسلى بالنظر إلى شعرة الضوء
المنسلّة من بصيص القفل
وأرسل خيط بصري الرفيع
في فتحة الإبرة
أريحُ عيني في فجوة ثقبٍ
وربما أتركها تنام هناك
تتوقف عيناي في سماكة الزجاج

وحدها على الوجه
وما أسرع ما زالت
ما من عنب مدوس هنا
لكن كل رائحة فاكهة غير مسماة
فانية تماماً
أم أن من هذه اللفافات الضعيفة
ولدت قوة هذا الترمل الفظيع
التي لم نحسن إخراجها
رغم فتح النوافذ في الحجرة

كأنما أتأمل في لبّ حدقتي
ما الذي رأته الجدة؟
حين انحنت على الزجاجة
حبسة لسانها أم بصرها
تلك القطرة التي لا غور لها
والتي صُنق صوتها فيها
تلك النظرة التي لا جفون لها
نظرةُ بعد الظُهر
نظرة الكلب الذي طارد طيلة النهار
دعسات تختفي فجأة
أو المرأة الباقية على صندوق
لا يتحرك شراعه إلى أي مكان
أم السأم الذي يحتاج وجهه
إلى عيون وشفتين
ليبدي اعتذاره
ماذا رأته الجدة
حين انحنت على الزجاجة
ما الذي رأيتُه في سماكة الزجاج
حين قَلَبْتُ الوسادة
على زجهها (وجهي) الآخر
كانت هذه الحبسة

鏡片的傷痕

我等待，在最小的房間裡
在最小的床上
我不是指節
也不是賣發麵的男孩
但我想著我祖母的眼鏡
鏡片上的那道傷痕
在它倆的水晶般的底面
每當我忘記了自己的視線
往那一看
那傷痕就從正面隱去
可它從景象背後折磨著她的視野
微弱地
彷彿在她雙眼的幻想中舞蹈
有時，她讓她的眼睛
在它裡面睡去
我則看著那道光的髮絲
從鎖眼中透出
我引著我細細的視線
穿過針鼻
我讓我的眼睛在孔隙中休息
或乾脆讓它在此入睡
我的雙眼在鏡片的厚度中停留
彷彿我在端詳自己的瞳仁
當祖母低頭看那鏡片
她看到了什麼？
是語塞還是「目塞」
那顆無底的
其中扼死了她的聲音的水滴
那沒有眼皮的目光
午後的目光
這樣一條狗的目光：
它整日追蹤一道足跡
而足跡卻突然消失
或是坐在的箱子上的
女人的目光
那箱子的風帆不朝任一方向移動
或是厭倦——
厭倦的臉，需要眼睛和嘴唇
來表達它的歉意
當祖母低頭看那鏡片
她看到了什麼？
當我將枕頭
翻到它（我）的另一面
祖母在鏡片的厚度中看到了什麼？
這語塞
獨自在臉上
它消失得多快
這裡沒有葡萄被踩碎
但任何一種未命名的水果香氣
都將完全消逝
或者，在這些軟弱的包頭中
生出了這可怕寡居的力量
而我們未能將它好好釋放
儘管屋的窗戶已經打開

A Glass Wound

I wait in the smallest room
on the smallest bed.
I am not a knot if fingers …
or the dough boy,
but I'm thinking of that wound
in the lenses of my grandmother's glasses
and how long I abandoned my vision
on the crystal floor.
The wound disappears from her
when she looks through them
but it pains her vision from behind the scenes
weakening it almost extinguishing it
as if it's dancing in the imagination of her eyes.
Sometimes she lets her vision
sleep inside the wound.
I amused myself looking at that hair of light
seeping from a keyhole
and I sent the thread of my vision
through the needle's eye
resting my eyes in the enclave within
and sometimes letting them sleep there too.
My eyes paused in the thickness
as if I'm witnessing in the interior of my eyes.
What did my grandmother see
when she bent to the glass?
Was it her tongue or her vision that became held
that became a bottomless drop
in which her voice was suspended?
That lidless stare
the afternoon look
the look of a dog who all day chases
steps that suddenly disappear
or the woman that sits on a box
whose sails never flutter
or the bored man whose face needs
eyes and lips
to begin a litany of excuses.
What did my grandmother see
when she bent to that glass?
What did I see in the thickness of it
when I turned the pillow
over on its other face (my face)?
Only this pause
on her face
and how quickly it lifted
whatever grapes were crushed there.
But the scent of every unnamed fruit
vanishes completely.
And perhaps these weak twists
bore the strength of this abominable
scent we were unable to get rid of off
even though we opened all the windows.

عطر الطريق

تصلين ووجهك رطب بالعرق
الذي سينشف
قبل أن تتكون حبيباته
آخذ منديلكِ
وأشمّ تحت خصلاتك
ذلك العطر الذي فقدته على الطريق
وربما أشمّ الطريق نفسه
حين لا أرى في انكماش الجبين الخفيف
والعينين المزويتين
سوى ناصية الشارع

路的香味

你到來，汗水濕了你的臉
它會風乾
來不及結成水珠
我拿了你的手絹
在你的頭髮底下，嗅到
你在路上散去的那種香味
或是嗅到路的本身
此時，我們在微皺的額上
和低垂的眼睛中
只看到街邊的人行道

Road Perfume

You arrive, your face moist with sweat
which will dry
before its beads take shape.
I take your handkerchief
and smell under your strands
that perfume you spread on the road.
Perhaps I'll smell the road itself
where we can't see
in the slight lift of the eyebrows
and the wayward eyes
anything except a sidewalk.

رسم

القوارب مرسومة على الماء
والماء لا يتحرك
حذرا منها

畫

小舟畫在水上
水不動
因對舟的戒備

A Sketch

The boats are drawn on the water,
and the water does not move
fearing them.

غيمة

أيتها الغيمة. منذ متى لا تشبهين الشعر. منذ متى نجدك في علبة كبريت بين العيدان الميتة. ثمة ما لا نستطيع إخراجه من المنزل. ثمة ما لا نستطيع أن ننزعه من بين العينين.

雲

雲啊，從何時起你不再像詩，從何時起我們看到你在火柴盒裡，在死的火柴中間。有些東西，我們無法從家中取出。有些東西，我們無法從兩眼之間抽去。

Cloud

Cloud, how long have you not resembled poetry. How long have we found you in the match box among dead sticks. There is something we cannot take out of house. There is something we cannot pull out of our eyes.

米若什·別德日茨基（波蘭），詩人、翻譯家與地球物理學工程師。常以筆名「MLB」出版作品，是波蘭「草稿一代」最著名的詩人。他著有十多本詩集，最近一本是波蘭語和英語雙語詩集《69》(美國西風出版社)。他的詩作被翻譯成加泰羅尼亞語、捷克語、英語、德語、意大利語、斯洛文尼亞語、西班牙語和俄語，他亦將斯洛文尼亞詩人托馬斯·薩拉蒙的作品翻譯成波蘭語。別德日茨基曾獲草稿格蘭披治詩歌獎、《文化時機》最佳首本詩集獎、新趨勢詩歌獎，以及克拉科夫城市藝術獎金。

Miłosz Biedrzycki (Poland), often publishing under the pen name "MLB," is a Polish poet, translator, and geophysical engineer. One of the best known authors of the "bruLion generation." His most recent Polish–English bilingual book of poems is *69* (Zephyr Press). His poems have been translated into Catalan, Czech, English, German, Italian, Russian, Slovenian, and Spanish. He translated poetry of Tomaž Šalamun into Polish. He is the winner of the Grand Prix of bruLion Poetry Award, the Best First Book of Poetry from *Czas Kultury*, the Nowy Nurt Poetry Award, and the City of Krakow Arts Fellowship.

米若什 · 別德日茨基

MIŁOSZ BIEDRZYCKI

中文翻譯：茅銀輝

English translation by Jennifer Croft and Frank L. Vigoda

Jesteś przestrzenią, jesteś gekonem

jesteś przestrzenią, jesteś gekonem
jesteś wszystkim tylko nie prostotą i spokojem

pod parasolkami zasnuwasz niebo
pod półtajnym numerem rozsuwasz story

co zrobić z takim wynalazkiem?
zacząć od piłeczki do ping-ponga, od obcasów?

bulgoce i wre pod pokrywką
mija wrzesień, poranki chrzęszczą, to samo

utytłany czy nieutulony
wkręcałbym się w odspojone warstwy

w komorze bezechowej
spadałbym jak suchy liść.

你是空間，你是壁虎

你是空間，你是壁虎
你是一切，除了簡單與平靜

在陽傘下，你遮蔽天空
在半秘密的數字背後，你畫出陰影

用這樣的發明能做什麼？
從一個小球到乒乓球，從高跟鞋呢？

蓋子下面的淙淙聲和沸騰聲
九月的汩汩聲，晨間的爆裂聲，同樣如此

髒了或傷心的時候
我會鑽進外連接地層

在消聲室裡
我會如枯葉般飄落。

You Are Space, You Are a Gecko

you are space, you are a gecko
you are everything but simplicity and peace

under garden umbrellas you cloud the sky
behind a semi-secret number you draw apart the shades

what can you do with an invention like that?
start with the ping-pong ball, with your heels?

gurgling and seething under the lid
September burbles by, the mornings crackle, the same

soiled or inconsolable
I would burrow into out-jointed strata

in an anechoic chamber
I would fall like a dry leaf.

(Translated by Jennifer Croft)

O doniosłości klasy robotniczej

myślisz, że nie widziałem tych tysięcy mężczyzn
z początkiem każdej zmiany przemieniających się
w brudnobure E.T. w gumiakach, z nonszalancją
odbijających karty w zegarze, uchylających
hełmów przed oleodrukowych kolorów św. Barbarą
w nadszybiu. te wagoniki z węglem w telewizji
to kamuflaż (o właściwym celu kopalń się
nie mówi) większość z nich pod ziemią po prostu
ustawia się w korytarzach, twarzami na zachód,
cierpliwie, na trzy zmiany, drepczą w miejscu.
(wiewiórka biegnąc w miejscu wprawia bęben w ruch)
nie pytaj mnie więcej, jak to jest, że się Ziemia obraca.

論工人階級的卓越地位

你以為，我沒見過那數以千計的男人
從每次換班開始就會變成
穿著骯髒的E. T. 膠靴，冷漠地
打著計時卡，在升降機井裡
聖巴巴拉彩色油畫像前脫掉
安全帽。電視上滿載煤炭的礦車
只是作秀（礦山的真正目的
從來無人提及）他們大多都在地下的
礦道裡，面朝西、
耐心地，三班倒、挪著小步邁向崗位。
（就像驅動輪子轉動不停奔跑的松鼠）
別再問我，地球是如何旋轉。

On the Preeminence of the Working Class

don't you think I haven't seen those crowds of men
at the beginning of each shift turning into
colorless E.T.s in work boots, casually
punching their time cards, tipping
their hardhats before oleographs of St. Barbara
in the elevator shafts. those cars full of coal on TV
are just for show (the real purpose of mines
is never mentioned) underground most of them
simply form lines, facing west,
they patiently walk in place in three shifts
(a hamster turns the wheel by running in place)
so stop asking me how the earth rotates.

(Translated by Frank L. Vigoda)

„najgroźniejsze jest jednak powietrze"

najgroźniejsze jest jednak powietrze, ostrzegają naukowcy
100% narkomanów zaczynało od wdychania powietrza.
osiem do dwunastu razy na minutę, dwadzieścia cztery
godziny na dobę. zaledwie kilka wdechów
może prowadzić do trwałego uzależnienia. pierwszy krzyk,
nagłe, krótkie zachłyśnięcie: wkrótce nie potrafią
bez tego żyć. prochy, opiaty, idee, samochody, poczucie
wyższości, poczucie krzywdy – potrzeba tylko czasu.
brama została otwarta. odwrotu nie ma.

niektórzy z narkomanów przedstawionych w programie
już nie żyją. wczoraj przez całą noc wiał halny,
niektórzy ze starszych narkomanów wdychających powietrze
umrą na serce. bez odwrotu. nie wszyscy musimy
mieć AIDS i żebrać: łyżka nad płomieniem gazowego
palnika – wytworna business kolacja w hotelu –
przyjemne popołudnie w gronie rodziny, przed telewizorem
– gorący, suchy wiatr pędzi październikowe liście
środkiem alei –

「最危險的就是空氣」

最危險的就是空氣，科學家們發出警告，
100% 的癮君子開始吸入空氣。
一分鐘八到十二次，二十四小時
一晝夜。只需吸上幾口
就能導致永久的依賴。第一聲尖叫，
來自突然、短暫的屏息：沒有它
馬上就活不下去。藥丸，阿片類藥物，想法，汽車，
優越感，傷害感——只是時間問題。
大門一旦打開。沒有退路。

我們計劃中的一些癮君子
已經死去。昨天山風刮了一整夜
一些吸食空氣的老年癮君子
會死於心臟病。沒有回頭路。不是每個人都必須
染上艾滋病再去乞求：在煤氣爐上
的勺子——在酒店中享受一頓精緻的商務晚餐——
與家人在電視機前共度一個美好的下午，
——炎熱、乾燥的風吹起十月的葉子
在大道中間——

"the most dangerous of all is air"

the most dangerous of all is air, scientists warn
100% of addicts started out inhaling air.
eight to twelve times a minute, twenty four
hours a day. even a few inhaled doses can lead
to permanent addiction. the first cry,
a sudden short choke—and you can't
live without it. pills, opiates, ideas, cars, feelings
of superiority, of being hurt—just a matter of time.
the gate has opened. there's no return.

some of the addicts featured in our program
are already dead. a chinook blew all night.
some older air addicts will die of a heart condition.
no return. not everybody needs to have AIDS
and beg: a spoon over a gas burner—a fancy
business dinner in a hotel—a nice afternoon
with the family in front of the tv—a hot
dry wind blows October leaves
down the alley—

(Translated by Frank L. Vigoda)

„jestem nocą która nie chce się skończyć"

jestem nocą która nie chce się skończyć
gorącą i suchą aż skleja się gardło
miękkie ściany wyściełane śluzem, kurzem

jestem metrowej wysokości literami IŁAWA GŁÓWNA
trupim światłem lamp sodowych
wściekłym świstem świetlówki w korytarzu

jestem bełkotem hipisa domagającego się
trzech tysięcy na herbatę
bo psy przed chwilą go puściły

jestem psami kulącymi się w przeciągu na peronie
z oczami czerwonymi z niewyspania
z głowami w kołnierzach mundurowych kurtek

jestem stalową rzeką pod mostem
jestem dudnieniem pociągu o kratownicę mostu
jestem rtęciowymi mgłami budzącymi się po polach

jestem urwanym oknem, podróżą bez morału
jestem urwanym oknem przez które mgły wdzierają się
do środka, jestem stukotem, drogą, nocą.

「我是一個不想結束的夜晚」

我是一個不想結束的夜晚
酷熱與乾燥鎖住咽喉
柔軟的壁上佈滿了粘液與灰塵

我是一米高的字母「IŁAWA GŁÓWNA」
我是鈉燈的蒼白光芒
我是走廊裡螢光燈憤怒的口哨聲

我是嬉皮士的胡言亂語
喝杯茶被宰了三千塊錢
只因為狗剛剛走失

我是平台上蜷縮的狗
因缺乏睡眠而紅了眼睛
把頭縮在制服的衣領裡

我是橋下的鋼鐵河流
我是橋上火車的轟鳴聲
我是在田裡醒來的水銀霧

我是一扇破窗，我是一段沒有道德的旅程
我是一扇破窗，擋不住霧氣
侵襲入室，我是喧鬧聲，我是路，我是夜。

"I am a night that doesn't want to end"

I am a night that doesn't want to end
so hot and dry my throat sticks
the soft walls coated by mucus by dust

I am the giant letters IŁAWA GŁÓWNA
the ashen glow of sodium lamps
the loud buzz of a fluorescent tube in the corridor

I am the mumbling of a hippie demanding
three thousand zlotys for a cup of tea
because the pigs only just let him go

I am the pigs on the platform hunched in the wind
eyes red from lack of sleep
chins tucked in the collars of their uniforms

I am the iron-gray river under the bridge
I am the clatter of a train on the bridge's grid
I am a mercury vapor rising above the fields

I am the broken window a trip without a moral
I am the broken window that lets the fog
seep in, I am the clatter, the travel, the night.

(Translated by Frank L. Vigoda)

Hymn

plamy po owadach są przejrzystym światłem, pełnym mocy.
szczątki owadów roztrzaskanych o przednią szybę, są przejrzystym światłem.
spieniona wybojami rzeka hucząca pod mostem ciężarówki, jest przejrzystym światłem.
przedni i tylny most ciężarówki, płynące nad zakrzepłą asfaltową rzeką, są przejrzystym światłem.
wielkie zaorane pole, białe od bocianów zbierających się do lotu, jest przejrzystym światłem.
pielgrzymka idąca skrajem szosy, zakonnica z megafonem na drągu, są przejrzystym światłem.
pielgrzymi w ukośnych sznurach deszczu, zakonnica z megafonem na drągu, są przejrzystym światłem.
bociany brodzące po brunatnym polu, ściernisko odwrócone twarzą do ziemi, jest przejrzystym światłem.
dzieci sprzedające zakurzone śliwki na poboczu, są przejrzystym światłem.
napięta skóra śliwek pod nićmi deszczu, dzieci tulące się do pnia pod gęstą koroną, są przejrzystym światłem.
grobla powyżej szosy, posiekane igłami deszczu lustro stawu, jest przejrzystym światłem.

szczelina czerwonego nieba pomiędzy deszczem i horyzontem,
dwa rzędy lip odprowadzające mokry piach do horyzontu,
czerwony odblask na drutach wzdłuż szosy.

聖歌

昆蟲的污漬是純淨的光，充滿力量。
撞在擋風玻璃上的昆蟲殘骸是純淨的光。
在卡車橋下泛著泡泡的喧鬧河流是純淨的光。
在卡車橋前後，流淌著凝固柏油的河流，是純淨的光。
大片的耕地，和聚集飛行白鸛，是純淨的光。
沿著路邊行走的朝聖隊伍，舉起掛著擴音器桿子的
　　修女，是純淨的光。
冒著雨簾行走著的朝聖者，舉起掛著擴音器桿子的
　　修女，是純淨的光。
在褐色的田野裡涉水而過的鸛，倒頭向下的秸稈，
　　是純淨的光。
路邊叫賣沾滿灰塵的李子的那些孩子是純淨的光。
雨中李子緊繃的果皮，背靠茂盛樹冠下枝幹的孩子們，是純淨的光。
公路之上的堤壩，池塘被雨滴敲碎的如鏡水面，
　　是純淨的光。

雨和地平線之間相隔的紅色天空，兩排菩提樹把潮
　　濕的沙子引向地平線，沿路電線上的紅色反光。

Hymn

smears from insects are pure light full of power.
remains of smashed insects on the windshield are pure light.
the river bubbling with potholes rolling under the bridge of our truck's
　　axle is pure light.
the front and rear axles floating over the solid asphalt river are pure light.
the big ploughed field white with storks gathering for flight is pure light.
the pilgrimage walking alongside the road, the nun with a bullhorn stuck
　　on a stick are pure light.
pilgrims in sideways ribbons of rain, the nun with a bullhorn stuck on a
　　stick are pure light.
storks wading in the brown field, stubble turned face down is pure light.
children selling dusty plums on the roadside are
　　pure light.
the plums' taut skin in the ribbons of rain, the children clinging to the tree
　　trunk under its thick crown are pure light.
the dyke above the road, the pond pinpricked with rain is pure light.

the slit of red sky between the rain and horizon
two rows of lindens leading wet sand to the horizon,
the red glow on the wires alongside the road.

(Translated by Frank L. Vigoda)

安娜・布蘭迪亞娜（羅馬尼亞），詩人、散文家、人權鬥士，亦是羅馬尼亞文化界的傳奇人物。著有十八本詩集、兩本短篇小說集、七本散文和一本長篇小說，她的作品曾被翻譯成二十六種語言出版，至今選編入八十本詩歌與散文集。1990 年，布蘭迪亞娜成為公民聯盟的聯合創辦人兼主席；同年她與一眾作家成立羅馬尼亞筆會，並當選主席。在歐洲共同體的支持下，布蘭迪亞娜創製了「共產主義受害人紀念碑」（1993），並獲嘉許「歐洲文化遺產標籤」。她獲獎無數，包括赫爾德獎、歐洲自由詩人獎及格里芬詩歌基金會終身成就獎。布蘭迪亞娜為歐洲文化作出了偉大貢獻，並英勇爭取人權，於2009 年獲法國頒發最高榮譽軍團勛章，以及在2014 年獲美國國務院頒發英勇女性大獎。

Ana Blandiana (Romania) is a poet, essayist and prose writer, civic right activist, and legendary figure in Romanian culture. She has authored eighteen books of poetry, two books of short stories, seven books of essays and one novel that have been translated into twenty-six languages and grouped into eighty books of poetry and prose to date. Blandiana was the co-founder and president of the Civic Alliance from 1990. She also refounded and became the president of the Romanian PEN Club in 1990. Under the aegis of the European Community, she created the Memorial to the Victims of Communism (1993), distinguished with the European Heritage Label. Her numerous international literary prizes include the Herder Prize, the European Poet of Freedom Prize, and the Griffin Trust for Excellence in Poetry. In recognition of her contribution to European culture and her valiant fight for human rights, Blandiana was awarded the highest distinction of the French Republic, the Légion d'Honneur (2009), while the U.S. Department of State distinguished her with the Romanian Women of Courage Award (2014).

安娜．布蘭迪亞娜

ANA BLANDIANA

中文翻譯：高興

English translation by Viorica Patea

Corabia cu poeţi

Poeţii cred că e o corabie
Şi se îmbarcă.

Lăsaţi-mă să mă urc pe corabia cu poeţi
Înaintând pe valurile timpului

Fără să-şi clatine catargul
Şi fără să aibă nevoie să se mişte din loc
(Pentru că timpul se mişcă
În jurul ei tot mai repede).

Poeţii aşteaptă, şi refuză să doarmă,
Refuză să moară,
Ca să nu piardă clipa din urmă
Când corabia se va desprinde de ţărm –

Dar ce e nemurirea dacă nu
Chiar această corabie de piatră,
Aşteptând cu încăpăţânare ceva
Ce nu se va întâmpla niciodată?

詩人船

詩人們認為他們是一條船，
並紛紛登上了船。

請讓我也登上詩人船
航行於時間的浪濤上，

不必搖動桅桿，
也無需移動船身
（因為時間正在
它周圍越來越迅速地移動）。

詩人們等待著，拒絕睡眠，
拒絕死亡，
為了不錯過那個
船岸分離的瞬間——

這條石船執著地
期待著某件
永不會發生之事，
這不是不朽，又是什麼呢？

Ship of Poets

The poets think it's a ship
And they get on board.

Let me get on the ship of poets
That sails through the waves of time

Without ever rocking its mast
And without ever having to move
(Since time moves around it
Faster and faster).

The poets wait and refuse to go to sleep,
Refuse to die,
So as not to miss that final instant
When the ship departs from the shore—

But what is eternity if not
This very ship of stone,
Obstinately waiting for something
That will never happen?

Îngeri bătrâni

Îngeri bătrâni urât mirositori
Cu iz stătut în penele jilave,
În părul rar,
În pielea scămoşată de insule de psoriazis,
Hărţi scrijelate adânc
Ale unor înspăimântătoare
Tărâmuri necunoscute.
Prea trişti pentru bunevestiri,
Prea slabi pentru sabia de foc,
Se lasă-ngropaţi dormitând
Ca nişte seminţe pe care le sameni,
Cu dureri reumatice la încheieturile aripelor
Tot mai ascunse-n pământ,
Tot mai moşnegi, tot mai oameni…

老天使們

老天使們惡臭難聞，
濕乎乎的羽翼間，
稀拉拉的毛髮中，
結著一塊塊牛皮癬的皮膚上
都散發出腐朽的味道，
他們的皮膚酷似
陌生土地那一幅幅
帶著深深劃痕的地圖。
他們已過於衰老，傳不出喜訊，
他們已過於虛弱，舉不動火劍，
他們打著盹兒任由自己被埋葬，
彷彿一粒粒種子撒進土裡，
翅膀關節處，風濕病疼痛難忍，
越來越陷入泥土，
越來越老，越來越像人類……

Old Angels

Old angels, stinking
With a rank smell in their humid feathers,
In their thinning hair,
Their skin peeling off in patches of psoriasis,
Maps of terrifying
Unknown lands,
Furrowed, scored and scratched.
Too sad to bring good news,
Too thin to wield the sword of fire,
They sink half asleep into the earth,
Like seeds being planted
In the rheumatic joints of wings,
Deeper and deeper in the ground,
Older and older, more and more human…

Un cal tânăr

N-am reuşit niciodată să ştiu pe ce lume sunt.
Încălecam un cal tânăr şi fericit ca şi mine
Şi în galop îi simţeam între pulpe
Inima zvâcnind
Şi inima mea zvâcnea în galop neobosită,
Fără să observe că între timp
Şeaua mea se sprijinea
Doar pe scheletul unui cal
Care în viteză se dezmembra risipindu-se
Şi eu continuam să călăresc
Un cal tânăr de aer
Într-un secol care nu mai era al meu.

一匹年輕的馬

我始終不清楚自己身處什麼世界。
我騎上一匹年輕的馬，牠同我一樣歡快。
奔馳中，我感覺到牠的腿肚間
那顆熱烈跳動的心。
我的心也在奔馳中熱烈跳動，不知疲倦，
絲毫也沒有注意到，不知不覺中
我的馬鞍只支撐在
馬的骨骼上，
急速中，那匹馬早已解體，揮發，
而我繼續騎著
一匹空氣之馬，
在一個並不屬於我的世紀裡。

A Young Horse

I've never figured out what world I live in.
I rode on a horse as young and as happy as I.
When he galloped I could feel his heartbeat
Against my thighs
And my heart pounded, unquenchable, with the speed.
Everything flashing by, I didn't even notice
That my saddle was resting
On the bones of a horse
That was rapidly falling to pieces on the trail
And that I was still riding
On a young horse made of air
In a century that wasn't my own anymore.

Animal Planet

Mai nevinovată, dar nu nevinovată,
În acest univers în care
Înseşi legile firii hotărăsc
Cine trebuie să ucidă pe cine
Şi cel ce ucide mai mult este rege:
Cu ce admiraţie este filmat
Leul placid şi feroce sfârtecând căprioara,
Iar eu, închizând ochii sau televizorul,
Am senzaţia că particip la crimă mai puţin,
Deşi ştiu că-n opaiţul vieţii
Trebuie pus mereu sânge,
Sângele altuia.

Mai nevinovată, dar nu nevinovată,
Am stat la masă cu vânători,
Deşi îmi plăcea să mângâi urechile lungi
Şi mătăsoase ale iepurilor
Asvârliţi, ca pe un catafalc, pe faţa de masă brodată.
Vinovată, chiar dacă nu eu apăsam pe trăgaci
Ci-mi astupam urechile, oripilată de zgomotul morţii
Şi de mirosul sudorii neruşinate a celor ce-au tras.
Mai nevinovată, dar nu nevinovată,
Totuşi mai nevinovată decât tine,
Autorul acestei perfecţiuni fără milă,
Care ai hotărât totul
Si apoi m-ai învăţat să întorc şi celălalt obraz.

動物星球

罪孽少些，但並非沒有罪孽，
在這個宇宙中
自然法則本身決定
誰必須殺死誰，
殺戮最多者是國王；
獅子沉著、殘忍地撕咬小鹿
人們拍攝這一鏡頭，興致勃勃，
而我，閉上眼睛，關上電視，
感覺自己參與犯罪少了點，
雖然我明白在生命的油燈裡
總得不斷添加血液，
他人的血液。

罪孽少些，但並非沒有罪孽，
我和獵手們坐在一起，
雖然我喜歡撫摸兔子長長的
絲一般的耳朵，那些兔子
被扔在繡花桌布上，就像被棄於靈柩檯上。
我是有罪的，即便我沒有扣動扳機，
即便在死亡噪音和兇手無恥的汗味中
我驚恐萬分，捂上了耳朵。
罪孽少些，但並非沒有罪孽，
不管怎樣，罪孽肯定比你少些，
無情的盡善盡美的作者，
是你決定了一切，
然後又教我轉過另一側面頰。

Animal Planet

Less guilty, though not innocent,
In this universe where
The laws of nature decide
Who should kill whom
And whoever kills most is king.
How admiringly they film
The placid and ferocious lion as it tears a fawn
to pieces!
And whenever I close my eyes or switch off the telly,
I feel that I participate less in the crime,
Even though the candle of life
Will always need blood to go on burning—
The blood of another.

Less guilty, though not innocent,
I sat at table with the hunters,
Nevertheless, I loved to caress the long and silky
Ears of hares
Lying in stacks. Like a tumulus
On top of an embroidered tablecloth.
Guilty, even though I didn't
Pull the trigger,
And I covered my ears
Horrified by the sound of death
And by the smell of the shameless sweat of the hunters that fired the shots.

Less guilty, though not innocent,
In any case more innocent than you,
The author of this pitiless perfection,
Who set up this design
And afterward, taught me to turn the other cheek.

Alb pe alb

Scriu cu alb pe alb
Deși știu că nimeni
Nu va putea să citească,
Nici chiar eu,
După ce voi fi uitat ce am scris.
Binele este întotdeauna
Greu de înțeles –
E mai ușor să accepți un eres
În paradis
Decât o jertfă benevolă omenească.

Mă încăpățânez
Să scriu alb pe alb
Deși mi se spune
Să folosesc cel puțin
Litere cu sclipici,
Când desenez ramuri de măslin
Sau fapte bune
Plictisitoare.

Dar,
Acum și aici
Nu am decât o culoare
Care poate
Să le cuprindă pe toate
Și scriu cu alb pe alb
În zadar.

白上白

我用白寫在白上，
雖然我知道誰也
無法閱讀，
包括我，
在忘了寫的什麼之後。
善總是
難以理喻——
在天堂，你更容易
接受罪孽
而非人類心甘情願的犧牲。

我堅持不懈地
用白寫在白上，
雖然人們建議我
至少使用
螢光字母，
在我描畫橄欖枝
或者令人厭倦的
好事的時候。

然而，
此時，此地，
我只有一種顏色，
一種包含
全部顏色的顏色，
而我還在徒勞地
用白寫在白上。

White on White

I write in white on white
Though I know nobody
Can read it,
Not even myself,
When I've forgotten what I wrote.
Good is always
Hard to understand—
It's easier to accept a blunder
Up in heaven
Than a noble human sacrifice.

I insist on writing
In white on white
Even if they tell me
To use bright
Letters at least,
When I sketch out olive boughs
Or boring
Good deeds.

However,
Here and now
I've just one color that contains
All the rest and I
Write in white on white
In vain.

鍾國強（香港），香港大學文學院畢業。曾獲多屆香港中文文學雙年獎、青年文學獎、中文文學創作獎、香港藝術發展獎藝術家年獎（文學藝術）等獎項。著有詩集《圈定》、《路上風景》、《門窗風雨》、《城市浮游》、《生長的房子》、《只道尋常》、《開在馬路上的雨傘》、《雨餘中一座明亮的房子》，散文集《兩個城市》、《記憶有樹》、《字如初見》，小說集《有時或忘》，文學評論集《浮想漫讀》等。

Derek Chung (Hong Kong) graduated from the Faculty of Arts of the University of Hong Kong. His numerous accolades include Hong Kong Biennial Awards for Chinese Literature, Youth Literary Awards, Awards for Creative Writing in Chinese, as well as Artist of the Year (Literary Arts) of Hong Kong Arts Development Awards. He has published many poetry collections, including *Delineation*, *Scenery on the Road*, *Doors and Windows and Wind and Rain*, *Urban Plankton*, *A Growing House*, *Nothing Unusual*, *An Umbrella Opened on the Road*, and *A Bright House in Residual Rain*; essay collections *Two Cities*, *Trees in Memory*, and *Words at First Sight*; novel collection *Sometimes One May Forget*; as well as literary critique *Floating Thoughts, Unrestrained Reading*.

鍾國強

DERREK CHUNG

English translation by Tammy Lai-Ming Ho

水井

那是老家瞪向天空的一隻眼睛
我親眼看見工人把泥從裡面掏出來
濕濕黃黃，黏黏纏纏，然後便有了水
從地層深處源源滲出，瞬間浸滿了
眼眶。我把木桶垂下，一把回聲
恍若恍若，迴旋著漣淪一圈一圈
向聚散的游雲，說另一世界的話

那是桌上一杯水，靜止，陰沉
玻璃杯沿像井口的圍欄，我趨前
呼出的氣息轆轤而下，貼著苔綠的內壁
停在影子幢幢的水面。周遭沒有一絲風
但我感到水的清冷，沿我的內壁源源滲下
於是透明，看見底層微微挪動的物質

我在支流裡停止，兩旁新舊的樓房在蹲看
一輛巴士夾在前面的路口，交警的白手套揮舞
在黑壓壓蓄勢翻湧的頭顱之上，像無人注意的一絲浪花
身邊的人向天張大了口，沒有聲音，沒有手勢
文字像遠年的苔蘚，滲出古綠的顏色。我閱讀著
這城市的內壁，滑到最深最深的地方，又從那裡緩緩攀升
河水流動。壩下的水捲起了漩渦。黑色的水有白色的泡沫
我們在石上蹲著，用鎚子，有節奏地鎚打枯枝似的魚藤
滲出奶白色的汁液，流進底下錚錚錝錝的繁響裡
於是在堤岸不遠，我們看見仰向天空的魚肚白
像浮沉著的陰雲，偶然兩邊翻動，展示著死亡和希望

我們擠過了瓶頸，三股支流匯成一道大河
有人用擴音器捕獵憤怒，有人在計算收成
有人張大了口，發出別人的聲音
河水越流越洶湧，陽光猛烈
直射河的最底層，沉著已久的淤泥和污砂
翻湧上升，邊緣閃著耀眼的光芒

我把一尾尾暈眩的魚撈起，放進河灘上的草簍
有些魚擱淺在石上，在草桿間掙扎翻身
我看著那些翕動的嘴巴，彷彿聽到牠們的聲音
在輪迴吐放的一個一個泡沫裡。我把一尾活像喝醉的魚
隔開，放進一隻盛著清水的小木桶裡
看牠勉力將肚子翻過來，如翻動一塊古遠的泥磚
一座搖搖欲墜的房子，一個被撂下的行囊
回家吃過鮮美的魚粥，吐著細細的
骨刺，便見牠在小木桶裡悠悠醒轉

河水流到下游，又迂迴分叉湧向四面八方的淺灘
有人傲立河岸，像口號不斷升高，在幢幢商廈間不斷迴響
天空在窗洞裡默覷，堤壩在聲音裡顫抖，泡沫在爆破
我看到聲音，看到聲音裡面巨大的沉默，如一張一張魚的嘴巴

我想把魚放回河裡，但河裡也不是美好的所在
我想把魚放進瓦煲裡，但我們吃魚還不夠嗎？

河水的聲音在身後響起，在身邊響起，在身前響起
蓋過草桿旁的漪淪，石隙間的呼息，泥巴上的鱗屑
簍筐裡的血絲。當河水染成氣球，岸上便有人宣告
聽，請聽，請聽河裡一把碩大無朋涵蓋一切的聲音

我雙手把魚捧到井口，向著一個深邃的影子
放下，然後靜靜聆聽，遠遠，一個，只屬於那魚的，回聲

我們都在發出聲音嗎？誰在聆聽？一道偉大行進的河
浩浩蕩蕩，沖激著堤岸，發出水井永遠發不出的聲音

我想像那魚，在老房子旁的水井裡，孤獨地轉悠身體
彷彿一隻鱗閃的眼睛，瞪著魚肚白的天空

2003 年 7 月 17 日

The Well

It's the old home's eye glaring at the sky
My own eyes see workers scooping out mud
Wet, yellow, sticky and tangled, then the water comes
Oozing from the deep earth, in an instant soaking
The eye's rim. I lower the wood bucket, and an echo
Speaks—as though, as though, circling round and round—
Another world's language to the passing clouds that gather and disperse

It's a glass of water on the table, still, gloomy
Its rim is like the well's fence, and I lean forward
My breath going down the windlass, sticking to the moss-green inner walls
And resting on the water where shadows flicker. Everywhere is windless
Yet I feel the chill of the water seep down my insides
So translucent, the substances below are seen to slightly wriggle

I stop at a tributary, old and new buildings squatting and watching from
    both sides
A bus stuck at the junction ahead, the traffic officer's white gloves waving
On a dark and surging skull, like an unnoticed ripple
Those beside me open their mouths to the sky, no voice,
    no gestures
Writing like moss from years ago, leaking ancient green. I read
The inner walls of this city, slide to its deepest place, then unhurriedly
    climb up

The river flows. The water below the dam rolls into whirls. Black water makes white
    foam
We squat on rocks, rhythmically hammering jewelvine like dead branches
The liquid oozing out is milky, and joins the complicated sounds beneath
Not far from the embankment, where white fish maw faces the sky
Like the dark clouds drifting along, its two sides occasionally stirring, revealing
    death and hope

We squeeze through the bottleneck, three tributaries converging into one great
    river
Someone hunts wrath with a loudspeaker, someone counts his harvest
Someone opens his mouth wide, and the voice is that of another
The river surges up, fierce sunlight
Directly reaching the river's lowest part, long sedimented sludge and filth
Rolling and rising up, edges shining bright

I dredge up the dizzy fish one by one, putting them in reed baskets on the beach
Some are stranded on the rocks, some struggle to turn over between grass stalks
I watch their mouths open and close, as if I could hear their voices
In the reincarnated bubbles. I separate one drunk-looking fish
From the others, placing it in a small wood bucket full of clear water
I watch it try to flip onto its stomach like turning an ancient brick
A crumbling house, a left-behind travel bag
Eating fresh fish congee at home, spitting out tiny
Bones, I see the fish languidly wake up, turning in the bucket

Downstream, the river divides circuitously into shallows that lead in all
  directions
Someone stands proudly on the riverbank, rising like a slogan echoing
  endlessly among office buildings
The sky observes window gaps in silence, dams tremble in sounds, bubbles
  burst
I see sounds, and see vast reticence in sounds, like the mouths of fish

I want to return the fish to the river, but the river is no fine place
I want to cook it in the clay pot, but have we not eaten enough fish?

The sounds of the river ring behind me, beside me,
  before me,
Overwhelming the ripples by the grass, the breaths in stone cracks, the
  scales on the mud
The wisps of blood in the basket. When the river is dyed balloons, someone
  on the shore will announce
Listen, please listen, listen to the river's thunderous sound, it encompasses
  everything

I cup the fish to the mouth of the well, toward a deep shadow
Put it in, and listen silently, as far away, the echo—the only echo—of one
  solitary fish

Are we all making sounds like that? Who is listening? A great river in
  motion
Majestic, crashing into embankments, creates a sound that wells could
  never make

And I imagine that fish, turning alone in the well by the
  old house
like a glistening eye, glaring at the sky as white as fish maw

17 July 2013

抽屜

那是一方僅容肉身的抽屜
從來沒有長大，從不陷進泥土
也毋需澆水；白天他穿梭於街巷
從瞎忙著的人群背後欠身而過
晚上拖著像掏空了的軀幹回去
插進一個亮著霓燈的，油膩的
把陰深的廊道完全敞開的裸身

他進出辦公室，商場，後巷和公廁
把一疊凌亂的A4紙抖開又閉合
沒有人看見內容，支票和輔幣
自動轉賬往他滿是刻痕的內壁
醫生從中摘掉三道疤，四顆瘜肉
銀行取回曾經承諾的數字，舊情人
刮去所有紀念日的紋身，和風景

沒有風景，便是閉合的，光潔的靈魂
他試圖擱在沙灘，斜靠在露天咖啡座
在戲院內遮擋別人的視線，在一樓一
讓年華還未完全老去的鳳姐無從下手
他努力擠出無可無不可的笑容
忙於吃，喝，排出一整族壁虎的乾屍
和依然保持體溫的，鮮軟的蟑螂卵

他瞪著肚臍的匙孔想像不曾有過的鑰匙
他試圖坦白，別人卻往他的身上丟零錢
試圖隱藏，埋在門牌的亂崗如失憶的墓碑
直至發覺自己忽然插不進昨夜的廊道
頹然跌進大街，剛好給一輛貨櫃車輾過
並來得及讓螢紅的尾燈照見什麼也沒有的
木質，展現一截一截仿如人體的肌理

2012年9月12日

The Drawer

It's a drawer that only holds flesh
It never grows, or sinks into soil
It needs no watering; during the day he passes through streets and alleys
Walking behind the purposelessly preoccupied crowd
At night he drags his emptied-out body back
And plugs it into a lit neon lamp, greasily
Opening his complete nakedness to the deep dark corridor

He walks in and out of offices, malls, back lanes and public toilets
Shaking out and closing a pile of disarrayed A 4 paper
No one sees their content, the cheques and coins
Transfer automatically to his scar-covered wall
The doctor pulls down three scabs and four adenomatous polyps
The bank retrieves the once promised figures, former lovers
Scrape off all their memorial tattoos and scenery

No scenery, only closed, cleansed souls
He tries to stand on the beach, recline in an open-air café
Block another's line of sight in the cinema, in a one-woman brothel
The hooker hanging onto the last of her youth can't lay her hands on him
He tries hard to squeeze out smiles that are neither here nor there
And busies himself eating, drinking, discharging a whole race of gecko corpses
And still warm, fresh and soft cockroach eggs

He stares at the keyhole on his stomach imagining a key that was never there
He attempts to be honest, but others throw coins at him
Attempts to hide the disorderly mound buried in his door plate like an
amnesiac tombstone
Until he notices he can no longer fit into last night's corridor
Disappointed, he falls in the street, where a truck runs him over
Just in time for the glowing red tail lights to shine on nothing
The wood displaying sections of body-like texture

12 September 2012

雨餘中一座明亮的房子

—— 向畢曉普（Elizabeth Bishop）的六節詩致敬

雷聲最響的時候也沒有驚動樹上的黃皮
雨水溜過一顆一顆，在末端凝聚重量
然後在失神的一刻倏然墜落，好像日子
逐一碎散。母親抬頭，還是聽不到任何聲音
偶然提起右手，顫顫指劃眼前的房子
像要在早前歷歷的怖慄中，重塑一個夢

母親那時仍堅持說，床邊的黑衣人絕不是夢
蝙蝠即使顛倒了日夜，黃皮依然是黃皮
她要提防纍纍的記憶逐一遠離房子
於是為菜肴下更多的鹽，為碗碟添加重量
不斷往返園門，撿回碎石與落葉的聲音
鎖起來，像月曆上，一個一個圈著的日子

父親又再重述，母親年輕時待在家鄉的日子
柴在灶裡，棺在樑上，糙米蒸出夾縫中的夢
那時母親剛學曉寫姓名，來信，須旁人讀出聲音
然後滯留廣州，蟬鳴過後，樹上還是酸澀的黃皮
抓一把泥，雨水中也不知增添多少重量
然後是磚牆，古得發綠，孤獨也像家鄉的土房子

如今這裡的十三呎半，也層層疊疊得有若那房子
田地在下，禽畜在中，根與血相連的那些日子
疊加一桌桌菜肴與狼藉，以及人散後空桌的重量
「去，去，去！」父親偶然也轉述母親的開口夢

然後給雷聲隱去，樹上是連飢鳥也不再吃的黃皮
在雨水中，諦聽園門內外，也只有雨水的聲音

母親回來的時候，像沒有回來般不發任何聲音
水井的漣淪也沒動，雨痂也沒有走進房子
然後電飯煲按了掣，蒜出香，箕側翻出一顆黃皮
然後是沒有剝離的咀嚼，連皮帶肉的日子
然後是清水，渠溝，碗歸碗碟歸碟，一床無夢
離去的步履也像回來，沒有增添更多重量

雷聲最響的時候天空有沒有一定的重量
打在人間？抽屜突然打開了，沒有聲音
照片冊也打開了，人工的描色褪回黑白的夢
一襲一襲都是黑衣人，穿過衣櫃，揹起房子
揹起那些不易走過也已走過的日子
走遠，成一道灰色的山線，淡去，一如黃皮

「帶回去吧。」夢中母親捧出剛摘的飽滿的黃皮聲音中有雨水的味
　　道，風雷光影交相鬱積的日子
是要繼續承載那重量嗎？雨餘中一座明亮的房子

2016年2月20日

A Bright House After Rain

—In honour of Elizabeth Bishop's "Sestina"

The loudest thunder cannot shake the tree's wampees
Rain passes through them one after another, endpoints gathering weight
To suddenly fall at a distracted moment, like days
Shattered one by one. Mother looks up, hearing no sound
By chance raising her right hand, and points tremblingly at the house
As though from former terror she reinvents a dream

Mother insists the bedside man dressed in black is not a dream
Even if bats reverse day and night, wampees stay wampees
She guards against accumulated memories leaving the house
So adds more salt to the food, and to the plates more weight
Constantly returning to the garden gate, she picks up stone and leaf sounds
To lock them up like a calendar's circled days

Father once again recounts how, when young, Mother kept to her village days
Firewood in the stove, coffins on the beams, brown rice steaming crevice dreams
Mother had just learnt to write her name, still needed someone to make her letters sounds
Then she was delayed in Guangzhou, after the cicadas sang, on the tree still bitter wampees
Grab some mud, who knows how much the rain has added weight
Then brick walls, so ancient they're green, as lonesome as a village earthen house

Now these thirteen and a half square feet, stacked up like that house
Field on the ground floor, poultry in the middle, roots and blood linked in those days
Disorderly dishes piled up; people dispersing after meals, leaving behind the empty tables' weight
"Go, go, go!" Sometimes Father relays mother's words in her dreams
Drowned out by thunder, even hungry birds on the tree won't eat those wampees
In the rain, listening carefully in and out of the garden, only rain sounds

When Mother returns, as though she had never returned—there's no sound
The ripples in the well don't stir, rain scabs don't enter the house
The rice cooker's on, the scent of garlic, in the winnow basket is a wampee
Chewing it without peeling off its skin, skin and flesh were one in those days
Then clear water, gutter, bowls returning to bowls, plates to plates, a bed without dreams
Footsteps of departure like those of returning, no added weight

When the thunder is loudest does the sky add any weight
To this world? The drawer is suddenly open, no sounds
The photo album is open, the artificial colouring fades into black and white dreams
All dressed in black going through the closet and carrying the house
Carrying those difficult bygone days
Walking far, forming a grey mountain line, fading like a wampee

"Take these home." Mother in the dream takes out the just-plucked plump
wampees
Her sound tastes of rain; wind, thunder, light, and shadows interweave on
stagnant days
Do I continue to bear the weight? After the rain, a bright house

20 February 2016

路易絲·杜普蕾（加拿大），作家和文學評論家。生於魁北克省，現居蒙特利爾。著有超過二十本書籍，其中十二本為詩集，獲獎無數。其詩集《高於火焰》和《縈魂之手》均獲得加拿大文學界的重要榮譽「總督獎」。杜普蕾是魁北克文學院院士和加拿大皇家協會院士。2014年12月，杜普蕾獲頒加拿大最高榮譽勛章，以表彰她作為詩人、小説家、劇作家、散文家與教授，對魁北克文學作出的偉大貢獻。

Louise Dupré (Canada) is writer and literary critic who was born in the province of Quebec and lives in Montreal. She has published more than twenty books, including twelve collections of poetry, which received many awards. Both *Plus haut que les flammes* (Beyond the Flames) and *La main hantée* (The Haunted Hand) won the prestigious Governor General's Award for poetry. Dupré is member of the Academy of Letters of Quebec and of the Royal Society of Canada. In December 2014, she was appointed to the Order of Canada for her contributions to Quebec literature as a poet, novelist, playwright, essayist, and professor.

路易絲．杜普蕾

LOUISE DUPRÉ

中文翻譯：樹才

English translation by Antonio D'Alfonso

Plus haut que les flammes (Extraits)

Et tu veux apprendre
à danser

sur la corde calcinée
des mots

te voici pur vouloir
pur dessein, détermination
violente

lancée
comme une flèche

ou un amour
trop vaste pour toi

te voici prête
à danser
par-delà ta peur

aveugle et sourde
aux craquements de tous les ciels

qui se sont cassés
depuis que tu sais lire

(...)

tu danses, l'enfant
collé contre tes seins

vous dansez
jusqu'à l'étourdissement
du jour

vous dansez la danse
comme une profession
de foi

une charité bien ordonnée

une supplication de fleurs
qui attendent
chez les marchands

un peu d'eau
pour les accueillir

tu crois le temps
venu
de consoler

la chair inconsolable
de cette douleur

que tu n'as jamais su
où loger
en toi

sinon en une faute
renaissant à chaque naissance

comme un appel
surgissant de la terre
ancestrale

lorsqu'elle se décide
à recracher ses entrailles

(...)

tu danses le jour
jusqu'à la grandeur de l'enfant
dans tes bras

ses questions déjà
blessées

et ton amour
qui ne pourra jamais répondre

tu n'as pas de leçon
à donner

pas de terre à promettre

tu n'es pas prophète
et tu le sais

seule une mendiante
de bonheurs

sans cesse tordus
comme des bouches
rouge Francis Bacon

une météorologue
aux aguets

dans l'œil d'un cyclone

si puissant qu'il peut arracher
les arbres et les rêves

mais tu te tiens droite
et tu danses

avec ces papillons
cachés dans ton cœur

à défaut de trouver
d'autres refuges

te voici assez forte
pour accueillir en toi

le monde
à jamais endeuillé

le porter, le bercer
aussi longtemps que tu vivras

malgré ton cœur
tropical
tu as encore assez de rythme

pour faire valser l'enfant
au centre du cyclone

car ici le temps
est bleu et nuit
avec étoiles

et tu veux voir
haut

plus haut que le mur
de ton œil

tu veux voir là où les visages
ressemblent encore
à des visages

et les villes, à des phrases
qui ne périssent plus
entre les lèvres

il y a bien une syntaxe
pour parler doux

au fin fond
de ton souffle blessé

ou devant les pierres
tombales

quand le sol devient si friable
que les morts se mettent à remuer
dans leur voix

tu peux alors entendre
se détacher
la plainte du monde

comme une physique
de la douleur

une science
à comprendre

avant tes dernières images

malgré ton cœur tropical
tu n'es pas trop vieille

pour la leçon
des vents qui t'encerclent

ils t'encerclent
mais tu danses

avec l'enfant et l'espoir fou
de répondre
au murmure de la terre

la terre n'attend pas
le repentir ni la prière

elle veut retrouver le cycle
des semailles
et des moissons

et l'eau humble
jetée sur le printemps

et les onctions en spirales
sur la tête des nouveau-nés

même tremblant, un geste
ressuscite parfois
la chair des mots

étouffés
sous la poussière

comme un testament
de l'ombre

que tu graverais
dans ta propre chair

la mémoire des morts
cherche une demeure

elle te demande
à boire
et à danser

et tu la fais valser
avec l'enfant

enivré par la joie
de ces cercles

que tu veux agrandir

jusqu'à ébranler
les parois indestructibles
de ta peur

peu importe la possible
vengeance des vents
ou des volcans

peu importe ta fatigue

dans tes bras
il y a l'enfant qui te regarde

et même sans bravoure
tu deviens une femme
de courage

une femme de fenêtres ouvertes

capable de déborder
le jour

tes os sont plus solides
que tu ne crois

ils ne te trahissent pas encore

et tu ne trahiras pas
le monde minuscule
accroché à ton cou

comme un mystère
qui t'implore
en riant

de continuer
à danser

高於火焰（節選）

而你想學
跳舞

在詞語的燒焦的
繩子上

瞧，你純粹的
心願，純粹的
打算，強悍的
決心

飛出去
像一支箭

或一場愛
太大了——對你

瞧，你已準備好
跳舞
克服那盲目的

無聲的恐懼
在天空的咔嚓聲中

天空斷裂
你聽得見

（……）

你跳舞，孩子
貼緊你的乳房

你們跳舞
直到讓白晝
暈頭轉向

你們跳著舞
像一次信仰的
立誓

一份命令好的慈悲

眾花的一種懇求
它們在商店裡
等待

一點點水
為了迎接

你相信
是時候了
去撫慰

這無從撫慰的肉體
這份痛楚

你從未弄明白
在你身上
它居於何處

或者居於某個錯誤
一次次重生

像一聲召喚
突然從祖先的土地
竄出

當土地下決心
再次吐出肺腑

（……）

你在白晝跳舞
直到孩子長大
在你的懷抱

他的問題
已經受傷

而你的愛
它無從回答

你沒有教訓
可給

沒有福地可許

你不是先知
這你知道

只是一個
幸福的乞討者

不停地扭曲
像一些嘴
紅色的弗朗西斯・培根

像一個氣象工作者
窺視

從一隻颶風的眼裡

颶風足以
扯斷樹和夢想

但你站得筆直
你跳舞

憑著藏在心間的
這些蝴蝶

因為找不到
別的避難所

瞧，你足夠強大
去迎接你身上的

世界
絕不哀傷

承載它，搖晃它
同你的生命活得一樣長

儘管你的心
熱烈
你仍有足夠的節奏

讓孩子在颶風中心
飛舞

因為此地時間
是藍色的，夜晚
攜著星星

而你想看到
高處

高於你眼瞳的
牆壁

你想看見那兒
那些臉仍然
同一些臉相似

而城市，像一些句子
不再在嘴唇之間
沉沒

一定有一種語法
把話說得溫柔

在你受傷的呼吸的
最幽微處

或者在滾落的
石頭前

當地面變得易碎
死者竟開始搖晃
在他們的聲音中

於是你聽到
對世界的怨言
脫落

像一具
痛苦的身體

像一門
可理解的科學

用你最後的形象

儘管你的心熱烈
你還不是太老——

可以給圍繞你的風
上一課

風圍繞你
你跳著舞

同孩子一起
同應答大地呢喃的
瘋狂的希望一起

大地不等待
內疚或祈禱

它想找回
播種和收穫的
節氣

還有撒向春天的
謙卑的水

還有抹在新生兒頭上
螺旋形的聖油

即使顫抖，一個手勢
仍然激活
詞語的身體

這些詞語窒息
在塵土下

像影子的
一份遺囑

你把它
刻進自己的肉裡

死者的記憶
尋找一處居所

它要求你
渴飲
跳舞

你讓它
同孩子一起旋轉

被這些人群的圓圈
所迷醉

你還想擴大圓圈

直到搖撼
你那恐懼的
無法摧毀的牆壁

不重要——
風或火山的
可能的復仇

不重要——

你疲憊的手臂
孩子正瞧著你

即使不英勇
你也成了
一位有勇氣的女性

一位敞開窗口的女性

有能力突破
白晝

你的骨頭比你想像的
更結實

它們還沒有背叛你

而你也沒有背叛
懸掛在你脖子上的
微形世界

像一種神秘
它笑著
挖掘你

Beyond the Flames (Excerpts)

And you want to learn
to dance

on the charred rope
of words

here you are sheer will power
sheer goal, violent
determination

soaring
like an arrow

or love
too vast for you

here you are
ready to dance
beyond your fears

blinded and deaf
to the creaking in every sky

that collapsed
as soon as you knew how to read

(...)

you are dancing
the child against you breast

you are dancing
till the day
becomes dizziness

you are dancing a dance
that is proof
of faith

well organized charity

plea of plants
waiting
in the flower shop

a few ounces of water
to welcome the petals

you believe this is
a time
for comforting

the inconsolable flesh
of this grief

you have not been able
to place
in you

is not as a fault
reborn with each birthing

like a calling
surging from the ancestral
earth

as it vomits
its bowels

(...)

you keep dancing in the daytime
until the child in your arms
achieves greatness

his questions already
hurting

and your love
can never find an answer

you have neither advice
to give

nor earth to offer as promise

you are no prophet
and you know it

you're a beggar
of joy

twisted and twisted
like Francis Bacon's
red mouths

a meteorologist
on the look-out

in the eye of the hurricane

powerful ripping
out trees and dreams

but you will not tip over
and you keep dancing

with butterflies
hidden in your heart

for they found
no other place of safety

and you are strong
enough to welcome

the world
in perpetual mourning

which you carry and cradle
until you die

in spite of your tropical
heart
you have the rhythm it takes

to waltz this child
in the eye of the hurricane

time here
is blue and night
has stars

and you want to glimpse
up

above the walls
inside your eyes

and see the place where
faces are still
faces

and cities where sentences
survive beyond
your lips

there surely exists a syntax
for the language of softness

deep inside
your hurting breath

and beyond
tomstones

where the soil is fragile
and the dead awaken
and their voices

you hear
rising above
the complaints of humankind

like a physics
of pain

a science
memorized

prior to images fading within you

in spite of your tropical heart
you are not old encugh

to learn the teachings
of the winds that circle around you

the winds circling
around you dancing

with this child and wild hope
provides answers
to earth's murmurings

the earth waiting for
neither repentance nor prayer

as it returns to cycle
of seed
harvest

and humble water
poured over the spring season

circling as unction oil
on the forehead of the newborn

though frightened a hand
can resuscitate
the flesh of words

smothered
by dust

like a testament
of shadow

that you engraved
on your own flesh

the memory of the dead
needs a home

and memory asks you
for water
and a dance

and you invite it
to waltz with you and the child

drunk with joy
and the twirling

you widen

as you break
the unbreakable walls
of you fear

though the wind
and the volcanoes
might wreak vengeance on you

though you are exhauted

in your arms
there is a child looking into your eyes

even if you are not brave
you become a woman
of courage

a woman of open windows

who lets
the day boil over

you have bones stronger
than you imagined

that have not betrayed you

like you will never betray
the small universe
hanging from your neck

for here is mystery
laughing
begging you

never to stop
the dance

弗羅斯特．甘德（美國），作家與翻譯家，擁有地質學和英語文學學位，曾於哈佛大學任教，現為布朗大學 A. K. Seaver 文學藝術與比較文學榮休教授。他的著作《來自世界的核心樣本》反思了我們跟外國接觸時如何被修繕和翻譯，這本書入選普立茲獎的最終名單以及全美書評界大獎。他的詩集《陪伴》贏得2019 年普立茲獎。甘德翻譯了大量拉丁美洲和西班牙作家的著作，合作翻譯過日本詩人野村喜和夫和吉增剛造的詩集，並致力於推廣多多、歐陽江河和翟永明等當代中國詩人的英譯本。

Forrest Gander (United States) is a writer and translator with degrees in geology and English literature. He taught at Harvard University and is now the A. K. Seaver Professor Emeritus of Literary Arts and Comparative Literature at Brown University. Gander's book *Core Samples from the World*, a meditation on the ways we are revised and translated in encounters with the foreign, was a finalist for the Pulitzer Prize and the National Book Critics Circle Award. His collection *Be With* won 2019 Pulitzer Prize. Gander has translated many books by writers from Latin America and Spain, co-translated books by Japanese poets Nomura Kiwao and Yoshimasu Gozo, and promoted English translations of books by Duo Duo, Ouyang Jianghe, Zhai Yongming, and other contemporary Chinese poets.

弗羅斯特·甘德

FORREST GANDER

中文翻譯：宋子江

Son

It's not the mirror that is draped but
what remains unspoken between us. Why

say anything about death, inevitability, how
the body comes to deploy the myriad worm

as if it were a manageable concept not
searing exquisite singularity? To serve it up like

a eulogy or a tale of my or your own
suffering. Some kind of self-abasement.

And so we continue waking to a decapitated sun and trees
continue to irk me. The heart of charity

bears its own set of genomes. You lug a bacterial swarm
in the crook of your knee, and through my guts

writhe helminth parasites. Who was ever only themselves?
At Leptis Magna, when your mother and I were young, we came across

statues of gods with their faces and feet cracked away by vandals. But
for the row of guardian Medusa heads. No one so brave to deface those.

When she spoke, when your mother spoke, even the leashed
greyhound stood transfixed. I stood transfixed.

I gave my life to strangers; I kept it from the ones I love.
Her one arterial child. It is just in you her blood runs.

兒子

並不是因為被遮起的鏡子，而是
因為我們之間仍有話未說。為何

要說死亡，此定然之事？為何
要說身體如何驅使無數蠕蟲

彷彿它是一個能夠把握的概念，而不是
令人燒心斷腸的實質？將之奉上，猶如

一篇悼詞或一個故事，關於我或你的
煎熬。這是某種自我貶抑。

如是我們繼續醒來面對被斬首的太陽和樹叢
繼續令我惱火。慈善的心臟

承受自己那組基因。你膝蓋的彎曲處
拖著洶湧的菌群，寄生蟲蠕動翻滾

穿過我的腸胃。有誰曾全然活出自我？
在大萊普提斯，你母親和我年輕時，看到

眾神的雕像，臉和腳都被破壞了。但是
那列美杜莎護衛的頭則無人膽敢抹污。

當她說話，當你的母親說話，就連拴著繩的
灰狗也會受驚呆立。我也會受驚呆立。

我把生命交給陌生人；不讓它接近所愛。
兒子，她唯一的血脈。只有在你身上，她的血才流淌。

Beckoned

At which point my grief-sounds ricocheted outside of language.

Something like a drifting swarm of bees.

At which point in the tetric silence that followed

I was swarmed by those bees and lost consciousness.

At which point there was no way out for me either.

At which point I carried on in a semi-coma, dreaming I was awake,

avoiding friends and puking, plucking stingers from my face and arms.

At which point her voice was pinned to a backdrop of vaporous color.

At which point the crane's bustles flared.

At which point, coming to, I knew I'd pay the whole flag pull fare.

At which point the driver turned and said it doesn't need to be

your fault for it to break you.

At which point without any lurching commencement,

he began to play a vulture-bone flute.

At which point I grew old and it was like ripping open the beehive with my
hands again.

At which point I conceived a realm more real than life.

At which point there was at least some possibility.

Some possibility, in which I didn't believe.

可能

到了哪個地步，我的悲聲才是從語言飛出的流彈。

猶如飄流的蜂群。

到了哪個地步，酸苦的沉默才隨後而至。

我被蜂群包圍，失去了意識。

到了哪個地步，連我也沒有出路？

到了哪個地步，我在半昏迷中度日，夢見自己醒來，

避開朋友，嘔吐，拔出臉上和手臂上的蜇針。

到了哪個地步，她的聲音才被針別在有如幻光的布幕上。

到了哪個地步，鶴的裙撐才反起。

到了哪個地步，正在醒轉，我才知道要付滿的士起步價。

到了哪個地步，司機才轉身對我說，它把你打倒了，

並不是你的錯。

到了哪個地步，不再有磕磕絆絆的畢業典禮，

他才開始吹奏鷹骨笛。

到了哪個地步，我老去猶如再度徒手掰開蜂巢。

到了哪個地步，我才感到幻境比生活更真實。

到了哪個地步，才至少有某種可能

某種我不信的可能。

Immigrant Sea

Aroused by her inaccessibility, he aches for more
of her life to live inside him. Watching

the waves, standing so close he can feel
heat coming off her wet scalp. What is

his relationship to this person
before him, so familiar and foreign? The way

he searches out her face, he searches out himself. Gusts
thrash crests of waves, spring grasses twirl circles

in the sand where they stand without speaking. She
wants him to know it's all charged, even grass

positive, pollen negative, so when the grass waves,
it sweeps the air for pollen. He feels electricity all around

as though the wild drama of the coming storm were already
aware of them, the foreigners on this shore. Little

sapphire-blue flowers speckle the dunes.
He wonders if he has let himself flatten out

into a depthless sheet, like escalator stairs, whether in the end
he'll disappear underground without the smallest lurch

of resistance. But when her lavish face turns toward him
unconcealed, beaming, the corners of her eyes wind-wet,

he yields to that excess, he reappears to himself.

流浪海

她的拒人千里喚起他的哀痛，渴望
她在他的心裡活得更長久。看著

海浪，站得那麼近，他能感覺到
熱力從她濕漉漉的頭皮流下。他

和站在他跟前的這個人有什麼關係？
如此熟悉，又如此陌生？他的眼神找尋

她的臉龐，又以同樣的眼神找尋自己。海上
陣風鞭鞭刮起浪尖，沙上春草圈圈

旋捲，他們站在此處，並不說話。她
要他知道，一切都充滿了電流，即使

草亦為正極，花粉亦為負極，草浪翻起，
為花粉驅趕氣流。他感到四周充滿電流

彷如一場鬧劇，彷彿即將到來的風暴早已
知曉他們的存在，海岸上的外來者。寶藍色

花兒點綴著座座沙丘。
他懷疑是否任由自己平復下去

成為一張毫無深度的白紙，是否就像扶梯踏板，
到頭來消失於地底，毫不抵抗，甚至沒有一下

最小的踉蹌。但是當她情感充沛的臉轉向他，
毫無掩飾，滿面笑容，眼角含淚，

他順應了這種過度的流露，他重現自我。

In the Mountains

If the November frost reaches her before your note does

If at your back door, the mushroom sprinkled with roving mites
turns the color of rodent teeth

Then her thighs will tremble, her head go light as she tries to stand

If her irises flare, if your collied face stares back dull as a sock

Then you share the sensation of being cored

If you sip Oothu tea slowly, trying to remember what to say

If she no longer feels the sludge of sadness gungeing-up her arteries

Then you will instinctively raise your knee as though to protect something

If the risks edge up behind you chattering

Then she will blindfold you and say: taste this

If it takes just one more crossed-out name to complete the bitterness

If dust in her throat comes from somewhere far off *y los voces no le*
responden en las calles desocupadas de sus sueños

Then whatever you gasp while she lies under you will sound like nonsense
from a dream

If you instantly choose whatever precludes thinking

Then she will cry out Oh no, Oh no as though surprised she can't stop it

If slow moving fog scarves the raw mountain

If she mistakes a tic in the corner of your left eye for your smile

If when she sets the basket on the counter, the ripest pear topples from
the peak

Then with the four hands of Shiva, you'll touch her everywhere at once

If local animals make themselves more nocturnal to avoid you, if swarms of
migratory birds no longer cross the summit

Then the barest gleam in her eyes in the dark will hook your eyes

But if this orange lichen gossiping across boulders blackens, curls, and
then goes silent?

山中

如果十一月的冰霜比你的筆記早一步觸到她

如果在你後門的蘑菇撒下飄浮的蟎蟲
改變了碩鼠牙齒的顏色

那麼她的大腿便會顫抖，她一站起來就會頭暈

如果她的鳶尾花綻放，如果你塵污的面孔回望，索然如一隻襪子

那麼你也有了心被掏空的感受

如果你慢慢酌飲烏塗綠茶，嘗試回想要説什麼

如果她不再感到濘滯的悲傷硬化她的動脈

那麼你便會下意識地抬起膝蓋，彷彿要保護什麼

如果風險喋喋不休，漸漸向你身後靠攏

那麼她便會蒙著你的眼睛，説：嚐嚐這個

如果只需要再一次劃去名字便能終結苦楚

如果喉嚨裡的塵埃來自遠方，夢裡寂寥的街道上無人應答[1]

那麼當她躺在你身下，無論你如何喘氣，聽起來都彷如夢囈

如果你瞬間選擇免卻思考

那麼她便會大叫「噢！不！」，「噢！不！」猶如對她無力阻止而
感到意外

如果瀰漫的霧靄吞噬粗樸的山嶽

如果她把你左邊眼角抽搐錯認為你的微笑

如果當她把購物籃放在收銀台上，最熟的梨從高處滾下

那麼你立即會化身濕婆用四隻手去抱她滿懷

如果當地動物讓自己更趨夜行以便避開你，如果群群遷徙的候鳥不
再飛越山峰

那麼她在黑暗裡以最赤裸的眼神勾引你的眼睛

那麼如果這片閒話扯過巨石的橙色地衣變黑，翻卷，繼而沉默呢？

1 「夢裡寂寥的街道上無人應答」：這句原文是西班牙文。

黃有源（南韓），詩人、翻譯家，於2013年獲得文學村出版社新藝術家獎。2015年出版的詩集《世間萬物最大化》獲得南韓最重要的詩歌獎金洙暎詩歌獎；2019年出版最新詩作《你應該看見我戴皇冠》。翻譯著作包括巴布・狄倫的《歌詞集：1961–2012》、美國作家赫爾曼・梅爾維爾的《白鯨記》，以及麥斯・波特、大衛・邵洛伊、約翰・加德納、卡理・紀伯倫和沃爾特・惠特曼的詩歌。黃有源現於東國大學攻讀哲學博士學位。

Hwang Yu-Won (South Korea) is a poet and translator. He made his debut as a poet, winning the Munhakdongne New Artist award in 2013. His book of poetry *Everything in the World, Maximized* (2015) won the Kim Soo-young Prize which is considered one of the most important poetry awards in South Korea. In 2019, Hwang published his latest collection *You Should See Me in a Crown* (2019). Among his works of translations are Bob Dylan's *The Lyrics: 1961–2012*, Herman Melville's *Moby Dick*, as well as the works of Max Porter, David Szalay, John Gardner, Kahlil Gibran, and Walt Whitman. Hwang is now completing his Ph.D. in Philosophy at Dongguk University.

黃有源

HWANG YU-WON

中文翻譯：陳佳琳

English Translation by Jake Levine and Jialin Chen

모두가 쏟아지는 햇살 속에 있었다

너는 사무실에서 식물을 기르고
나는 불광천변에 벚나무를 기른다

또 어느 날 너는 논에서 올챙이를 길러
그게 개구리가 되는 걸 보고
개구리는 논물이 석양에 물드는 것을 본다

내가 잘 기른 천둥 하나
네가 잘 기른 하늘에 울려 퍼지더니

빗줄기 쏟아지고

어둠의 한복판에 개구리 울음 쏟아진다
나는 그걸 그해 여름 하동에서 너희들과 함께 들었지

비가 그치면
강원도의 해녀들은 바다가 세상에서 가장 큰 개인 수영장이라고 말하며
오늘도 그 속으로 뛰어든다

오늘은 날씨가 참 좋아
봄이 잘 길러 낸 여름이 되었고

바람은 나무가 한 계절 잘 기른 머리를 쓸어 넘겨 주고 있다
나무는 그걸 몹시 좋아해
그 나무는 우리가 길러 낸 것이고

때로는 씨엠립에서 앙코르 와트 사이에 반얀나무를 길러보기도
서울에서 반얀트리 호텔을 길러보기도 한다
누구나 지구 위에서 자기를 기르고 있는 중일 테지만

늦은 밤 호텔에 체크인한 외국인이
자기를 다른 나라에 잠시 심어 두고 잠든다

그 쓸쓸함은 내가 기른 것이고
네가 길렀다 바람에 창밖으로 놓쳐버린 것

길게 기른 머리 바람에 휘날렸다
가라앉고 있었고
네가 기른 긴 플레어스커트도 바람에 펄럭였다
가라앉고 있었다

바람이 기른 건 바람이 죽으면
바람과 함께
차분히
죽고

우린 이제 각자의 길을 걸어간다

네가 걷고 있는 길은 내가 길렀고
내가 걷고 있는 길은 네가 기른 것

一切皆在傾灑的陽光中

你在辦公室中種下一株綠植
我於佛光川邊植一棵櫻樹

某日，你在稻田養育一隻蝌蚪
看著牠長成青蛙
青蛙看著稻田染上斜陽

我悉心養育的一聲驚雷
在你悉心養育的天空中散動

驟雨來臨
青蛙笑聲傾灑在黑暗的正中央
那年夏天，我曾與你們一起在河東聆聽

驟雨初歇
江原道的海女們將大海稱作世上最大的私人泳池
即便在今日，她們也躍入其中

今日天氣甚好
春天孕育的夏日來臨

風拂過樹木積蓄了一整個季節的頭髮
樹木愛極了那撫摸
那樹木為我們所植

有時，我也在吳哥窟和暹粒之間種下榕樹
或者種在首爾悅榕庄假酒店裡
誰人不是在地球上將自身種植

在深夜裡入住酒店的外國人
將自身暫時地種植在異國之後安然入睡

那樣的孤單我也曾種下過
你也曾種下過，而後你任清風從窗外將之帶走

蓄長的頭髮在風中飄揚
而後下沉
留長的喇叭裙亦在風中飛揚
而後下沉

若是清風死去，它養育的一切
也將與清風一起
沉靜地
死去

我們現在，在各自的路上行走

你正走著的路，為我所造
我正走著的路，為你所造

Everything Soaked by the Rays of the Sun

You grow plants in your office and
I grow cherry trees near the Bulgwang Stream.

Some day you grow a tadpole in a rice paddy
and watch it become a frog
and the frog watches the rice paddy get dyed by the sunset.

You raise a thunder
that claps in the sky,
in the sky I made and
the rain slashes and

in the very center of the darkness, croaking frogs.
Remember, we listened together, that summer in Hadong County.

When the rain stops
all the women divers in Kangwon-do
say the sea is the biggest, private pool in the world
and even today, they jump right in.

Isn't the weather fucking great?
The Spring did a good job raising this Summer and
the wind over there is petting the hair
of a tree that grew its hair for the season.
The tree fucking loves it.
That tree is something we grew and

sometimes I also grow banyan trees between Angkor Wat and Siem Reap or
I grow a Banyan Tree Hotel in Seoul.
Although it is true everyone is in the middle of growing themselves on this earth,

a foreigner who checks in late at night at the hotel
temporarily plants herself in a foreign country and goes to sleep.

That loneliness the foreigner feels is a loneliness that I grew too,
and so did you, but after you did
you set it next to the window
and it was taken out, taken away by the wind.

The hair grown long whipped in the wind and
settled down,
and the long, flared skirt you grew also flapped in the wind
and settled down.

If the wind dies, the things the wind grows
also, together
with the wind,
calmly
die, and

we now walk our own two separate paths.

Your walking path is something I paved and
the road I walk on is something you mapped.

(Translated by Jake Levine)

한산 (寒山) 에서

겨울엔 발이 차다
마음은 안 시리고
양손도 따뜻한데
찬 발이 떼로 시리다
그날 퇴근길에 괜시리 걸어봤던 동호대교
얼어붙은 한강 위에 서 있다 일렬로 날아오르던
새 떼들 생각을 한 것도 아닌데
찬 발이 겨울 같다
네가 십 년 전에 사준 등산양말을 나는 아직도
겨울마다 꺼내 신는다
방 안에서만
밖에서는 안 신고
발이 시린 방 안에서만 신다가
겨울이 사라질 것 같으면 다시 벗는다
시린 발로
내가 가본 모든 차가운 나라라도 다시 가본다
발이라도 차야 한다
마음이 안 시리면
양말이라도 벗어야 한다
그러다 문득 다시 밀려오는 새벽에 발이 시리면
나는 어디도 갈 수 없을 것만 같고
나는 어디로도 갈 수 있을 테지만
어디로 가도 여기서 벗어날 수 없을 것만 같아
시린 발이 새벽 같다
모든 새벽의 발이 시리고
모든 새벽의 발이 양말을 신길 꺼리는 것 같다
늦은 새벽 술자리에서 꼰다는
자꾸 내게 너는 시인이니까
멋진 마무리 멘트나 하나 해보라는데
시인은 그런 거 대신 그저 양말이나 벗고
시린 맨발이나 보여줄 수 있을 뿐이다
밤새 미친놈처럼 맨발로 혼자
겨울 산에나 오를 수 있을 뿐이다
정신 못 차릴 정도로 멋진 생각이 떠오를 때까지
그 생각 읊어줄 생각에 이가 다 시려올 때까지 !
그러다 발이 사라질 것 같을 때쯤
정신이 번쩍 들어
이제는 발목 다 늘어난 양말 양손으로 벌려
그 속으로 너무 늦게 들어가보기도 한다
사라질랑 말랑 하던 발이
양말 속에서 말랑말랑해질 때까지
선배 시인 한산 (寒山) 도
산중의 추운 밤이면
옛날에 누가 사 준 양말 꺼내 신고 잤을까
알 수 없지만
벌써 십 년이란 세월이 흘러갔지만
나는 아직 잊지 않았다
이제 이 양말은 전신이 축 늘어져
집에서밖에는 신을 수 없게 돼버렸지만

在寒山中

冬天雙腳冰涼
心未冰冷
雙手尚溫
冰涼的腳化作飛鳥
那日在下班路上莫名架起的東湖大橋
矗立在封凍的漢江之上
未加思索，群鳥一列升空
冰涼的雙腳像冬天一樣
你在十年前為我買下的登山襪
如今每到冬日我還會拿出來穿
只穿在屋內
不曾在屋外穿過
只在冰冷的屋內將之穿在腳上
冬日若消逝便再次脫下
用那雙冰涼的腳
我再次前往曾經踏足的寒冷國度
儘管雙腳會被凍僵
只要心臟未涼
定要將襪子脫下
如此一來，在突然重新湧現的凌晨，若是雙腳冰涼
我便彷若無處可去
儘管看似何處皆可去
儘管看似無論去何處都無法脫離此處
冰涼的腳似凌晨一般
所有凌晨的腳皆是冰涼
彷彿所有凌晨的腳都不穿襪子

在深夜酒席上老人常對我說
你是詩人
便試著祝辭作為完美的收尾吧
詩人並未祝辭，只能脫下襪子
露出冰涼的赤足
只能整夜像狂人一般獨自赤足
攀登冬日的山
無精打采直到思如泉湧為止！
直到牙齒為那呼之欲出的靈感發寒為止！
如此一來在雙腳彷若要消失時
猛然清醒
在此刻用雙手撐開在腳踝處變長的襪子
遲遲地將雙腳伸入其中
直到那似是要消失的腳
在襪中變得柔軟為止
先輩詩人寒山
在山中寒冷的夜裡
也會拿出往日誰人為之買下的襪子穿著入眠嗎？
儘管無從得知
儘管已是十年歲月飛逝
但我還未曾遺忘
此刻襪子伸長至全身
儘管徹底變得無法在屋外穿

On the Cold Mountain

In winter, my feet feel cold,
but my heart doesn't,
and my hands are still lukewarm.
So cold my feet transform into birds.
That day on my way home after work, I saw Dongho Bridge
was hanging over the frozen Han River.
Without thought, a flock of birds rise to the sky.
My feet are as cold as winter itself.
The hiking socks you bought me ten years ago,
I take them out and wear them in winter every year,
but I only wear them inside the house
never outside
I only wear them inside the house where I feel cold.
I take them off as soon as winter ends.
My feet that once felt cold
will step on all the warm places they stepped on before.
Even though my feet feel cold,
as long as my heart does not,
I will take off the socks.
In the dawn that breaks in a sudden, if my feet feel cold,
I would as though have nowhere to go.
Although I seem to have everywhere to go
I cannot escape no matter where I go.
My feet are as cold as the dawn.
The feet of all the dawns feel cold,
as if none of them wear socks.
At a midnight drink, old people often say:
You are a poet.
You end the drink with a note.
But the poet does nothing but takes off the socks
and shows his cold bare feet.
He can only climb the winter mountain alone
all night long with his bare feet like a wild man,
low-spirited until inspiration channels
until his teeth chatter for the inspiration about to burst
At the moment the feet are to vanish
the poet sobers up
pulls the socks that have slipped to the ankles.
He slowly stretches his feet inside
until the vanishing feet
soften in the socks.
Did the ancient poet Han Shan
take out the socks that someone bought for him
and wear them in bed at a cold night on the mountain?
Though no way to tell,
and it has been ten years,
I haven't forgot
the socks have stretched to cover my whole body
cannot be worn outside the house.

(Translated by Jialin Chen)

毛子（中國大陸），本名余慶，湖北宜都人，現居宜昌。出生於六十年代，當過工人、推銷員、個體戶、編輯。曾獲得《揚子江》詩刊年度詩人獎、聞一多詩歌獎、李杜詩歌獎等獎項。出版詩集《時間的難處》及《我的鄉愁和你們不同》。

Maozi (Mainland China), the pen name of the poet Yu Qing, was born in the city of Yidu in Hubei Province in the 1960s. She currently resides in Yichang. She used to be a worker, a saleswoman, a freelancer, and an editor. Her numerous accolades include *Yangtze River* Artist of the Year, Wen Yiduo Poetry Prize, and Li Du Poetry Awards. Her published poetry collections include *The Difficulties of Time* and *My Homesickness Is Different from Yours.*

毛子

MAOZI

English Translation by Matt Turner and Haiying Weng

圓

圓從蒼穹、果實
和乳房上
找到了自己

它也從炮彈坑、傷口
窮人的空碗中
找到了
殘損的部分

漣漪在擴大，那是消失在努力
而淚珠説
—— 請給圓
找一個最軟的居所

所有的弧度都已顯現
所有的圓，都抱不住
它的陰影……

Roundness

Roundness, from
The heavens and the fruits and
Breasts, found itself

In bomb blast craters, wounds
In the empty bowls of the poor
Found
The broken part

Ripples are expanding, the effort of vanishing
And the tears say
—Please find for roundness
The softest place it can live

All arcs have appeared
No roundness can hold
Its shadow...

那從庸常中升起的……

果皮箱的語言
勝過首飾盒的語言。
地動儀
勝過地球儀。

從靈魂裡轉身，巴塔耶凝視
糞便和一切排泄之物。
他視乎要從這確鑿的證據中
建立人的哲學……

詩歌也是從這作嘔的基礎中
升起的。就像吉爾伯特
回憶少年的小鎮。
一個發瘋的老女人，整日的狂躁、咆哮
當他有一次路過，發現她撅起屁股
在草叢裡安靜撒尿。
那一刻，他為我們奉獻出
一個醜陋的聖母。

Those that Rise from Mediocrity

The language of the trash can
Is better than the language of jewelry displays.
A seismograph
Is better than a globe.

Turning away from the soul, Bataille gazed
At shit, at excrement.
He seems to have established a human philosophy
draw from hard evidence...

Poetry also rises from this condition
Of nausea, like Gilbert's
Memories of a town from his youth.
A mad old woman, howling hysterical
He passed once, and saw her ass-out
Pissing quietly in the grass.
At that moment, he dedicated to us
An ugly Virgin Mother.

賭石人

在大理的旅館，一個往返
雲南與緬甸的採玉人
和我聊起他在緬北猛拱一帶
賭石的經歷
—— 一塊石頭押上去，或傾家蕩產
或一夜暴富

當他聊起這些，雲南的月亮
已升起在洱海
它微涼、淡黃
我指著它說：你能賭一賭
天上的這塊石頭嗎？

這個黝黑的楚雄人，並不搭理
在用過幾道普洱之後，他起身告辭
他拍拍我的肩說：朋友
我們彝族人
從不和天上的事物打賭

The Gambler

At a hotel in Dali, a man who goes back and forth
Between Yunnan and Myanmar looking for jade
Tells me about his gambling for it
At Maogong, northern Myanmar
—A piece is laid down, and you might lose everything
Or maybe you'll get rich overnight

When he talked, the moon in Yunnan
Rising over Erhai Lake
Was cool, and yellowish.
I pointed at it and said: Can you bet on this
Bit in the sky?

This dark person from Chuxiong ignored me
After several rounds of *pu'er*, he rose to say goodbye
Patting me on the shoulder he said: Friend
We, the Yi people
Never bet with Heaven

失敗之心

扎西説，詩，還是少寫為宜
是的，寫來寫去，無非是小天賦，小感覺
無非生米做成熟飯，巧婦
做無米之炊

月亮在天上，寫不寫
都是古代的漢語
它爬進雲層，就像王維進了空山
山，在他那裡，就是不見人

我有一個拍紀錄片的朋友
去了一趟西藏，呆了數月，卻始終沒有打開鏡頭
他説，哪怕打開一點點，就是冒犯，是不敬
是譫妄中的不誠實

謝謝這些膽小的人，持齋戒的人
謝謝他們在一個二流時代
保留著一顆失敗之心

The Heart of Failure

Of poetry, Zhaxi said, it's better not to write too much
Really, all that writing, it's just a little bit of talent or feeling
Raw rice can be cooked, and a skillful woman
Can cook without rice

The moon in the sky. whether or not you write about it
It's all ancient Chinese words
Climbing into the clouds, just like Wang Wei in the empty mountains
He saw no one, as far as he was concerned

I have a friend who makes documentaries
He went to Tibet, stayed for months, but never removed his lens cap
He said that even using it a little bit would be offensive and disrespectful
Was delirious dishonesty

Thank these cowardly, fasting people
Thank them for keeping the heart of failure
In this second-rate era

退化之詩

爸爸從空氣裡來，又停在空氣中
我肉眼看不見

畜生們看見了
一頭老水牛打了一個響鼻
狗也覺察到異象
對著天空一陣狂吠

它們嘰嘰哼哼，比我還著急
—— 你怎麼不和自己的父親說話啊？

那些畜類啊
我有難處，有業障

想從前，我們也不進化，四肢妥貼
我們互蹭皮毛，原地打轉
有靈敏的嗅覺

A Poem of Devolution

Dad comes from the air, and he stops in the air
I can't see him with the naked eye

But the animals saw
An old buffalo hit its nose
Dogs also perceive unusual visions
And bark into the sky

They hummed, being more anxious than I was
—why don't you talk to your father?

Those animals!
I've got problems, bad karma

Considering the past, we aren't evolving, our limbs fit us well
We've rubbed each other's fur, turned around in place
And have a keen sense of smell

馬圖拉（愛沙尼亞），原名為馬格斯．拉提克，是愛沙尼亞年輕一代最有才華的當代詩人。曾榮獲古斯塔夫．蘇特詩歌獎及維魯文學獎。馬圖拉的文選已翻譯成多種語言，包括英語、芬蘭語、希伯來語和西班牙語；他本人亦致力翻譯德里克．沃爾科特的詩作。馬圖拉經常替愛沙尼亞國家廣播公司撰稿，並為愛沙尼亞作家聯盟成員。

Mathura (Estonia) is the pen name of writer and translator Magnus Lattik, who is among the most talented contemporary Estonian writers. He is the winner of the Gustav Suits Poetry Award and Virumaa Literary Award. His own work has been translated into a dozen languages, including book-length selections in English, Finnish, Hebrew, and Spanish. He is also the translator of Derek Walcott's poetry. Mathura contributes regularly to the Estonian National Broadcasting service and is a member of the Estonian Writers Union.

馬圖拉

MATHURA

中文翻譯：劉安廉

English translation by Mathura and Ilmar Lehtpere

Tursaneemel

Tuletorn
räsitud muuli tipus

nagu latern
karastunud peos

käsib mul olla valvel
ega ütle sõnagi sellest,

kuhu seada oma siht.
Ometi

nüüd,
kui oled kaugel—

ja vahel tundub,
et kadunud sootuks—,

seilan ühtelugu
sadamast sadamasse,

leidmaks uuesti valgust,
mis annaks mulle suuna.

Karide eest
see kaitsma ei peagi.

燈塔

一座燈塔
佇立於風暴中碼頭前端

就像一盞燈籠
握在一隻僵硬指掌中

它告訴我，要時刻警覺，
卻一字不提

前往到底是何方
不過，

此時你身在遠處——
有時

看似
完全消失——

我常常遠航
從港口到港口，

藉以尋找光
指引我方向。

縱然遭逢擱淺
亦無需保護我。

Lighthouse

A lighthouse
at the tip of a storm-swept pier

is like a lantern
in a hardened hand:

be alert, it tells me,
but not a word

what heading to take.
And yet

now that you are far—
sometimes

it seems you're gone
forever—

I keep on sailing
port to port

in search of light,
a sense of vision.

No need even to protect me
from running aground.

Maastikusse minek

Wolf Kahnile

Kusagil armastuse ja oskustöö piiril
sünnib midagi,
mida võiks nimetada kunstiks.
Aga nüüd

hõõru laiali need sõnad
ja vaata, mis jääb
äsjaöeldust alles.

Leheräbu, kivitolm.
Pelgalt taustatoon.

Kõik ülejäänu on kingitus, and,
ootamatu terendus hommiku roosas hahetuses—
noored viljapuud,
veel viljatud, aga siiski täis lootust

nagu maastik, mis ootab
mõtestust,

nagu silm, millel on oma
eiramatu janu.

走進風景

致沃爾夫・卡恩

就在愛與技藝之間
我們稱為藝術的事物
誕生。
但此刻

把這些字眼塗抹
再看看剛才所說的
還剩下什麼。

枯葉、碎石。
不過是底色而已，

其餘一切均是餽贈、禮物、
從沒見過晨曦時的幽暗粉紅——
青澀果樹
　　　　縱無果實，仍滿懷希冀，

就像一幀風景
等待它的意義；

就像一隻眼睛感覺到自己
無法否認的乾渴。

Entering the Landscape

to Wolf Kahn

It is somewhere between
love and craftsmanship
that something we call art
is born.
But now

scrub these words to a blur
and see what then holds up
of things just said.

Crumbling leaves, the rubble.
Nothing but an undertone,

all else a bestowal, a gift,
a vision that you've never seen before,
a young orchard
looming pink at dawn—
　　　　fruitless yet so hopeful,

a landscape
awaiting its meaning,

an eye with its own
undeniable thirst.

Meri. Üheksa akvarelli

Anders Zornile

Ühes paigas siiski kohtub kõik
see pole surnuaed see on meri

*

Ikka jälle ikka jälle üle kahvatu vee
liigub mu mõte oota mind veel

*

Vihmast nõretav maastik
lapse pisarais palg

*

Tõusuvees polegi midagi näha
tuul rapsib huupi kõik on nii hall

*

Hõõrutud hall piserdatud hall
väljauhutud hall hall hall hall

*

Pilliroog kooldub pritsmete udus
ainult laintemüha ja ei ühtegi huiget

*

Päike on ainult täpike vett
murdlaine varjus helgatab miski

*

Varsti torm taandub ja siis juba muutub
ka sinu palett

*

Vahel mõtlen et kõik ongi ainult
veega joonistatud vesi

大海。九色水彩

致安德斯•佐恩

有一個給萬物相遇的地方
不是墓園，而是大海。

*

跨過蒼茫海水，一次次，
我的想法隨即遠逝，並在彼方等著我

*

雨水沾濕風景
一名小孩淚流滿面

*

上升的水面隱藏一切
狂風亂舞，萬物成灰

*

磨刷成灰、撥撒成灰、
洗淨成灰　　　灰、灰、灰

*

蘆葦在雨灑的陰霾中彎身
浪濤咆吼，卻無法聽到叫喊

*

太陽頓成一點水滴
在碎浪暗色中閃耀發光

*

這場風暴即將退卻，然後
你將換過一塊調色板

*

有時我想，萬物不過是
繪於水上的水

The Sea. Nine Watercolours

to Anders Zorn

There is a place where everything will meet—
it's not a graveyard, it is the sea

*

Across pale waters, time and again,
my thoughts will pass, wait for me there

*

The tearful face of a child,
landscape dripping with rain

*

The rising water hides it all, the wind just
bustles at random, and everything is grey

*

Scrubbed grey and sprinkled grey,
washed-out grey　　　grey grey and grey

*

Reedbeds bend in the haze of spray
waves roar, no whoops to be heard

*

The sun is now a dot of water
something shimmers in the breakers' shade

*

Soon this storm will recede
and your palette will change

*

Sometimes I think that everything is
water painted in water

Rothko

See rahutu
vaikus

ehmatus
ja janu

üks pilv
üks ruum

üks pilguheit
tühjuse taha

liikumine
üha lähemale

mõõtmatusele
kus võid olla

kruus
ja olla tühi

seejärel olla
tühjem veel

羅斯科

在那片
不安

驚慄的
乾渴

空間
或濛霧的沉默中

觀照空無以外
的一瞥

一種
趨近那

廣袤無量之流動
於該處你可化為

一隻
空杯

繼而
更空

Rothko

In that silence
of unease

startled
thirsty

space
or mist

a glance beyond
all emptiness

a movement
near to that

immensity
where one can be

a cup
be empty

and thereupon
still emptier

Kividena

Kõik, mis on olnud,
on kunagi olnud
ega tule enam uuesti,
või kui, siis mitte samamoodi.
Pärast tuhandet aastat settimist
uhub meri meid välja
helesinisele rannale,
me ei tea oma raskust
ega ümarust,
oleme tuimad nagu
raidkuju käsi.
Meil on vaja raamatut,
mis ütleks, et oleme saladused,
aga lehed liimuvad kokku
nagu aastaringid puus,
nii et me näeme neid
ega näe nende sisse;
meil on vaja seaduste kogu
unustatud ilust,
surma jõledast palgest,
aja kihutavast vankrirattast,
aga ilu
jääb kirjutamata raamatuks,
nagu elugi,
päevad, päevad,
valged õied,
udu merel,
leheküljed pudenevad,
täis midagi,
eimiskit.

如石

一切曾存在的，
皆曾存在
並將不復存在，
縱或假如存在，將不再以
相同的方式存在。
沉澱千年過後
大海把我們沖到
一個淺藍色的岸邊，
對我們的重量與圓潤
一無所知，
我們呆滯得彷如
一尊雕像的手掌。
我們需要一本書
去告訴我們本身就是個秘密，
但就像樹的年輪
書頁都黏在一起，
我們看著書頁
卻讀不進裡面；
我們需要一套
關於失傳的美、
死亡的可怖面容、
以及時間之輪的律法，
而美
仍是一部未及寫成的書，
恰似人生。
日子、日子
白色鮮花，
海上迷霧，
書頁脫落，
寫滿
什麼，
或是一無所書。

As Stones

Everything that has been,
has been
and will not be again,
or if it is, it will not be
in the same way.
After a thousand years of settling
the sea washes us out
onto a light blue shore,
oblivious of our weight
and roundness,
we are as numb as
a statue's hand.
We need a book
to tell us we are secrets,
yet the pages stick together
like the yearly rings of a tree,
we see them
but not into them;
we need a set of laws
about forgotten beauty,
death's repulsive face,
the racing wheel of time,
yet beauty
remains an unwritten book,
like life.
Days, days,
white blossoms,
mist on the sea,
pages fall out,
full of something,
or nothing.

塞爾希奧·萊蒙迪（阿根廷），其詩集《公民詩歌》標誌著二十世紀末阿根廷客觀主義詩歌的高峰，更深深影響了廿一世紀阿根廷詩歌寫作。他的詩集《批評性辭典》獲古根漢基金獎及德意志學術交流中心獎。萊蒙迪於2002年榮任阿根廷國立南方大學當代文學教授，2011至2014年擔任布蘭卡港市政府文化部長。

Sergio Raimondi (Argentina) is the author of *Poesía civil*, which is considered the apex of Argentinian objectivist poetry in the end of the twentieth century and has exerted significant influence on the poetry writing in the twenty-first century in Argentina. His book of poems *Para un diccionario crítico de la lengua* received the Guggenheim Fellowship and also DAAD Fellowship. In 2002, Raimondi became a professor of contemporary literature at the National University of the South in Argentina. From 2011 to 2014, he served as the Secretary of Culture in Bahía Blanca.

塞爾希奧·萊蒙迪

SERGIO RAIMONDI

中文翻譯：胡續冬
中譯校對：袁婧
English translation by Ben Bollig

Sileno en la Estación de Ferrocarril

Acostado de lado, con un codo incómodo
apoyado en el cemento y la cabeza
tirada hacia atrás, duerme. Rodillas dobladas,
pies contra el culo, al aire la panza enorme,
boca abierta al cielo, chata nariz.
Esto es obra de dos o tres tetra-brik.
Si fuera de mármol estaría expuesto
en un museo de Roma, Londres o París
como ejemplo de arte helenístico.
Y no le molestarían las moscas.

火車站的西勒努斯[1]

側躺著，一隻手肘彆扭地
撐在水泥地上，頭
向後扭著，呼呼大睡。膝蓋彎曲，
雙腳抵著屁股，袒露著大肚子，
嘴巴朝天空張開，扁平的鼻子。
這是一件兩三個利樂包裝盒[2]的作品。
如果他是大理石做的，他將會在
羅馬、倫敦或者巴黎的博物館裡
被展出，作為希臘藝術的典範。
不會有成群的蒼蠅來攪擾他。

Silenus at the Railway Station

Lying on one side, with an awkward elbow
leaning on the cement and his head
tipped back, he sleeps. Knees bent double,
feet against his arse, airing his big belly,
mouth open to the sky, squat nosed.
This is the work of two or three litres.
If he were marble he would be displayed
in a museum in Rome, London or Paris
as an example of Hellenistic art.
And the flies wouldn't fuss him.

1 西勒努斯（Silenus），古希臘神話裡職司森林的神祇之一，是酒神狄奧尼索斯的伴侶和導師，形象邋遢，常與狄奧尼索斯共飲，很容易喝醉。

2 利樂包裝盒（Tetra Brik），是指採用瑞典利樂公司的全無菌生產線生產的複合紙質包裝盒，常見的有液態牛奶和飲料包裝盒，也有一些酒類使用利樂包裝盒。此處根據上下文，應指用利樂包裝盒包裝的廉價酒。

Qué es el mar

El barrido de una red de arrastre a lo largo del lecho, mallas de apertura máxima, en el tanque setecientos mil litros de gas-oil, en la bodega bolsas de papa y cebolla, jornada de treinta y cinco horas, sueño de cuatro, café, acuerdos pactados en oficinas de Bruselas, crecimiento del calamar illex en relación a la temperatura del agua y las firmas de aprobación de la Corte Suprema, circuito de canales de acero inoxidable por donde el pescado cae, abadejo, hubbsi, transferencias de permiso amparadas por la Secretaría de Agricultura, Ganadería y Pesca; ahí: atraviesa el fresquero la línea imaginaria del paralelo, va tras una mancha en la pantalla del equipo de detección, ignorante el cardumen de la noción de millas o charteo, de las estadísticas irreales del INIDEP o el desfasaje entre jornal y costo de vida desde el año mil novecientos noventa y dos, filet de merluza de cola, SOMU y pez rata, cartas de crédito adulteradas, lámparas y asiático pabellón, irrupción de brotes de aftosa en rodeos británicos, hoki, retorno a lo más hondo de toneladas de pota muerta ante la aparición de langostino (valor cinco veces mayor), infraestructura de almacenamiento y frío, caladero, eso.

什麼是海

沿著床掃過的拖網，
網眼開到最大，油箱裡的七十萬升
柴油，儲藏室裡一袋一袋的土豆和洋蔥，
三十五小時的輪班，四小時的睡眠，咖啡，
布魯塞爾的那些辦公室簽署的協議，
阿根廷魷魚數量的增長和水溫以及
最高法院簽署的文件之間的關係，
不鏽鋼隧道在漁業衰落地帶的環繞，
黑線鱈、無鬚鱈，受農牧漁業部支持的
執照轉讓。在那裡：
深海捕魚船穿過想像中的平行線，探尋著
監視器屏幕上的一塊污點，
魚群不瞭解距離或者特許令的概念，
不瞭解國家漁業研究所的虛假統計數據或者
一九九二年以來工資和日常花銷之間的鴻溝，
尖尾無鬚鱈魚片，漁民協會和鼠尾鱈，
偽造的信用證，燈，亞洲的權宜船旗，[1]
英國牛群中口蹄疫的大爆發，長尾鱈，
返回最深處的成噸的死墨魚
此時對蝦（五倍的價值）湧現，
存儲與冷藏的基礎設施，漁場，如此種種。

What the Sea Is

The sweep of a trawler net across the length of the bed,
mesh at maximum, in the tank seven hundred thousand
litres of diesel, down below bags of potatoes and onions,
shifts of thirty-five hours, sleep for four, some coffee,
agreements signed in offices in Brussels, increasing
illex squid in proportion to the water temperature
and the approvals signed in the Supreme Court, circuit
of stainless steel channels where the catch falls,
pollock, hake, permit transfers with the support
of the Ministry of Farming and Fisheries; there:
the fishing boat crosses the imaginary parallel, goes
after a stain on the screen of the detector machine,
the shoal ignorant of the notion of miles or charter,
of the made-up Fisheries Institute stats or the gap
between wages and cost of living since the year 1992,
long-tailed hake fillet, Seamen's Union and rattail,
faked credit letters, lamps and Asian flag of convenience,
outbreak of foot and mouth in British herds, hoki,
chuck back to the very depths tons of dead cuttlefish
when langoustine (five times greater value) appears,
storage infrastructure and cold, fishing ground, that.

1 權宜船旗是一種商業慣例，船公司或船東將其所擁有的船舶登記於其他國籍，該國籍因標準較低，可以達到降低成本之效果。

Hoy cocina Matsuo Bashō

El maestro dijo "pimienta más alas igual libélula",
no al revés, no se trata de sacar alas a la libélula
para abandonar en el aire un aromático grano
que por su propio peso caería, sino de dar vuelo
al fruto a fin de que lejos se eleve desde la mesa.
Pero a veces urge cualquier picante para otorgar
gusto a la salsa que sobre la hornalla hierve
y no hay más que esa libélula o figura de lenguaje
dando vueltas por ahí y hasta molestando un poco.
El maestro, ya con delantal, debería abandonar
la elegancia de la anécdota para tener en cuenta
tanto su propio apetito como el de los comensales;
el juicio poético podrá o no condenar la acción,
pero el estómago sabrá agradecerlo en la cena.
Y no es de extrañar que, de ser la cocción justa,
la digestión se cumpla entre platos, ollas y vapores
con el sentimiento preciado de gracia y levedad.

今天松尾芭蕉掌勺

大師說「辣椒加翅膀等於蜻蜓」
而不是相反，這並不意味著從蜻蜓身上拔下翅膀
以在半空中留下如若順其自然必會墜地的
一顆芳香的穀粒，而是為了讓水果
飛翔，讓它從桌子上高高升起。
但有時候需要任意一種辣椒，來給
在火爐上沸騰的湯汁添加味道
只有這隻蜻蜓或語言形象
在周圍飛來飛去，甚至有些討厭。
大師已繫上圍裙，他將拋棄
軼聞中的優雅，一心惦記
他自己和食客們的胃口；
詩歌的判斷力會或者不會譴責這一行為，
但是晚餐時胃將懂得感激。
不要感到驚訝，只要烹飪得當，
消化會在鍋、碗和蒸汽之間完成
帶著彌足珍惜的優雅和輕盈感。

Today Matsuo Bashō Cooks

The Master said "pepper plus wings equal dragonfly"
not the reverse, it's not about plucking its wings
to leave in mid-air an aromatic grain
that on its own would fall. No, the trick is
to give flight to the fruit so it rises from the table!
But at times something spicy is needed to give
taste to the sauce that's boiling on the hob
and there's nothing but that dragonfly or conceit
flying around and even bothering a little bit.
The master, now with his apron, should give up
the elegance of the anecdote to keep in mind
as much his own appetite as that of those dining;
poetic judgment may condemn—or not—the act,
but the stomach will appreciate it in the dinner.
And it's no surprise that, if the cooking is right,
digestion takes place among plates, pans and steam
with a pleasant sense of grace and lightness.

El poeta menor ante el nacimiento de su hijo

Luego de hallar, tras días de búsqueda, el lápiz
en la cabina del camioncito de los bomberos,
y de comprobar la independencia de juicio
del heredero, que rompe las páginas predilectas
e intactas deja las indiferentes, el poeta menor
decide dialogar con su mujer sobre un tema clave:
la organización espacial y temporal de su labor,
en la casa, luego del nacimiento del hijo.
A lo largo de la conversación se tocan varios temas:
compra de comestibles y artículos de limpieza,
pago de impuestos, turnos para el cuidado,
diversión, alimentación e higiene del niño,
ausencia de cuidado, diversión, alimentación
e higiene de la pareja, necesidad de registrar
sus primeros pasos, frecuencia de uso del
—vulgarmente denominado—chupete,
amables formas de imponer distancia a los abuelos.
Cuando una mutua mudez evidencia el final,
el poeta menor comprueba que su inquietud
ha sido desplazada en vista de otras urgencias.
Esa noche, como un inspirado romántico
que aprovechase el silencio de los mortales
para dejar fluir el carácter alado de sus versos,
canta durante horas una canción de cuna.

兒子降生之際的小詩人

找了幾天之後，他在
玩具消防車的車艙裡找到了鉛筆，
他目睹了他的繼承人獨立的意志：
撕爛了他最喜歡的書頁
他不喜歡的卻完好無損，小詩人
決定和他妻子討論一個關鍵性問題：
兒子出生以後，在家中
他的工作在空間和時間上該如何組織。
討論過程中觸及了好幾個話題：
購買生活物資和清潔用品，
交税，輪班帶孩子，
小寶寶的娛樂、營養和衛生，
兩個大人的被關懷感、娛樂、營養
和衛生的缺失，記錄孩子邁出第一步
的必要性，被俗稱為安撫奶嘴
的那個東西使用的頻次，
和爺爺奶奶們保持距離感的友好方式。
當討論最終陷入雙向的緘默，
小詩人意識到他的焦慮
已被另外一些迫切性所替代。
那一夜，似有浪漫的靈感
利用世人的沉默
讓他長有翅翼的詩行得以流動，
他一連幾個小時都在唱搖籃曲。

The Minor Poet on the Birth of His Son

Having found, after searching for days, his pencil
in the cabin of the little toy fire truck,
and witnessing the independent judgment
of his heir, who tears up the preferred pages
and intact leaves the rejects, the minor poet
decides to discuss with his wife a key question:
the organisation of time and space for his work,
at home, after the birth of their son.
And this talk touches on various questions:
purchasing groceries and cleaning products,
revenue payments, turns to give the child
care, entertainment, food and hygiene,
the lack of care, entertainment, food
and hygiene for the couple, the need to record
his first steps, how often to use what is known
—by the vulgar masses—as a dummy,
nice ways of keeping the grandparents at bay.
When a mutual muteness marks the end,
the minor poet realises that his concerns
have been displaced by more pressing needs.
That night, like an inspired romantic
taking advantage of the mortals' silence
to give space for his verses to take flight,
he sings, for hour after hour, a lullaby.

Fish Block

Porque por supuesto aún la misma fluidez del pez en el agua
a ver, más específicamente: ese vértice agudo y extendido
de la merluza de cola magallánica útil para moverse en orden
múltiple a cien dos tres cuatrocientos metros de profundidad
vuelta otra vez a las capas altas del Atlántico y Pacífico sur
ha de terminar compactada solidificada congelada embalada
para asumir así la forma vigente de la producción industrial

paralelogramo premium de siete kilos y medio de filet de hoki
medida estandarizada y universal de la lengua y las máquinas
comercio y transporte a través de parelelogramos semejantes
ángulos sin imperfecciones y una superficie alisada de vacío
exacta para diluir los movimientos de la mano que enviscera
extrae el epitelio y se dispone ya a realizar el despinado fino
a bordo de un arrastrero cuya bandera no importa demasiado.

冷凍魚塊

因為，很顯然連水中魚的流動
——好吧，更具體一點：南美尖尾無鬚鱈
鋒利、狹長的頂端，有助於牠們做多階移動
從一二三四百米的深度
回到大西洋或者南太平洋的水面——
也會終結為壓縮、凝固的冷凍包裹
以迎合工業生產的流行樣態

七點五公斤的長尾鱈優質四方塊
舌頭和機器的標準化、全球化尺碼
貿易和運輸都在相似的四方塊中進行
毫無瑕疵的棱角，真空般光滑的表面
恰好掩蓋了摘取內臟、
剝皮和去骨的手部動作
在拖網漁船上掛誰的旗幟並不那麼重要。

Fish Block

Because of course even the flow of the fish in the water
well, more specifically: that sharp and extended vertex
of the Patagonian grenadier, useful for moving in multiple
order at one two three four-hundred metres' depth
back at the higher layers of the Atlantic or South Pacific
will end up compacted solidified frozen packaged
in order to adopt the usual form of industrial production

a premium parallelogram of 7.5 kilos of filet of hoki
standardised and universal measure of taste and machines
commerce and transport across similar parallelograms
angles without imperfections and a vacuum smooth surface
exact to dilute the movements of the hand that eviscerates
extracts the epithelium and starts the fine deboning
on board a trawler whose flag doesn't matter that much.

安娜・里斯托維奇（塞爾維亞），生於貝爾格萊德，著有九本詩集，獲獎無數。2005 年獲胡伯特・布爾特詩歌獎（頒給德國的歐洲青年詩人），其後獲頒塞爾維亞兩項重要的詩歌大獎，分別為迪索瓦那格拉達詩歌獎（2014）及德珊卡瑪西摩維奇詩歌獎（2018）。里斯托維奇於2018 至2019 年在德意志學術交流中心任駐留作家。她的詩集經翻譯為英語、德語、匈牙利語、馬其頓語、斯洛文尼亞語及斯洛伐克語，並在世界各地出版。

Ana Ristović (Serbia), born in Belgrade, has published nine books of poetry and is the recipient of numerous poetry awards including Hubert Burda Preis (an award for young European poets in Germany), and two of the most important poetry prizes in Serbia: Disova nagrada (2014) and Desanka Maksimović Prize (2018). Ristović was the 2018–2019 writer-in-residence at the DAAD in Berlin. Her poetry books have been translated and published in English, German, Hungarian, Macedonian, Slovenian, and Slovak.

安娜 · 里斯托維奇

ANA RISTOVIĆ

中文翻譯：黃峪、Marija Todorova、馬文康

English translation by Maja Teref and Steven Teref

Супружници за тастатурама

(страх од близине)

Седећемо у истој спаваћој соби,
ћутећи, свако за својим столом,
и слати једно другом најпре опширна,
а онда врло штура писма
преко интернета.

На крају ни то, већ само потписе
уз питање
Јеси ли за кафу, чај, пољубац,
или ни за шта.

Екрани ће горети и зујати
од вишка памћења онога
што смо оставили у ходнику
гласне ранобрачне историје.

Утискујући се целим телом
у белину стакла као некада у снег
правићемо пале анђеле
тежине милион гигабајта
од којих се руши и најчвршћи систем.

Оно што ће преживети биће плаво
као око гиљотине.[1]

Оно што проговори:
столови, столице, пепељаре и подови
надгласаваће једно друго
позајмивши само облик
наше некадашње близине.

1 Адам Загајевски, *Референдум*.

鍵盤上的配偶

（對親密關係的恐懼）

我們睡房裡寂靜，
我們在分開的桌前坐著，
給對方發送冗長
而後稀疏的電子郵件。

到了最後，郵件只以一個問題
作結：我能給你咖啡、茶、一吻，
或是別的什麼？

我們的屏幕發光哼鳴
只因走廊裡殘留了
過多內存
我們聒噪婚姻的開始。

我們將這身體
印入屏幕的空白
好似印入白雪，
賦形出墜落的天使
千萬兆字節大小
使最強力的系統崩潰。

「幸存的任何東西都是藍色
如同斷頭台之眼。」[1]

任何說話的物體，
桌子，椅子，煙灰缸和地板，
把彼此溺斃
向我們過去親密關係
借來的不過是形體。

1　出自Adam Zagajewski《全民公投》。

Spouses at Keyboards

(fear of intimacy)

Silent in our bedroom,
we sit at separate desks,
and send each other lengthy,
then sparse emails.

In the end, only closings
with a question: Can I get you
coffee, tea, a kiss,
or anything?

Our monitors glow and hum
from the excess memory
of what's left in the hallway:
our noisy marital beginnings.

We imprint our bodies
into the screen's whiteness
as in snow,
create fallen angels
a million gigabytes' worth and
crash the most powerful computer.

"Whatever survives will be blue
as a guillotine's eye."[1]

Whatever speaks,
desks, chairs, ashtrays and floors,
drowns one another,
borrows only the shape of
our past intimacy.

1 From Adam Zagajewski's poem *Referendum.*

Спавати са медведима

(страх од „подетињити“)

Имам тридесет и четири године
и почињем да спавам са медведима

Јуче претурах по кеси у којој је
стајало шћућурено
неко плишано доба, годинама

Вече скоро да препалаках, јер открих –
једном је уместо носа
деценијама била забијена црна чиода

Извадих је, нежно, пинцетом, онда

ставих меко дугменце, нађох ћебенце

И до у ситне сате гледах кратке
ТВ документарце
о плишаним медведима још из 19. века
и о специјалним болницама у Лондону
у које их шаљу на лечење од прашине
па на поновно интензивно пуњење

И видех:једном, мом, усахлом,
глава лежи на раменима; испразних
стомак од тридесет година старих крпа,
напуних га сунђерастим улошцима
за push-up брусхалтере, које сам
дуго чувала у разним орманима

И потроших пола бојлера
потапајући у лавор три медведа;
сапуница је била црна
и све време ми је било жао

И док сам их држала под водом
дошло ми да им у њушку ставим
сламчицу, да би могли
барем мало ваздуха да сишу

И када су на површину испливали
остаци сунђера и нешто
мрке пиљевине, схватих,
увелико на моја плућа дишу

Да су стајала мирно деценијама
сигурно би била другачија,
без облака, мрље, та, гарава,
понекад кркљава плућа
а ипак моја

И после сушења, заспали смо
тише, чак и мирније
него остарели љубавници
у све ближем, вечном загрљају
сасвим монотоних боја

Док нам је над главама
кружила невидљива игла,
двоумећи се кога ће
прво морати да зашије

與泰迪熊同眠

（對重訪童年的恐懼）

三十四歲的我
還與泰迪熊同眠

昨天，我在一個口袋裡摸索
我有段長毛絨時期的生活
在袋裡擠躺了好些年

那晚我幾乎哭了一夜當我發現——
其中一隻熊的鼻子沒了
只剩一支黑色大頭針

輕輕地，我用鑷子把它拔出來

在上面縫了個小小的軟鈕扣，還找到一張小毯子

那天夜裡，我看了
幾部短紀錄片
說的是十九世紀以來的長毛絨泰迪熊
還有那些倫敦的特殊醫院
為毛熊們掃塵
重填內裡

我瞥看我的一隻小熊，瘦弱憔悴
它的頭往肩下縮：我清空了它
肚子裡面三十年的舊破布

充填以從壁櫥裡翻出的
豐胸胸罩的填料

我用掉燒水壺裡一半的水
洗著三隻小熊：
黑沉沉的肥皂泡
讓我難過

把它們沒入水中
我想把一根吸管
插進它們口鼻之中讓它們呼吸

當他們與胸罩襯墊的殘餘
浸透的碎木屑一同浮出水面
我幡然領悟
它們通過我的肺部來呼吸

晾乾它們之後，我們靜靜地
睡著了，比舊情人們
還更平靜
在一個親密的，永恆的擁抱中
帶著單色調的陰影

在我們頭頂
一枚看不見的別針繞圈
考慮著先縫合
我們中的哪個

Sleeping with Teddy Bears

(fear of revisiting childhood)

At thirty-four
I still sleep with teddy bears

Yesterday, I rummaged through a bag
where a plush period of my life
lay huddled for years

I cried almost through the night when I found—
one of them had a black pin
where its nose used to be

I pulled it out, gently, with tweezers,

sowed a soft little button on it, found a little blanket

Late into the night, I watched
short documentaries
about plush teddy bears from the 19th century
and the special London hospitals
where they were dusted off
and re-stuffed

I look over at one of mine, emaciated
its head slung against its shoulder: I emptied out
its stomach worth thirty years of old rags,

I stuffed it with padding
from a push-up bra taken from my closet

I used up half the water from the boiler
washing three teddies:
the black soapsuds
saddened me

Submerging them
I wanted to insert a straw
into their muzzles so they could breathe

When they resurfaced
along with the remains of bra pads
and sodden sawdust it dawned on me
they breathe through my lungs

After drying them, we fell asleep
quietly, more peacefully
than old lovers
in an intimate, perpetual embrace
of monochrome shades

Over our heads
an invisible pin circled
wondering which one of us
to sew up first.

Црнаротква

Рендамцрнуроткву
докнапољу
пада
ситансснег,

вејемљутксасте, белепахуље
надаскуодбамбусовогдрвета
аонепрштеинаононаштанебисмеле:
насто, столице, кухињскипод, руке.

Кадпосечемпрст
капкрви
упијебелина.

Богија, упосленисличним,
ујединствутрајнеразлике:
онбезрасипањапријатнељутине,
јабезједнекапикрви
којаљутинублажи
адатоганисамнисвесна.

Итако, рендамодуго
иједноидруго,
иједнодруго,
докнаснесавлада
ипак, увекиста
глад.

Анапољу, мећава
изваннасодавнотраје
итаколако,
безикаквебриге,
пометесваки
паизаједнички
праг.

黑蘿蔔

我把黑蘿蔔磨碎
就像神磨碎雪。

我在竹子切菜板上
揉出辛辣雪花
它們落在餐桌
椅子、廚房地板，我的手上。

我切到了手指
那純然之白
將鮮血吸盡。

神和我
一齊研磨：他不會丟失
任何美味
而我少了幾滴血
緩解著我不在意的
一種高熱。

我們這樣研磨
他和我
彼此研磨
直到我們都
因同樣的飢餓
精疲力盡。

Black Radish

I grate a black radish
as God grates snow,

I rub the spicy flakes
on the bamboo cutting board
they shoot onto the table,
the chairs, the kitchen floor, my hands.

I cut my finger
the whiteness
soaks up the blood.

God and I grate
in unison: He without losing
any delightful zest,
and I minus a few drops of blood
soothing a heat
I'm oblivious to.

So we grate,
He and I,
and grate one another,
until exhausted
by the same
hunger.

Outside, the blizzard
howls, with ease
and without a care,
buries our
mutual
threshold.

Оконуле

Независне смо жене.
У ишчекивању нове љубави
дишемо астматично. Хранимо се пилулама
неиспуњених обећања. Тонемо у мутне снове.
Двадесет и четири часа болно водимо љубав
са мигреном
и опраштамо јој јер је женског пола.

Независне. Својим мушкарцима
кувамо јела којима су нас научили
њихови претходници.
Макароне у облику клиториса.
Кечап што клизи као менструална крв
и обећава само лизање тањира.
Ал још увек верујемо у тријумфалне капије
које расту између постеље
и кухињског стола.

Пуштамо им музику коју смо слушале
при губљењу невиности и девојаштва.
Међу заводљивим вешом
сетно чувамо примерке
са невидљивим трагом претходних сперми.
Њишемо бедрима као да окрећемо млин:
после извесног времена цури
још само лепљива жуч.

И кажемо, да не верујемо више
у заједнички ваздух
који се може делити између уста и уста,
а све чешће остајемо без даха.

И кажемо, да центрифугу веш машине
користимо само кад се на њој
може одиграти добар сношај.
А у програм претпрања и цеђења
све чешће, уместо рубља, убацујемо
парче по парче своје истањене коже.

Независне жене. Цензуришемо
своје одвећ меке речи.
Подупиремо ревизију осећања и теорију
по којој је прво настала недужна Ева,
а Адам загризао отровну јабуку
јер је пожелео да му Бог
од змије створи још два фалуса:
мислио, јадничак, да му један
довољан неће бити.

Независне, кажемо, више но икад.
А у осамљеним ноћима, у уску вулву
спуштамо свој чудесни прстић све чешће,
као да убацујемо метак у пушчану цев

која опалити неће.
И смешимо се, с тугом, у сну без снова.
И рука је на сигурном, док кружи
око меке нуле.

圍零畫圈

我們是獨立的女性
我們等待新的愛情時
呼吸深喘不已。我們吃著未實現諾言的
藥丸生活下去。我們沉溺於暗鬱的夢。
一天二十四小時我們痛苦地
和偏頭痛做愛且原諒她
因為她是女性

獨立。為我們的男人
我們做他們前輩教給我們的菜式
陰莖形狀的麵食
茄汁滴落就像經血
但只允許把盤子舔了又舔
然而我們仍然相信凱旋門
升弧在床單和廚桌之間

我們為他們播放
破處時聆聽的音樂
在誘人的內衣之間
深思，我們保存著帶有
舊精液隱痕的內褲
我們扭動臀部似乎在轉磨坊風車：
過一會後它滴下的
只是粘稠的苦痛

但我們也宣告自己不再相信
分享嘴巴之間
同樣的呼吸
更常見的是我們無法呼吸
卻聲稱我們用了洗衣機的
離心之力
只因我坐在上面的時候
悅人的性交有可能發生
在預清洗和洗滌過程中
洗的是我們變薄的皮膚
而不是扔進去的衣物

獨立婦女。我們審查
我們所有溫柔過分的話語
我們支持對情感的修改
以及無辜的夏娃而非亞當
先被創造的理論，還有是亞當
咬了一口墮落的蘋果
因他希望上帝從大蛇上
創造出另兩條陽具：
可憐的東西，他覺得一條
還不足夠

獨立，我們宣稱，從未如此獨立
但在寂寞夜晚，我們把一根神奇手指
一次又一次，插入緊緻的外陰裡
就像把一粒子彈置入
拒絕開火的槍膛
而我們帶著感傷在無夢的夢裡微笑
而這安全的手，圍著
柔軟的零畫圈

Circling Zero

We are independent women.
We breathe asthmatically
while waiting for new love. We pop pills
of unfulfilled promises. We drown in murky dreams.
Twenty-four hours a day we painfully make love
to a migraine and forgive her
because she's female.

Independent. For our men
we cook dishes taught to us
by their predecessors.
Clitoris-shaped pasta.
Ketchup dripping like menstrual blood
yet promising only the licking of plates.
But still we believe in the *arc de triomphe*
which rises between the bed sheets
and the kitchen table.

We play them the music
we lost our virginity to.
Pensive among seductive
lingerie, we keep underwear
with the invisible track of old sperm.
We gyrate our hips as if turning a mill:
after a while it drips
only sticky bitterness.

Yet we claim that we no longer believe
in sharing the same breath
between mouths
and more often we're left breathless
yet claim we use the centrifuge
of the washing machine
only when delightful intercourse may occur.
In the prewash and rinse cycles
instead of clothes we throw in
pieces of our thinned out skin.

Independent women. We censor
our all too soft words.
We support the revision of feelings
and the theory arguing that innocent Eve
was created first, and that Adam
bit into the poisoned apple
because he wished for God to create
two more phalluses from the serpent:
poor thing, he thought one
wouldn't be enough.

Independent, we claim, more than ever.
Yet during lonely nights, in our tight vulva
more and more, we insert a small magical finger,
as if placing a bullet into the chamber
which refuses to fire.
And we smile with sadness in dreamless dreams.
And the safe hand, circling
the soft zero.

薩奇達南丹（印度），是當代印度獲翻譯得最多作品的詩人，發表過三十一本翻譯詩集，共十九種語言，包括阿拉伯語、漢語、英語、法語、德語、愛爾蘭語及意大利語，以及印度的主要語言如坦米爾語、孟加拉文和印度語。他曾為英語教授，歷任印度國家文學院院長、英迪拉甘地公開大學翻譯學院總監、印度高級研究所國家研究員，亦是喀拉拉邦文學院成員，曾多次代表印度參加國際文學節及書展，並於不同國家贏得四十七項文學獎。

K. Satchidanandan (India) is perhaps the most translated of contemporary Indian poets, having thirty-one collections of translation in nineteen languages including Arabic, Chinese, English, French, German, Irish, and Italian besides all the major Indian languages like Tamil, Bengali, and Hindi. He was a professor of English in Kerala and later became the Secretary (Chief Executive) of the Sahitya Akademi (Indian National Academy of Literature), the Director of the School of Translation Studies, Indira Gandhi Open University, a National Fellow of Indian Institute of Advanced Study, Shimla, a Fellow of the Kerala Sahitya Akademi. Satchidanandan has won forty-seven literary awards from different countries around the world.

薩奇達南丹

K. SATCHIDANANDAN

中文翻譯：鄭政恆

Stammer

Stammer is no handicap.
It is a mode of speech.

Stammer is the silence that falls
between the word and its meaning,
just as lameness is the
silence that falls between
the word and the deed.

Did stammer precede language
or succeed it?
Is it only a dialect or
a language itself?
These questions make
the linguists stammer.

Each time we stammer
we are offering a sacrifice
to the God of meanings.

When a whole people stammer
stammer becomes their mother-tongue:
just as it is with us now.

God too must have stammered
when He created man.
That is why all the words of man
carry different meanings.
That is why everything he utters
from his prayers to his commands
stammers,
like poetry.

口吃

口吃不是殘障。
這是一種言說的模式。

口吃是沉默落在
言辭及其含義之間，
正如跛腳是
沉默落在
言辭和行動之間。

口吃在語言之先
還是之後呢？
它本身只是一種方言
還是一門語言？
這些問題令
語言學家口吃。

每次我們口吃
我們正在向
意義之神獻祭。

當全體族群口吃
口吃成為他們的母語：
就像我們現在一樣。

上帝創造人時
也一定有口吃。
因此人類所有的言辭
帶有不同含義。
因此祂所說的一切
從祂的祈禱到祂的誡命
口吃，
如詩。

The Mad

The mad have no caste
nor religion. They transcend
gender, live outside
ideologies. We do not deserve
their innocence.

Their language is not of dreams
but of another reality. Their love
is moonlight. It overflows
on the full moon day.

Looking up they see
gods we have never heard of. They are
shaking their wings when
we fancy they are
shrugging their shoulders. They hold
even flies have souls
and the green god of grasshoppers
leaps up on thin legs.

At times they see trees bleed, hear
lions roaring from the streets. At times
they watch Heaven gleaming
in a kitten's eyes, just as
we do. But they alone can hear
ants sing in a chorus.

While patting the air
they are taming a cyclone
over the Mediterranean. With
their heavy tread, they stop
a volcano from erupting.

They have another measure
of time. Our century is
their second. Twenty seconds,
and they reach Christ; six more,
they are with the Buddha.

In a single day, they reach
the big bang at the beginning.

They go on walking restless for,
their earth is boiling still.

The mad are not
mad   like us.

瘋子

瘋子沒有種姓
也沒有宗教。他們超越
性別，自外於
意識形態。我們不配
他們的清白。

他們的語言不屬於夢
而屬於另一個現實。他們的愛
是月光。它湧溢
在滿月的日子。

他們抬頭看見
我們從未聽説過的神明。他們
拍動翅膀
當我們認為他們
聳聳肩膀。他們堅持
就連蒼蠅都有靈魂
還有蚱蜢的綠色神明
用瘦腿跳起。

有時他們看到樹木流血，聽見
獅子在街上咆哮。有時
他們看見天堂在小貓的眼中
閃閃發光，就如
我們。但只有他們可以聽到
螞蟻合唱。

拍打空氣的同時
他們正在控制
地中海上空的旋風。
他們沉沉踩踏，他們阻止
一座火山爆發。

他們有另一種
時間的計算。我們的世紀是
他們的一秒。二十秒，
他們來到基督面前；再過六秒，
他們和佛陀在一起。

一天之內，他們到達
原初的大爆炸。

他們繼續焦躁行走，
他們的地球仍在沸騰。

瘋子不
瘋　如我們。

To Meet My God

To meet my God
I rode a bee's buzz and
followed the road of the word.
A roaring black tiger kept me company.
That road led me
to death in the battle field.

To meet my God
I got into a dry leaf's vein and
followed the road of Silence.
A dumb camel kept me company.
That road led me
to death in the desert.

To meet my God
I mounted a silkworm's hair and
followed the road of Order.
An army of guards kept me company.
That road led me
to death in the mountain-snow.

To meet my God
I rode a whirlwind's back and
followed the road of Disorder.
People, scared, gave me way.
That road led me
to death in the deep woods.

To meet my God
I hung on to an eel's gills and
dived into the mid-sea.
A whale swallowed us and
led us into the netherworld.
From the barred darkness there,
I heard my God cry
guarded by seven god-men
with flaming swords.
I freed him.

Since that day
I have been in Hell,
unable to know who sent me here,
God or the god-men?

見我神

見我神
我騎著蜜蜂的嗡嗡聲
沿著言辭之路。
一隻咆哮的黑虎作伴。
那條路引領我
在戰場上死亡。

見我神
我進入乾葉的葉脈
沿著沉默之路。
一隻愚蠢的駱駝作伴。
那條路引領我
在沙漠中死亡。

見我神
我爬上蠶的一撮毛
遵循秩序之路。
一隊守衛作伴。
那條路引領我
在雪山中死亡。

見我神
我騎著旋風歸來
沿著無序之路。
人們害怕，給我讓路。
那條路引領我
在深林中死亡。

見我神
我掛在鰻魚的鰓上
潛入海中央。
一條鯨魚吞噬了我們
帶領我們進入陰間。
從那被堵塞的黑暗，
我聽到我的神在哭
由七位神人
和火劍守衛。
我釋放了他。

從那天起
我去過地獄，
不知道是受誰派遣，
是神還是神人？

How to Go to the Tao Temple

(From the sequence, *Northern Cantos*)

Don't lock the door.
Go lightly like the leaf in the breeze
along the dawn's valley.
If you are too fair,
cover yourself with ash.
If too clever, go half-asleep.
That which is fast
will tire fast:
be slow, slow as stillness.

Be formless like water.
Lie low, don't even try to go up.
Don't go round the deity:
nothingness has no directions,
no front nor back.
Don't call it by name,
its name has no name.
No offerings: empty pots
are easier to carry than full ones.
No prayers too: desires
have no place here.

Speak silently, if speak you must:
like the rock speaking to the trees
and leaves to flowers.

Silence is the sweetest of voices
and Nothingness has
the fairest of colours.

Let none see you coming
and none, going.
Cross the threshold shrunken
like one crossing a river in winter.
You have only a moment here
like the melting snow.

No pride: you are not even formed.
No anger: not even dust
is at your command.
No sorrow: it doesn't alter anything.
Renounce greatness:
there is no other way to be great.
Don't ever use your hands:
They are contemplating
not love, but violence.

Let the fish lie in its water
and the fruit, on its bough.
The soft one shall survive the hard,
like the tongue that survives teeth.

Only the one who does nothing
can do everything.

Go, the unmade idol
awaits you.

(*Tao Temple, Chu-Fu*)

如何去道觀

（選自《北方詩章》系列）

不要鎖門。
輕輕離去如微風中的葉子
沿著黎明的山谷。
若你太美麗
便用灰塵掩蓋自己。
若太聰明，便矇矓。
那走得快的
會累得快：
走得慢的，慢如止水。

如水無形。
處下，莫圖往上。
莫圍繞神靈：
空無無方，
無前亦無後。
莫以名呼喚，
其名無名。
無供奉：空罐
比滿罐更易攜帶。
也無祈禱：慾望
於此無立足之處。

默言，如要說你須：
如石對樹
如葉對花。

沉默是最美妙的聲音
而空無有
最美麗的色彩。

無人見你來
無人見你去。
越過門檻時退縮
就像冬天過河。
你在這裡只有片時
如融雪。

無驕：你甚至沒有成形。
無怒：甚至灰塵
也不受你的掌握。
無悲：它不改變任何事。
棄偉大：
沒有其它方法可以偉大。
永不要用你的手：
他們正在冥思
不是愛，而是暴力。

讓魚兒靜止在水中
讓果實靜止在樹頭。
柔持久於剛
如舌持久於齒。

唯不作之人
能作一切。

去吧，未成之偶
等著你。

（楚府道觀）

One Grief

One grief smells my feet
like a puppy, finds I am not his man
and rushes to my neighbour, wagging his tail.

A bark. A cry.

A joy caresses my cheeks
like a kitten: until another grief
comes crawling by
and winds around to choke me

一次悲傷

一次悲傷聞我的腳
就像小狗發現我不是牠的主人
又衝向我的鄰居，搖著他的尾巴。

一聲吠叫。一聲叫喊

一種喜悦撫慰我的臉頰
就像小貓：直到另一次悲傷
爬行而來
然後四周的風教我窒息

Learning Languages

I would love to learn languages,
Santali, Balochi, Catalan, Slovenian.
In all these tongues
we can say "love";
we can say "kill" too.

It is too late;
no time even to design a time-piece
may be, I can design a verse-piece

Languages walk past the age of love
bent over a walker.

I too will go,
to the land where I have plenty of time
to learn languages
and then
I will kill you with love.

學習語言

我喜歡學習語言，
桑塔利語，俾路支語，加泰羅尼亞語，斯洛文尼亞語。
在所有這些語言中
我們可以說「愛」，
我們也可以說「殺」。

為時已晚；
沒時間設計一個計時器
也許，我可以設計一個寫詩器

語言俯身於助行器
走過愛的時代。

我也會去，
到我有充足時間
學習語言的土地
然後
我會用愛殺你。

馬丁・索羅楚克（斯洛伐克），生於布拉提斯拉瓦，在斯洛伐克柯美紐斯大學研究美國詩歌並取得博士學位，目前在此校任教。首部詩集《沉默的戰爭》（1997）獲得斯洛伐克文化基金最佳新人獎，隨後著有《磨》（2001）、《萬有引力的浮游生物》（2006）及《愛情故事：代理人與病人》（2007）。索羅楚克譯作等身，翻譯過薩繆爾・貝克特、謝默斯・希尼、查爾斯・希米克、約翰・阿什貝利、泰德 休斯與大衛・安提的作品。索羅楚克現為詩藝國際詩歌節和出版社的總監。

Martin Solotruk (Slovakia), born in Bratislava, obtained his Ph.D. in American poetry from Comenius University, Bratislava, where he currently teaches. Solotruk's first book of poetry *Silent Wars* (1997) won the Slovak Literary Fund Best Debut Award. It was followed by *Grinding* (2001), *Plankton of Gravity* (2006) and *Lovestory: Agent and Patient* (2007). Solotruk has also translated the works of Samuel Beckett, Seamus Heaney, Charles Simic, John Ashbery, Ted Hughes, and David Antin. He is also a Director of Ars Poetica International, a poetry festival and publishing house.

馬丁 · 索羅楚克

MARTIN SOLOTRUK

中文翻譯：趙四
English translation by Zuzana Starovecká

Mraãenie v poläase rozpadu

Stále hovorí‰, Ïe sa mraãím,
No ja pritom len v duchu
pobehujem medzi t˘m
v‰etk˘m, ão som si napozeral.

Utekám pred t˘m
ako beÏec na vzduchu
pred zbiehajúcimi sa mraãnami.

Tak rád by som Èa
presvedãil,
Ïe sa nemraãím
—aspoÀ pri milovaní.

Akosi ma to zaãína braÈ.

Mraãím sa, lebo sa neviem
zbaviÈ pocitu,

Ïe obãas tak prudko plynieme,
aÏ sme pomaly len skrytou
reklamou seba sam˘ch.

Vidite º ní iba v kaÏdom
zlomku ãasu, ktor˘ je men‰í,
neÏ si vie mozog uvedomiÈ.

Ïe plynieme tak prudko,
aÏ zaãíname cítiÈ svoj poläas.
A pritom by sme sa chceli
len sústrediÈ a zostaÈ sústredení.

MilovaÈ sa a poãúvaÈ praãku,
jej nekoneãn˘ program,
ten rytmus Ïivotaschopnosti
najprostej‰ích vecí, ão nám obãas
zaklope na hlavu,
ako heuréka.

Ikonoklazmus mraãenia
proti solárnym mraãnám
protuberanciám atomárnych dvojíc
protuberanciám nukleárnych rodín

obrovské so‰né NIE so‰nosti
zauÏívanej reality

d˘chanie vanúce od mraãenia
k so‰nosti sústredenia.

To ono tvorí architektúru
t˘chto protuberancií
protuberanciami zamraãeného telesa,

ktoré sa tak sústredene,
do vypätia koneãnej ºahkosti
dychu, s drobn˘m frflaním
zbavuje neãistoty neistôt z toho,
ão si poãaÈ s voºn˘mi radikálmi,
bez najmen‰ieho rizika implózie.

SÈahujem zo seba
svoje mraãenie sa
To mraãenie sa priedu‰nej koÏe.
SÈahujem sa
zo starej do novej.
To z mraãenia vstávam.

Z mraãenia, pod ktor˘m je jasno.

Mraãenie ma prená‰a,
robí subtílnej‰ím.
Mraãím sa ako v stæpe prachu,
ktor˘, ako sama najlep‰ie vie‰,
nikdy celkom nevyÏenieme.

Neodchádzam ním, to tu len,
obãas rozpaãito, no predsa
neustále, pristávam
tebe na oãiach

i za chrbtom
pristávam

a zostávam s tebou.

Tak povedz, e‰te sa mraãím?

皺眉在半衰期

你說我總在皺眉，
但在我看來
我只不過是在我看到的
每件事物中跑來跑去。

我逃離它
像一個空中的奔跑者
在正聚攏而來的雲面前。

我很想
說服你
我沒在皺眉
——顯然沒皺，在做愛時。

這開始讓我坐立不安。

我皺眉因為沒法
擺脫這種感覺：

有時我們流動得太快了
以至我們所獲除了一個秘密的
自我廣告外均告落空。

僅在比我們的大腦能想像到的
更小的每一時間
片斷中可見。

我們奔流得太快了
我們能感到自己的半衰期。
我們想要的全部就是集中注意力
和保持注意力集中。

做愛，聽著洗衣機轉，
聽它沒完沒了的節目單，
最簡單事物的
生命力節奏
有時來敲我們的腦袋，
「有了！」

——皺眉頭的偶像破壞
反對太陽皺眉，
原子夫妻的突起，
核家庭的突起，

平凡現實之強健的
巨大壯碩的「不」。

皺眉刮起的微風
是自由離子的呼吸。

那就是正在創造出
這些突起的結構程序，
一具黑暗軀體的突起物

那軀體如此一心一意地清除懷疑之污垢
用最終耗盡的呼吸之輕盈
和一聲瑣碎的抱怨：
該拿這些有最低內爆風險的
自由基怎麼辦呢。

我在剝離
我的皺眉。
能滲水的皮膚的皺眉。
我正在
從舊我走進新我。
正是自皺眉中我升起。
其下是一片明朗的皺眉
使我心蕩神移

正是這使我更其精微。

我皺眉彷彿身在一柱塵土中，
（你是對此再清楚不過的人）
我們永遠也不能徹底驅散它。

我沒有留在它裡面，我只是在這裡，
有時候膽怯，但會
不息不止地
著陸在你眼中

或在你身後
我在這兒著陸

並且陪在你身邊。

現在告訴我，我還在皺眉嗎？

Frowning in Half-Life

You say I'm always frowning,
But in my mind
I'm only running about
amidst everything that I've been watching.

I'm running away from it
like a runner on air
before clouds that are coming together.

I'd love
to convince you
that I'm not frowning
—surely not when making love.

It's beginning to upset me.

I'm frowning because I can't
get rid of the feeling

that sometimes we flow so rapidly
that we come to nothing more than a secret
commercial of ourselves.

Visible only in every
fraction of time smaller
than our brain could ever imagine.

That we're flowing so rapidly
we can feel our half-life.
And all we want is to concentrate
and stay concentrated.

Make love and listen to the washing machine,
to its endless program,
the rhythm of vitality
of the simplest things,
which sometimes comes knocking at our head,
eureka

—iconoclasm of frowning
against solar frowns,
protuberances of atomic pairs,
protuberances of nuclear families,

a huge sturdy NO of the robustness
of ordinary reality.

It's the breath of free ions
that breezes from the frowning.

That's what's creating the architecture
of these protuberances,

the protuberances of a dark body
which is so intently getting rid of the dirt of doubts
with the final strain on the lightness
of breath and a petty grumble
uncertain what to do with the free radicals,
with minimal risk of implosion.

I'm peeling off
my frowning.
The frowning of permeable skin.
I'm moving
from the old one into a new.
It's the frowning I come rising from.

From frowning under which it's bright.

That's what transports me
making me ever subtler.
I'm frowning as if in a column of dust,
which (you're the one knows this best)
we'll never disperse completely.

I'm not leaving in it, here I just,
sometimes timidly, yet
ceaselessly
land in your eyes
or behind your back
I land here

and I stay with you.

Tell me now, am I still frowning?

Improbable Balance of Roots

waiting for a bit of emptiness
in the pool to swim in creates
the lapse in time of push and pull
that we have happily tried avoiding by rooting
　　　for the balance of roots
that have been waiting
for our immersion by deepening choirs
which have offered us the shade
of the improbable deep to the soil

of the unknown

(Written by the author in English)

根之間不大可能的平衡

等待一點池中空
以便泳游其間，創造了
在推拉時光中的時間流逝
我們愉快地植根於為了保持根之間的平衡
而試圖躲開的時間流逝
我們一直以來通過沉鬱唱詩班的聲調
想要等來的浸禮其中
提供給我們下到未知
之國土那不大可能的深處

之蔭蔽

Lousiness

struck by the inarticulate lightening
I have emerged aloof,
on the back foot scrutinizing
what the back makes
the sense of commonness
that I have yet to appreciate
to be able to draw inspiring
support from the ground
that made me hesitate
and you angry
by the apparent lack of
recognition
"can't you see what you're wasting trotting?,"
"don't you see, it's a given opportunity?,"
grounded window of opportunity
"you could fall through
alike Alice into wonderland"
but I just replied
"I'm just amazed at the wake of
approach that keeps sinking
into the moment of falling
through at bay
of the game of time."

(Written by the author in English)

生蝨

被口齒不清的閃電擊中
我冷淡地出現，
在後腳不利位置細查
是什麼背後製造出了
普通之意義
那普通——我尚不必感激
能從地面汲取的
鼓舞人心的支持
那使我猶豫
令你生氣的
因為明顯缺乏
受賞識
「難道你看不出你正在浪費於奔波嗎？」
「難道你沒發現那是個天賜良機？」
機運的接地窗
「你有可能掉進去
和愛麗絲掉進仙境一樣」
但我只是回答
「我只是驚奇於這接近路徑
留下的尾跡：一直沉浸在
掉落進時間遊戲
之海灣裡的
掉落一刻。」

Being Just Like Having Nothing

having a being
being a title
to the most intimate
sense of having
sleepless snoring
having split mind
being the condition of
being half—
awake half asleep being
wakeful in the fierce trial
towards always tentative
rest
nonetheless
starting from this having this performative
sonorous
sound of alive and kicking having being being having
said that
that being a noisy embedded something
nosing self—
propelled thrusting via any thing
being in a position of just quietly having a
boring boeing—
like jetting but being timely and time and time
again capable
of jettisoning a fixed idea of having split
but rather being aboard with
some being, intimate though distant,
rising to uncharted heights
being propelled
by a self snoring out some mind-boggling
noisy stuff governed by the glory
of the zone above
the sleep indulging
the sovereign noise of the schizophrenic struggle
for the control of the free skies
being
the one ready to embrace any noise
being worth the word
and hold it for eternity
just like having nothing
just being that.

(Written by the author in English)

就像一無所有那樣存在

有一個存在物
是擁有鼾聲隆隆的失眠
分裂的心靈
這種最私密
感覺的
所有權
是處在半
醒半睡
這種狀態是
朝著總要嘗試性
去休息的
激烈考驗中的睡不著
儘管如此
始於這擁有這富有表現力的
鏗鏘
在世之聲和踢向存在之「有」擁有存在
說出那
作為一個聒噪的嵌入式事物
自動推進的
鼻息運動突入任意一物
處在一個正巧悄然擁有一架無聊
波音飛機的地位
像是噴氣機飛行但能夠及時地，一次
又一次地
扔棄要擁有分裂的執念
而和某些存在
待在飛機上，雖遙遠但私密，
升至無人涉足的高度
被一個外部的鼾聲隆隆的自我
所推動，一些令人難以置信的
喧鬧東西被睡眠之上
地帶的榮光
所支配，為了控制自由天空們
主動沉溺於作反覆無常掙扎的
無上權力的噪音
成為
一個樂於擁抱任何噪音的人
那語詞擁有價值
為了永恆持有它
就像一無所有
就那樣存在。

阿列斯・斯特格（斯洛文尼亞），詩人、小說家和散文家。著有七本詩集、三本長篇小說及兩本散文集。曾獲法國藝術與文學勳章，並為德國文學院成員，比內克國際詩歌獎、皮特拉克詩歌獎（歐洲青年作家）、維羅妮卡詩歌獎及Rožanc獎。他的作品被翻譯成十五國語言在世界各地出版，包括中文、捷克語、克羅地亞語、德語、匈牙利語及西班牙語。他亦是一名視覺藝術家，最近在印度科茨穆奇里斯國際藝術雙年展展出大型裝置藝術作品。他也曾與多位音樂家和電影導演合作。

Aleš Šteger (Slovenia) is a poet and prose writer who has published seven books of poems, three novels, and two collections of essays. He has received the title "Chevalier des Artes et Lettres" from France and is a member of the German Academy for Language and Literature. He has earned the International Bienek Prize for Poetry, the Petrarch Prize for Young European Authors, the Veronika Award, and the Rožanc Award. His works have been translated into fifteen languages, such as Chinese, Czech, Croatian, German, Hungarian, and Spanish. Šteger is also a visual artist. His installations have appeared at the International Kochi-Muziris Arts Biennale in India. He has collaborated with musicians and film directors.

阿列斯 · 斯特格

ALEŠ ŠTEGER

中文翻譯：梁麗真

English translation by Brian Henry

Dragi moj oče

Dragi moj oče, saj veš, da vem,
Kar ve moj mali sin, da nič ne ostane,
Nobena beseda, nobeno telo.

V tvojem živi spomin na truplo tvojega očeta,
Ki ni mogel pozabiti mladostnega prizora,
Ki so gomazeli iz lobanje njegovega očeta.

Jaz gledam tebe, glava v povezah, na bolniški postelji,
In vem, moj dragi oče, da je zaman, vse zaman,
Nič ne ostane, ne beseda ne telo.

Koža zgnije, organi se utekočinijo,
Tkiva in mišice gredo v kompost
In kmalu so kosti le prah.

Ti si sin mojega spomina, oče, jaz sem zadnja priča
Tvojega očeta, moj sin je porok tvojega razpada,
Ki bo trajal, dokler bo živel človek, ki ga pomni.

Tako odhajajo v nič telesa in besede.
Ves trud zaman. Ničevo. In groteskno vso
Naprezanje, da bi trajali za hipec dlje.

Včeraj so te operirali, skrili mrtev vijak
V tvojo polomljeno čeljust, črvička iz titana,
Ki bo nekoč, kot edini preživeli pričal

O izginulem sinu in izginulem rodu
In o kraju izginulem, kjer so nekoč se, dragi oče,
Srečevale pozabljene besede in telesa

V pogubi.

我親愛的父親

我親愛的父親，你知道我明白
我的小兒子懂得的，不會有任何存留，
詞彙不會，身體不會。

你的身體裡活著你對你父親的屍身的記憶，
你的父親不會忘記兒時看見蠕蟲
爬出他父親頭顱的情景。

我看著你，你的頭纏裹繃帶，你在醫院病床上，
我明白，我親愛的父親，已是枉然，一切徒勞無功
不會有什麼存留，既不是詞彙也不是身體。

皮膚腐爛，器官液化，
組織和肌肉成為混合肥料，
很快，骨骼是塵埃。

你是我的記憶的兒子，父親，我是你的父親的
最後一名目擊者，我的兒子是你的衰朽的核保人，
你的衰朽將持續到一個男人生命的最後，如果他記得這衰朽的生氣。

就這樣一些軀體和詞語遁進空無。
一切徒勞無功。次要而微薄。我們所有
荒唐的勉力只夠維持一個稍長的片刻。

他們給你動手術，在你斷裂的頜骨裡
埋進一顆沒有生命的螺釘，一隻鈦金屬做的小蟲，
有一天，作為消失的兒子和消失的血統

與這消失的方位中的唯一生還者，
它將作證，在那個地方，親愛的父親，
遭淡忘的詞語和身體曾經相遇在

萬念俱寂。

My Dear Father

My dear father, you know that I know
What my small son knows, that nothing remains,
Not the word, not the body.

In your body lives the memory of the corpse of your father,
Who could not forget the childhood scene with the worms
That crawled out of the skull of his father.

I look at you, your head in bandages, on a hospital bed,
And I know, my dear father, that it is in vain, all in vain,
Nothing remains, neither the word nor the body.

Skin rots, organs liquefy,
Tissue and muscles become compost,
And soon the bones are only dust.

You are the son of my memory, father, I am the last witness
Of your father, my son is the underwriter of your decay,
Which will last as long as a man who remembers it will live.

Thus bodies and words go into nothingness.
All effort in vain. Paltry. And all this grotesque
Exertion of ours to last a brief moment longer.

Yesterday they operated on you, concealed a dead screw
In your broken jaw, a worm made of titanium
That one day will testify as the only survivor

Of the vanished son and the vanished lineage
And the vanished place where, dear father,
Forgotten words and bodies once met

In perdition.

Mati moja

Mati moja,
Ki si v telesih,
Razdejanje je tvoje ime.
Pridi vsaj k meni,
V tvoje izgnanstvo,
Zgodi se tvoje nasilje
V revščini in izobilju.
Navrzi vsaj danes
Kakšno puhlo drobtino
In odpusti mi
Trenutke šibkosti,
Ko poskušam ukrasti življenju
Več, kot nameniš.
Ne odpelji me ponovno v praznino,
Naj se zdrobé moje kosti,
Ko me pobožaš,
Mati.

我的母親

我的母親
在不同的身體裡，
崩毀是你的名字。
至少，從你的流亡，
來到我身邊，
從貧困和豐饒裡，
綻出你蠻荒的威嚴。
至少，今天，
扔一塊菲薄的麵包屑，
原諒我
在那些虛弱的時刻，
試圖從生活裡偷竊
那比你想要活得更多的。
請不要再次將我帶進空無，
當你撫摸我
願我的骨頭被碾碎，
母親。

My Mother

My mother
Who art in bodies,
Devastation is your name.
Come to me at least
In your exile,
Your brutality occurs
In poverty and plenty.
Toss today at least
A worthless crumb
And forgive me
My moments of weakness,
When I try to steal more from life
Than you intend.
Don't lead me once more into emptiness,
May my bones be crushed
When you caress me,
Mother.

Moj mali bog

Ob rojstvu
Se je v mene skril
En mali bog.

Jaz se spreminjam,
On pa je ves čas
Le samosvoj.

Ne prekrivava se scela.
Pogosto ga kličem,
Pa ga ni.

Včasih seže iz mene,
Boža bogove drugih,
Ne da to opazim.

Ni slab ta moj mali bog,
Četudi nerazumljen in sam.
Smili se mi.

Ne bi bil rad v njegovi koži.
On pa je v moji,
Zato sem mu hvaležen.

我的小神

出生時
一位小神
藏在我的身體裡。

我總在變化，
祂一直
就是祂自己。

我們並不完全重合。
我常呼喚祂，
祂不在。

有時祂會從我裡面伸出手
摸摸其他人的神，
而我毫無察覺。

祂不糟糕，我的小神，
儘管祂被誤會，孤伶伶。
我可憐祂。

我並不想在祂的皮膚裡。
可祂就在我的皮膚裡，
那麼我感謝祂。

My Little God

At birth
A little god
Hid inside me.

I change,
He is always
Only himself.

We don't totally overlap.
I often call him,
He isn't there.

Sometimes he reaches out of me
And strokes others' gods
Without me noticing.

He isn't bad, my little god,
Though misunderstood and alone.
I pity him.

I wouldn't want to be in his skin.
But he is in mine,
Thus I am grateful to him.

Moje telo je centralni komite

Moje telo je centralni komite.
Kri partijska celica za verska in ideološka vprašanja.
Preveč materialistično sanjaš,
Se mi posmehujejo tovarišice komsomoljke.
Da bi bil boljši, pograbim svojo dušo
In jo zaženem čez prag.
Do naslednjega kongresa naj izgine, samo da bo mir.
A kmalu prifrfota nazaj, tava naokrog,
Prevrača stole in lista knjige mojih kitajskih tovarišev.
Rad bi bil eden od njih in umrl gladko.
Tako pa se moram ukvarjati
Z uničevanjem neoprijemljive zarote bodočnosti.
V naslednjem življenju si bom izbral druge prednike,
Bolj uglajeno okolje, se prehranjeval s koreninicami,
Umiral kot kamen na rešetkah hidroelektrarne.
Evropejca pa se me duša drži
Kot izvensodni poboji za moda revolucije.
Vrača se iz cerkve. Pravi, da je plamen nagrobne sveče lep.
Zaženem jo v krematorij. Osmodi si peruti.
Vrne se pretresena, kriči, da je ogenj strašen razredni sovražnik.
Zaženem jo v zadnji krog pekla.
Od tam nobenih znamenj ne sporočil.
Kar uči dobra praksa in eoni:

1. Partija mora izglasovati
   Večni moratorij na vračanje duš umrlih.
2. Partija mora nagrajevati
   Samovžig in druge naslade telesa.
3. Partija mora napram smrti postati
   Tako mistična, kot je moje ime v razmerju
   Do celic, iz katerih izginja,
   Ne da bi v njih kdajkoli prebivalo.

我的身體是一個中央委員會

我的身體是一個中央委員會。
血液是黨為宗教和意識形態問題建設的基層組織。
你的夢過於唯物論，
我的共產主義青年團的同志們戲弄我。
為了變得更好，我一把抓住我的靈魂
將它拋上門檻。
讓它在第二次代表大會之前消失，只有這樣才有和平。
可很快它撲扇翅膀回來了，四下徘徊，
撞翻椅子，亂翻我的中國同志的書籍。
它希望成為它們中的一本，並且死得安穩。
這樣我就必須著手
挫敗有關我們未來的不容易捉摸的圖謀。
來世我會選擇另一群祖先，
一個更彬彬有禮的環境，以根鬚為食，
像水電站格柵上的一塊石頭那樣去死。
可作為一個歐洲人我堅守我的靈魂
就如同大規模殺戮牢牢把握住革命的睪丸。
靈魂從教堂返回。它説葬禮上蠟燭的焰苗很美。
我把它扔進火葬場。燒焦它的翅膀。
它回歸後已動搖，大喊著火是一個可怕的階級敵人。
我把它拋進地獄的最後一層。
打那裡再看不見它有任何表達溝通的動靜。
良性的實踐和萬古教導我們：

1. 黨應該實施
   對返回的死者們的靈魂的永久凍結。
2. 黨必須獎勵
   自焚和其他身體愉悦。
3. 黨必須對
   死亡採取神秘主義的態度，就像我的名字
   跟基層組織的關係，還沒來得及在其中活命，
   它已消失得無跡無痕。

My Body Is a Central Committee

My body is a Central Committee.
The blood is the Party's cell for religious and ideological questions.
You dream too materialistically,
My Komsomol comrades tease me.
In order to be better, I grab my soul
And hurl it over the threshold.
Let it disappear until the next Congress, only so there's peace.
But soon it flutters back, wanders around,
Knocks over chairs and leafs through the books of my Chinese comrades.
It would like to be one of them and die smoothly.
Thus I must deal with
Destroying the intangible plot of our future.
In the next life I will choose other ancestors,
A more courteous environment, feed on roots,
Die like a stone on the grate of a hydroelectric plant.
But as a European I hang onto my soul
Like mass killings hang on the testicles of revolution.
The soul returns from church. Says that the flame of the funeral candle
is beautiful.
I hurl it into the crematory. Scorch its wings.
It returns shaken up, shouts that fire is a dreadful class enemy.
I hurl it into the last circle of hell.
From there it communicates no signs.
What good practice and eons teach:

1. The Party must adopt
An eternal moratorium on the souls of the dead returning.
2. The Party must reward
Self-immolation and other bodily pleasures.
3. The Party must become mystical
Toward death, like my name is in relation
To cells, from which it disappears
Without ever living in them.

Zid

Ne mine dan, ko ne pomisliš,
Da so tudi tebe zazidali ven iz sveta.
Ti vzeli perspektivo. Izobčili.

Ne mine jutro, ko si ne zaprisežeš,
Da danes razrušiš ta zid, in ne večer,
Ko se vrneš razrušen. Tvoj upor je brez pomena.

Nikogar ni, ki bi ti podeljeval varnost nasprotja.
Opeke se same razpro, mehko kot ure.
Spustijo te skozi, še preden se jih dotakne dlan.

Čeprav ni nobene druge strani, nobenega drugega kraja.
Nikamor ne prispeš in nič te nikjer ne drži.
Brez zidu si, kjer bi se vse to končalo.

In nikjer nikogar nikdar je tvoj zid.

牆

沒有一天過得去，如果你不想起
你和世界之間那面被安放的牆。
擋住了你的遠景。放逐了你。

沒有一個早上過得去，如果你不發誓
今天你就拆掉這面牆，沒有一個夜晚過得去，
如果你不是支離破碎地歸來。你的反抗毫無意義。

沒有任何人能准予你對立面的安全。
牆磚獨自移換，輕柔如同時間。
它們容你穿過，在手掌觸到它們之前。

縱使沒有另一面，縱使不存在另一個地方。
你從不抵達，也從沒有盤桓的理由。
你的存在裡沒有牆，所有這一切原本可在那裡結束。

而你的牆是無名之地從來無人。

Wall

Not a day goes by when you don't think
That a wall was put between you and the world.
Took your perspective. Banished you.

Not a morning goes by when you don't swear
That today you will tear down this wall, and not an evening
When you don't return torn down. Your revolt is meaningless.

There is no one who will grant you the security of an opposite.
Bricks are shifting alone, softly like hours.
They let you through, before the palm touched them.

Even though there is no other side, no other place.
You arrive nowhere and nothing holds you anywhere.
You are without a wall, where all this would end.

And your wall is *nowhere no one never.*

瑪麗亞・斯捷潘諾娃（俄羅斯），詩人、散文家與記者，著有十本詩集和三本散文集。曾獲多項俄羅斯與國際文學獎，包括俄羅斯Bolshaya Kniga大獎、NOS大獎及安德雷・貝利獎。她的詩作被翻譯成多種語言，包括英語、法語、德語、希伯來語和意大利語。她的小說《悼念記憶》糅合回憶錄、檔案和散文，匯成史詩式敘述，2017年11月以俄語出版，於2018年12月榮獲大書獎。斯捷潘諾娃創辦並主編眾籌網上日誌COLTA.RU，報導俄羅斯與世界各地的文化、社會和政治生活，每個月的瀏覽量達到六十萬人次。

Maria Stepanova (Russia) is a poet, essayist, and journalist. She is the author of ten poetry collections and three books of essays, and a recipient of several Russian and international literary awards, including the Bolshaya Kniga Prize, the Russia's main literary award, as well as the NOS Prize and Andrey Bely Prize. Her poems have been translated into many languages, including English, French, German, Hebrew, and Italian. Her novel *Pamiati pamiati* (In Memory of Memory), which blends memoir, documents and essays into an epic narrative, came out in Russian in November 2017 and received the Big Book Prize in December 2018. Stepanova is the founder and editor-in-chief of COLTA.RU, a crowdfunded online daily covering the cultural, social, and political life in Russia and in the world. It attracts an audience of 600,000 unique visitors per month.

瑪麗亞 · 斯捷潘諾娃

MARIA STEPANOVA

中文翻譯：張猛

English translation by Sasha Dugdale

«Нету разницы между»

нету разницы между
первою и второй
отечественной и отечественной
великой и тихой
атлантической
мировой

все равно они падают
на единственной, на гражданской
где заря в золе копошится

извлекает наконечники копий

леш а леш
огоньку бы
говорит убитому убитый
убитый говорит убивцу

「這兩者之間沒有差別」

這 兩 者 之 間 沒 有 差 別
第 一 次 和 第 二 次 的
衛 國 的 和 衛 國 的
偉 大 的 和 寂 靜 的
大 西 洋 的
世 界 的

無 論 如 何 他 們 都 降 落 在
統 一 的 ， 公 民 的
朝 霞 在 草 木 灰 裡 蠕 動 的 地 方

抽 取 出 複 印 件 的 端 頭

廖 什 啊 廖 什
如 果 被 殺 者 能 從 被 殺 者 身 上
如 果 殺 人 犯 能 從 被 殺 者 身 上
感 受 到 火 光

"No difference between first and second"

no difference between first and second
patriotic or patriotic
great or pacific
atlantic
world

all the same they fall
to the only the civil
where sunrise quivers in the cinders

draws out the spear-tips

mate eh mate
giss a light
says the dead to the dead
says the killed to the killer

«Цветок умирает под кожей стекла»

цветок умирает под кожей стекла
роток почернел и культя затекла
земля за убитых, она сохранит их
и в должное время представит тела

разумные звери выходят на суд
свидетельский ящик – прозрачный сосуд
там тёмно и тёкло, дорожка намокла
и видно как суку щенята сосут

судья поднимает глаза с полировки
на низкую лампу дневного огня
берет распечатки ориентировки
и спросит присяжных прощать ли меня

и не прерывая уже разговора
вчерашние братья выходят из бора
в обугленных шкурах, в болотной грязи
садятся в телегу, а ну-ка вези

туда, где поляна палатку держала
стянули тропу травянистые жала
и держат как стропы дорогу назад
чтоб даже надежду она не рожала

а как оправдаться? язык едока
покажет отчетливый след молока
древесные кольца покажет бумага,
следы топора и слова дурака

про магна имаго

「一朵花正在玻璃的皮膚底下死去」

一朵花正在玻璃的皮膚底下死去
嘴巴變黑，殘肢發腫
大地站在被殺者一方，她保護他們
並在恰當的時間把身體展示出來

理智的野獸走上法庭
證人的抽屜是透明的容器
那裡的幽暗處流淌，小路濕透
看起來就像小狗們在吮吸母狗

法官從拋光處抬起雙眼
望向白日焰火的低矮枱燈
拿起方位的打印件
問陪審員們是否寬恕我

沒有打斷談話
昨天的兄弟們從松林中走出
皮膚燒焦，身上帶著褐綠色污泥
坐到了馬車上，啟程吧

去往林中空地撐起帳篷的地方
草上的刺束緊小路
抓緊了身後的道路宛若吊繩
為的是讓她甚至連希望也不要分娩

那該怎樣為自己辯護？一個人的舌頭
會展示牛奶清晰的痕跡
一張紙會展示樹木的年輪，
斧頭的印記和傻瓜的話

關於成蟲馬戈納

"The flower dies under a skin of glass"

the flower dies under a skin of glass
mouth blackens stumps trickly crust
earth takes the dead she keeps them
and brings them up when she must

the sensible animals hold court
the witness box is a transparent lung
dark and trickled the way is damp
the bitch suckles her young

the judge lifts its eyes from the bench
to daylight's low-hung bulb
holds up wanted posters
and asks the jury if I am absolved

barely pausing their talk
yesterday's brothers emerge from the copse
in charred pelts, mud-crusted
get up on the cart, whip on the horse

to where the meadow holds an awning,
pins a path of stinging plants and thorns
the way back is belted down
even hope is stillborn

how to justify this? on the greedy tongue
milk writes in curds,
and paper is marked by tree rings
traces of axe   a fool's words

magna imago

«Человеческое тело»

человеческое тело
не расходится как мыло
в напомаженной воде
оно никогда не бывает было
оно всегда сейчас и где

оно светимо сквозь валежник
его уничтожить мудрено
оно пробьется как подснежник
сквозь углеродное пятно

и все что в нем едва существовало
но изнывало взаперти
рванется в черные провалы
чтобы опять произойти

новая жизнь восходит когда не чаешь
знать не можешь чем ее повстречаешь

「人的身體」

人的身體
不會像肥皂
在塗了油膏的水中消失
它從沒有過「曾經」
它總是「現在」和「在哪裡」

穿過枯樹枝它被照亮
要將它摧毀很困難
它像雪花蓮一樣
衝破碳灰開始生長

它體內的一切勉強存在
卻在囚禁中疲憊不堪
它將衝出黑色的塌陷
為了再次的重生

新生活將會出現當你不再抱著期待
你無法知道，你將會拿什麼來迎接它

"The human body"

the human body
is not soap wearing thin to a hole
in the scented water bowl
nor is it ever wholly
of the past, always of the here and now

glows through the deadwood
not easy to dispatch
it creeps up like a snowdrop
through the carbon patch

and what was pining, barely alive
shut away within its bony cage
now floods into the dark recesses
to happen again

new life emerges when hope is no more
and you stand there, empty-handed and unsure

«Жизнь ты прореха нуждающаяся в починке»

жизнь ты прореха нуждающаяся в починке
смерть ты тесто стосковавшееся по начинке

「生活你是亟待修理的破洞」

生活你是亟待修理的破洞
死亡你是懷念餡兒的麵團

“Life, you are a gash in need of stitching”

life, you are a gash in need of stitching
death, you are a crust that yearns for filling

«Те, кто держит во рту»

те, кто держит во рту, сперва осторожно, головы с глазами

те, кто трогал в уме газету, как мама учила не, никогда, и руки отмой

те, кто рвут на лету, переносят из дома в дом, размазывают по стеклам

тупорылое тело пробуют установить на колеса

и катить, наставляя жерло, поплевывая в направленьи

те и эти
но в большей степени эти

для них самобранкою новобранцы
раскидывают зеленые руки
им ложатся в ноги
тупыми березовыми стволами
чтобы понравиться карне
по желанию жли
по веленью баяна
под побудку аккордеона

и о, голоса детей, поющих, где было купол
в нечистом поле
в окруженьи хлебов и пугал

「那些一開始小心翼翼」

那些一開始小心翼翼，把頭顱和眼睛銜在嘴裡的人

那些在心中觸摸報紙的人，像媽媽曾叮囑永遠不要的那樣，也觸碰了我的手

那些在飛翔中掙脱，從一個房子遷移到另一個，在玻璃上塗抹的人

試圖將嘴臉蠢笨的身體安裝到車輪上

然後驅使，裝上炮口，不時朝著前進方向吐唾沫

那些人和這些人
但在極大程度上這些人

對他們來説新兵們用桌布
攤開綠色的手臂
將它蓋到腿上
彷彿笨拙的白樺樹幹
為的是讓短號喜歡上
按照日力的願望
按照大手風琴的要求
伴隨著手風琴的起床號

哦，孩子們唱歌的嗓音，那裡曾有圓頂
在不潔淨的田野
在糧食和稻草人的環繞中

"Those who carry in their mouths"

those who carry in their mouths, at first with care, heads with seeing eyes

those who touched newspaper print in their heads, as mother said never to do,
never, wash your hands

those who rip apart in flight, carrying from nest to nest, smearing on the glass

attempt to mount the blunt-snouted body on a set of wheels,

set it trundling, throat outstretched and spouting fire

yes, them and these, too
but actually more these

for them conscripts spread their green arms wide
like a tablecloth plentifully spread
lie heaped at their feet like birch logs
to please the valkyries
at the harpies' hearts desire
to the bayan's thrum
the accordion's reveille

and O, those children's voices, singing where once there was a dome
in the soiled field
surrounded by corn and scarecrows

托絲・克里斯蒂娜（匈牙利），匈牙利最受歡迎及最著名的詩人之一，曾獲葛雷夫斯獎、德里・提波爾獎及約瑟夫・阿提拉獎，更榮獲匈牙利文學最高榮譽的桂冠獎等。托絲至今著有十本詩集、七本散文集，包括長短篇小説與詩歌，經翻譯成十五國語言出版，包括捷克語、英語、芬蘭語、法語、德語、波蘭語、西班牙語及瑞典語等。

Tóth Krisztina (Hungary) is one of the most popular and best known Hungarian authors and the recipient of the Graves Prize, the Déry Tibor Prize, and the Attila József Prize. She has also been awarded the Laureate Prize, one of the highest recognitions in Hungarian literature. She has published ten volumes of poetry and seven volumes of prose to date. Her works have been translated into fifteen languages. Her novels, short stories, and poems can be read in Czech, English, Finnish, French, German, Polish, Spanish, and Swedish among others.

托絲 · 克里斯蒂娜

TÓTH KRISZTINA

中文翻譯：余澤民

English translation by Ottilie Mulzet and Antony Dunn

Kelet-európai triptichon

I

Nevünket mondja a hangosbemondó
és mi felpattanunk. Nevünket
rosszul írják és rosszul ejtik,
de mi készségesen mosolygunk.
A szállodákból elhozzuk a szappant,
az állomásra túl korán megyünk.
Nehéz bőrönddel, bő nadrágban
mindenütt ténfereg egy honfitársunk.
Velünk mennek a vonatok rossz irányba,
és ha fizetünk, szétgurul az apró.

Határainkon félünk, azokon túl
eltévedünk, de felismerjük egymást.
Felismerjük a világ túlfelén is
a lámpaláztól átizzadt ruhát.
Alattunk áll meg a mozgólépcső, szakad le
a teli szatyrok füle, és mikor
távozunk, megszólal a riasztó.
Bőrünk alatt, mint egy sugárzó ékszer
ott a bűntudat mikrochipje.

II

Tudom, hol laksz, ismerem azt a várost.
Ismerem azt a fekete vízesést.
Anyád a tetőre járt napozni,
nyáron a bányatóban fürödtetek.
Ismerem azt a láb nélküli embert
aki a kapualjban lakik,
ismerem azt az országot, ismerem
vonatait, sírását, klór egét,
savas esőit, lassú havazását,
túlöltöztetett, sápadt csecsemőit.

Tudom, hol laksz. Hiába élsz akárhol,
csonkolt akácok szegélyezte út
kísér álmodban, hogyha hazagondolsz.
Ünnep múltán, mikor mint túl nehéz
halottat, lábánál fogva vonszolják a fát,
megállsz, nézed, ahogy többihez lökik.
Tudom, mit látsz. Emberi testek kusza halmát
kinyújtott, sárga karjukon egy-egy
ottfelejtett ékszerrel: kék-arany
kifosztott szaloncukorpapírral.

III

A nevem Alina Moldova.
Kelet-Európából jöttem,
magasságom 170 centiméter,
várható életkorom 56 év.
Fogaimban amalgámtömést,
szívemben öröklött szorongást hordok.
Angolomat nem értik,
franciámat nem értik,
akcentus nélkül
csak a félelem nyelvét beszélem.

A nevem Alina Moldova.
Szívbillentyűm őrizetlen sorompó,
ereimben mérgek keringnek,
várható életkorom 56 év.
Tíz éves fiamat elbírom,
szerzek lisztet, mozgó vonatra szállok.
Megüthetsz, rázogathatsz,
csak a fülbevalóm zörög,
mint levált alkatrész
a még forgó motorban.

東歐三聯畫

一

擴音喇叭裡點我們的名字
我們迅速站起。我們的名字
被人寫錯並唸錯，
但我們還是熱忱地微笑。
我們帶走酒店裡的肥皂，
早早就趕到火車站。
到處都能見到拖著沉重皮箱、
穿著肥大褲子的我們的同胞。
列車載著我們駛向錯誤的方向，
我們付款時，零錢滾落一地。

我們在邊境上害怕，在邊境外
迷路，但是我們能夠彼此認出。
即使在地球的另一半我們也能認出
因怯場而被冷汗濕透的衣裳。
滾梯在我們腳下，裝滿東西的塑料袋
斷了提手，我們離開商店時，
防盜器發出刺耳的蜂鳴。
犯罪感的芯片，像一件閃光的首飾
植在我們的皮下。

二

我知道你的住址，我熟悉這座城市
我熟悉那黑色的瀑布，
你媽媽去屋頂曬太陽，
夏天你們在礦湖裡游泳。
我認識那個沒腿的人，
他住在大門洞裡。
我熟悉這個國家，熟悉它的那些
火車、哭泣、漂白粉味的天、
酸雨、緩慢的飛雪、
穿得過多、面色蒼白的嬰孩。

我知道你住在哪裡。不管你活到何地，
只要一想家，路兩邊枝斷葉枯的
槐樹，就會在夢中陪伴你。
節日過後，你拖著聖誕樹，
就像抓著腳拖一具很沉的屍首，
你站住，環顧，把它跟別人的扔到一起。
我知道你看到了什麼。你看到成堆的人體
堆成小山，在他們枯黃的胳膊上有一個個
被遺忘的首飾：藍色和金色的
皺巴巴的糖紙。

三

我的名字叫奧莉娜·摩爾多瓦。
我來自東歐，
身高170釐米，
預期壽命56歲。
我嘴裡有用銀汞補的牙，
我心裡揣著與生俱來的焦慮。
我不懂英語，
也不懂法語，
我只能不帶口音地
講恐懼的語言。

我的名字叫奧莉娜·摩爾多瓦。
我的心瓣是無人看守的攔路桿，
毒素在我的血管裡流淌，
我的預期壽命56歲。
我能抱著十歲的兒子，
拎著麵粉，跳上開動的列車。
你可以毆打我，推搡我，
只有我的耳環會嘩啦作響，
像個鬆動的零件
在還旋轉的馬達裡。

East-Europe Triptych

I

The loudspeaker calls out our names
and we jump up. Our names are
misspelled and mispronounced,
but we smile graciously.
We take the soap from the hotel,
and arrive too early at the station.
With heavy suitcases, in baggy trousers,
everywhere one of our compatriots loitering.
The trains go with us in the wrong directions,
and if we pay, the small change rolls everywhere.

At our borders we're afraid, and beyond that
we get lost, but recognize each other.
We know the other side of the world,
the sweat-drenched clothes beneath the coat.
Below us stands the escalator, the handle
of the shopping bag filled to bursting rips, and when
we leave, the alarm goes off.
Beneath our skin, like a radiating jewel,
is the microchip of a guilty conscience.

II

I know where you live, I know that city well.
I know that black waterfall.
Your mother used to sunbathe on the roof,
in the summer you swam in the quarry lake.
I know that man, his legs amputated,
who lives in the entranceway.
I know that country, I know
its trains, its cries, its chlorine heavens,
its acid rains, its lingering snowfalls,
its pale overly-swaddled infants.

I know where you live. No matter where it is,
if you happen to think of home, the road bordered
with the stumps of acacia trees
haunts you in your dreams.
After the feast, when they drag in
the tree, like a dead man, too heavy, grabbing at the foot,
you stop and look, as it is cast out to the others.
I know what you see: the disheveled heap of human bodies,
on every one of their extended yellow hands
a forgotten jewel: plundered
blue and gold Christmas-candy wrappers.

III

My name is Alina Moldova.
I come from Eastern Europe,
I am 170 centimeters in height,
my life expectancy is 56 years.
I have amalgam fillings in my teeth,
in my heart I carry an inherited dread.
When I speak English, no one understands me,
when I speak French, no one understands me,
it is only the language of fear
that I speak without an accent.

My name is Alina Moldova.
My heart valves are an unmanned rail-crossing,
poisons circulate within my veins,
my life expectancy is 56 years.
I support my ten-year-old son,
I get hold of some flour, step onto moving trains.
You can hit me, you can shake me,
but my earring only jangles a little,
like a loosened part
in a motor still running.

(Translated by Ottilie Mulzet)

Az egérről

A költő könyvében, aki már nem él,
a vers mellett, melyben egy nőről ír,
aki nem él már, mint egy sárvirág
megőrződött a macskám lábnyoma:

odalopódzott mindig, mert nagyon
izgatta őt a lapok közti rés,
várta, hogy egyszer kijön az egér
(régen elveszett az a macska is),

és tényleg, ott a papíralagút
mélyén valami folyton imbolyog:
elteszünk ezt-azt a lapok közé,
lepréselni a véletleneket.

老鼠

在詩人的書裡，她已不再活著，
詩外的文字裡，寫了一個女人，
她已經死了，就像一朵蒲公英
守護的我的貓的足印：

牠總是悄然湊近，因為
紙頁間的縫隙使牠興奮，
等待，突然從裡面鑽出一隻老鼠
（這隻貓也已丟了很久），

果真，在那紙隧洞的
深處有什麼東西一直晃動：
我們在紙頁間放這放那，
為了壓扁偶然。

After a Mouse

In a book by a long-dead poet,
by the poem in which he fixes a woman
long-dead, is a flowerhead of mud
pressed flat; the foot-stamp of my cat.

Forever sniffing round, she was
transfixed by lurking-space between the pages,
and froze there, once, for the out-race of a mouse
(and now my cat, my pet, is long-gone, too),

And true enough, in the spine-dark deep
of the paper hidey-holes there's something trapped:
we're forever slipping this or that between the sheets
to keep a hold on all, our every accident.

(Translated by Antony Dunn)

苡若瑪・恩梅彬憂（尼日利亞），生於拉各斯，《給艾達的問題》作者，2016 年非洲最重要的文學節Writivism 稱她為當代非洲頂尖新晉詩人之一。她的詩作被翻譯成法語、葡萄牙語、俄語、西班牙語和土耳其語。此外，她的詩歌印刷本遍佈世界各地，在國際社交媒體上也具有極高的人氣。恩梅彬憂應邀於庫伯聯盟學會作TEDx 演講，試圖理解與拆解沉默的傳統。

Ijeoma Umebinyuo (Nigeria), born in Lagos, is the author of *Questions for Ada*. In 2016, Ijeoma was named one of the top contemporary poets emerging from Africa by the Writivism, which is one of the most important literary festivals in Africa. Her works have been translated into French, Portuguese, Russian, Spanish, and Turkish. Widely disseminated in print, her poetry also enjoys popularity on international social media. Ijeoma was invited to give TEDx talks in the Cooper Union and her talk seeks to understand and dismantle the tradition of silence.

苡若瑪・恩梅彬憂

IJEOMA UMEBINYUO

中文翻譯：吳詠彤

The Delicate Acts of Survival

you must bring your daughter to church
the devil used her to tempt her uncle
it is the devil that has possessed her fourteen-year-old body.
when she tells you she hurts,
scold her for tempting men,
make her feel ashamed of her body.
you must bring her to church for deliverance.
when she is seventeen
and the boys enter her room she does not go to you the next day,
your daughter bathes with her pain her tears a eulogy for their crimes.
the day she sat on the couch somewhere in London
screaming at the therapist begging for help
she never mentions it to you.

when she is twenty-three standing
with a degree in her hand
and an unsmiling face
between you and uncle,
she flinches when he moves closer
your daughters sit sharing memories one after the other,
revealing a timeline of secrets.
they are not silent
like their mothers
and they hold their hearts, curing their pain with love.
your daughter is twenty-five
she called me
begging me to make the depression go away. go away. go away.
go away. go away. go away.
when your daughter turned thirty you begged her to make you
a proud mother.
she married him.
broken heart, broken ribs two miscarriages later

the days she says "no"
he yells ownership of her body and she lets him.
and she lets him.
and she lets him?
but, remember
your daughter was fourteen and you begged her
and you begged her
to learn the language of silence.

委曲求全之道

你一定要帶你的女兒到教堂去
是魔鬼利用了她來誘惑她的叔叔
是魔鬼附上了她十四歲的身軀。
當她對你說覺得受傷害，
你要因為她曾誘惑男人而責備她，
讓她為自己的身體感到羞恥。
你一定要把她帶到教堂裡讓她得救贖。
到她十七歲的時候
那些男孩進了她的房間而她並沒有在第二天
把這事告訴你，
你的女兒卻把她的傷痛和淚水浸泡成頌詞歌頌他們的惡行。
那天在倫敦某處她坐在沙發上
向著她的治療師尖叫著乞求幫助
而她從來沒有向你提起此事。

到她二十三歲的時候她站著
手上拿著大學畢業文憑
卻沒有笑
在你和叔叔中間，
當他移近她就不安地閃避
你的女兒們坐著把一個又一個回憶道出，
揭開了一連串藏在時光裡的秘密。
她們並不沉默
不像她們的母親
她們捧著自己的心，以愛治療著她們的痛楚。
到你的女兒二十五歲的時候
她致電我
求我把抑鬱帶走。帶走。帶走。
帶走。帶走。帶走。
當你的女兒三十歲你懇求她讓你能做一個
驕傲的母親。
她嫁給了他。
心碎了，肋骨碎了，在兩次小產之後

那天她說「不」
他對她的身體宣示主權，而她由得他。
而她由得他
她由得他？
但，請你記得
當你的女兒十四歲的時候你曾求她
你曾求她
要學懂沉默。

Conversations with Broken Girls

she calls you on the telephone screaming for help
begging you to come visit her you sit
she tells you how she loved him you listen
as she carries herself to memories she has a faraway look
her skin begins to glow
she says
"men take and take"
you nod in agreement
you hold her hand
as she searches your eyes
for an answer you cannot give
she is smiling as you bring her soup
she has on her lazy smile and her half-moon gaze men have always loved her
for her sugar smile, consuming her high
you ask her if it hurts
she does not respond
she says
"he loved how my skin felt against his"
she has a distant look,
gathering her pain
for another lonely night
you ask her again
she does not respond
she says with pain stretching her voice
"i already had baby names"
and you hear the walls wail.

與心碎的女子談話

她致電你，在電話的另一端呼喊求援
懇求你前來探望於是你坐下
她告訴你她怎樣愛他於是你聽著
她凝望遠處把自己帶到回憶裡去
她的皮膚開始發亮
她説
「男人予取予求」
你點頭同意
你牽著她的手
這時她凝視你
希望找到一個你不能給的答案
當你端過湯來，她微笑著
她有慵懶的笑容和如月半彎的雙眼
男人們常喜歡、常沉醉於
她如糖一般甜的微笑
你問她痛嗎
她沒有反應
她説
「他喜歡感覺到我的肌膚貼著他的」
她若有所思
收起她的痛楚
準備度過另一個孤單的長夜
你再問她
她仍是不反應
她的聲音透著痛楚説
「我已在想孩子的名字」
而你聽到牆壁哭泣。

Trigger

He said
"How can you be a virgin?
There are no virgins in Nigeria!"
you watch him quietly
He puts his fingers in
And you flinch
"Be a big girl," you told yourself
At twenty-five, you should know
a man will leave
if you do not offer him some sugah
So, he unzips
and you hear yourself cry
But you never made a sound he will not understand
He said
"How can you be a virgin? There are no virgins in Nigeria!"
And you hold on
rushing to the bathroom
to scrub his smell away
Now, you plant cactus on your skin preparing for the men
who will come
for some of your sugah.

誘

他說
「你怎麼可能是個處女？
尼日利亞是沒有處女的！」
你靜靜地看著他
他把指頭插入
你閃躲
「我已長大了。」你告訴自己
二十五歲的時候，你該知道
如果你不讓一個男人嚐到些好處的話
他會離開
所以，他解開衣鏈
你聽見自己的哭聲
但你沒有一種聲音是他聽不明白的
他說
「你怎麼可能是個處女？尼日利亞是沒有處女的！」
而你堅持著
跑到浴室
要把他的氣味洗去
現在，你在自己的皮膚上種了仙人掌，準備
招架那些為了得到好處
來找你的男人。

Splinter

Your father does not carry pain like most do.
He puts it in bottles
and throws it at your mother till she screams for God,
kneeling in church
seeking refuge in the arms of the unknown.
Your father
came back from the war; now
He's always crying at night
and without saying a word
your mother strips naked
as he
holds her body,
whispering
"thank you"
before drifting off to sleep.

斷裂

你的父親並不如一般人一樣處理痛楚。
他把痛楚藏在瓶子裡
把瓶子扔向你母親直至她呼喊上帝，
在教堂裡跪下
尋找一個她看不見的避難所。
你的父親
從戰後回來；現在
他每晚都哭泣
不發一言
你的母親一絲不掛
當他
抱著她的身體，
輕聲說
「謝謝」
然後才沉沉睡去。

Things We Lost in the Fire

The gentle reminders
as you leave some patches of your spirit
around the corners of my soul,
freeing yet binding me to you.

The way my name rolled off your tongue
as though you were whispering it to God.

Late-night calls
as you peel words,
sprinkling them with desire for me to taste.

Forgive me, how did your soul forget so soon?
The way we held on to heaven,
carrying our moans as offerings to
The Universe scratching our souls,
mapping our conquest.

The way we thought
our world would never end.

那些我們在火中失去的事物

你留下溫柔的提醒
把你靈魂的方塊
貼在我心靈的角落，
把我們倆釋放又捆綁著。

我的名字自你口中滑落
彷彿你對上帝這樣默念著。

深夜在電話裡
你把每一個字的表皮剝開
在它們身上輕灑你的渴望盼我能逐一品嚐。

原諒我，為什麼你的靈魂那麼快便忘記了？
我們是這樣堅持著踏上天路，
要以我們的呻吟為祭
給那抓傷我們心靈的宇宙
看見我們要征服它的決心。

我們曾這麼以為
屬於我們的世界永不滅亡。

譯成二十種語言出版。他亦曾翻譯中國詩人李賀的詩歌作品。威斯托尼迪斯曾獲任雅典奧運會申辦材料的主筆。現為希臘最重要的報紙《論壇日報》撰稿，居於雅典。

Anastassis Vistonitis (Greece) was born in Komotini, Northern Greece. He studied Political Sciences and Economics in Athens and Philosophy in Thessaloniki. From 1996 to 2001, he was a member of the board of the EWC (The Federation of European Writers). From 2003 to 2007, he was the Vice-president of the EWC. Vistonitis has published twelve books of poetry, four volumes of essays, five travelogues, a book of short stories, and a book of translations of the Chinese poet Li He. Vistonitis was the General Editor of the candidature file of Athens for the Olympic Games of 2004. His writings have been translated into 20 languages. He writes for the leading Greek newspaper *To Vima* and lives in Athens.

安納斯塔西斯 · 威斯托尼迪斯

ANASTASSIS VISTONITIS

中文翻譯：錢穎超

English translation by Anastassis Vistonitis and George O'Connell

Ars Poetica

Το ποίημα δεν είναι σαν τα φύλλα
που ο άνεμος σέρνει στους δρόμους.
Δεν είναι η ακίνητη θάλασσα,
το αραγμένο καράβι.
Δεν είναι ο γαλάζιος ουρανός
και η καθαρή ατμόσφαιρα.

Το ποίημα είναι ένα καρφί
στην καρδιά του κόσμου.
Ένα φωτεινό μαχαίρι
μπηγμένο κάθετα στις πόλεις.
Το ποίημα είναι σπαραγμός,
κομμάτι γυαλιστερό μέταλλο,
πάγος, σκοτεινή πληγή.
Το ποίημα είναι σκληρό,
πολυεδρικό διαμάντι.
Συμπαγές – λαξευμένο μάρμαρο.
Ορμητικό – ασιατικός ποταμός.

Το ποίημα δεν είναι φωνή,
πέρασμα πουλιού.
Είναι πυροβολισμός
στον ορίζοντα και την Ιστορία.
Το ποίημα δεν είναι άνθος που μαραίνεται.
Είναι βαλσαμωμένος πόνος.

詩藝

詩歌不像樹葉
可以由風吹落至地面。
也不像靜止的海面，
可以停靠船隻。
詩歌不是蔚藍的天空
和清新的空氣。

詩歌是刺透世界心臟的
那根木樁。
是筆直穿透城市的
那把亮刀。
詩歌是精神的傷痛，
是反光的金屬碎片，
是冰塊，是發黑的傷口。
詩歌是堅硬的
多面鑽石體。
是純色的——雕琢完好的大理石。
是洶湧澎湃的——亞洲河流。

詩歌不是聲音，
是飛鳥的痕跡。
詩歌是海平線和歷史上的
運行軌跡。
詩歌不是枯萎的花朵。
是不腐的傷痛。

Ars Poetica

Not like the leaves
windswept through the streets.
Nor still in the sea,
a tethered boat.
A poem is not the sky's azure,
its lucid air.

A poem is a stake
through the world's heart,
a glinting blade
driven through the towns.
A poem is pain,
a bright splinter of steel,
ice, a blackened wound.
A poem is obdurate,
its facets diamond.
Graved stone.
A surging Asian river.

A poem is neither voice
nor winged passage.
It's a rifle shot
at history, the skyline.
A poem is no withering bloom.
It is anguish, embalmed.

Το φεγγαρι στο ποτηρι

I

Αυτό
το αβέβαιο τραπέζι
πολώνει την ερημιά, θυμίζει πεθαμένους φίλους.
Με μια λάμπα παγώνει το σκοτάδι.

Όμως δεν είναι έτσι το φως.

Εγώ το είδα παιδί μέσα στις πεδιάδες
να βγαίνει έξω από τα χρώματα.
Στρογγυλό φεγγάρι, χάρτη των ανοίξεων,
πάνω από τις καλαμποκιές και τα σιτάρια.

II

Τώρα
Το κρύο μεταμεσονύκτιο
είναι μια λίθινη επιγραφή πάνω από τα σπίτια
κι η θάλασσα ένας χώρος άδηλης αναπνοής.
Αδιέξοδα, θλιβερές αποφάσεις,
σπαταλημένο αίμα των αγαπημένων,
γεμίζει τούτο το τραπέζι ξύλινα δόντια,
καμένες προσωπίδες, ίσκιους που φλέγονται
και στο κέντρο ένα ποτήρι νερό
με το φεγγάρι βουλιαγμένο στον πάτο.

瓶中之月

I

這張
晃動的桌上
鋪滿了孤獨，使人想起死去的摯友。
一盞燈的光解凍了整片黑暗。

但這並不是光。

孩童時期我看到光在平原上
從無數的色彩中升起。
是玉米田、麥田上方的
圓月，春之圖。

II

當下
午夜的寒冷
是屋頂上的石碑
和大海某處模糊的呼吸聲。
絕境，痛苦的選擇，
失血過多的愛人，
堆滿木齒的桌子，
燃燒的面具，陰影
在一杯水中央燃燒
而月亮沉入杯底。

The Moon in the Glass

I

This
wobbly table
sets wildness at odds with itself,
summons friends from the dead.
Its lamp gels the dark.

So unlike light.

As a boy I saw how it rose
from the plains of color,
full moon over wheatfield, cornstalks,
a map of wellsprings.

II

Tonight
midnight's chill,
a stone scribed over rooftops,
the sea breathing unseen.
Dilemmas, the agonies of choice,
the lost hemorrhaging of those one loves,
this table strewn with wooden teeth,
scorched masks, shadows aflame
surrounding a water glass,
at its bottom
a drowning moon.

Πετρα

Βαθιά στη σκοτεινή πυρίτιδα
που τη λένε μνήμη
μ' ένα βαρόμετρο κόκκινο,
πιο κάτω η θεόρατη πέτρα,
το τυφλό παραμύθι,
η σκιά του πατέρα μου,
είμαι ακόμη εδώ,
κάτοικος του νεκρού βασιλείου,
στα ερείπια φτερά παγονιού,
το χιόνι φράζει το σπήλαιο,
στη φωνή του βασάλτη ένα τρίξιμο,
φιμωμένη καρδιά,
μαύρη ελευθερία.

石頭

黑火藥的深處
人們稱之為記憶
還有紅色的氣壓表，
再往下是巨大的石頭，
難以理解的傳說，
父親的陰影，
我仍然在此，
死亡王國的居民，
廢墟裡的孔雀翅膀，
堆滿山洞的雪，
玄武岩裂開聲中，
蒙蔽的心，
黑色的自由。

Stone

Deep in the black gunpowder
called memory,
below the massive stone,
blind fable, I'm still here
with a red barometer,
my father's shadow,
last of a plundered kingdom.
Amid these ruins,
strewn peacock plumes.
Snow stops the cave mouth,
fissure in the grammar of basalt,
blinkered heart, dark freedom.

Μεταφορα

Ξαναβλέπω μετά από χρόνια τ' αστέρια.
Νύχτα ασέληνη, μητέρα των τεράτων,
ουρανός γεμάτος στροβίλους,
ηλεκτρικά ποτάμια, κοιλάδες,
ίσκιοι του πυρετού κι ορύγματα
στην πίσω πλευρά του κρανίου.
Έρχονται άσπρες εικόνες –
το αραιό χρώμα των ψευδαισθήσεων.

Καλοκαίρι γεμάτο μούχλα και τσιγάρα
και μόνο σκουπίδια εδώ και πενήντα χρόνια.

Η φωνή σου, η αναπνοή σου, λεπτή
γραμμή της αράχνης κι η ψυχή σου
έντομο κρεμασμένο στο κενό.

Μέσα μου τρέμει μια γριά φαντασία.

隱喻

多年後我再次看到了星星。
沒有月亮的夜晚，噩夢之母，
佈滿漩渦的天空，
電流之河，山谷，
頭骨背後
狂熱的陰影和溝渠。
白色的畫面——
那是幻覺的褪色。

充斥著霉菌和香煙的夏天
堆放了五十年的垃圾。

你的聲音，你的呼吸
如蜘蛛的細線而你的靈魂
如懸在空中的昆蟲。

老婦人的幻想在我內心晃動。

Metaphor

Years, then once more I see the stars.
Moonless, monster-spawning night,
eddying sky,
valleys of electric rivers,
fever's shadows, behind the skull
entrenchments.
Blanched forms materialize,
the pale shades of illusion.

Summers of mold, dead cigarettes,
the trash of fifty years.

Your voice, your breath a silken
strand of spider web, your soul
an insect snared over the abyss.

Inside me, an old dream
trembling.

Το τελος του χρονου

Εκατομμύρια τόνοι καμένο καύσιμο
για τα βιβλία, για τις στατιστικές και την Κλειώ,
την αγέλαστη βασίλισσα του παπύρου.

Σε μερικούς αιώνες θα 'χουμε γεμίσει το Γαλαξία
με είδωλα αόμματα κι αόρατα ταμ ταμ.
Ίσως κάποια μέρα ο χρόνος
να μην είναι πλέον μια υπόθεση
και κάποιος να διατυπώσει τον ορισμό του,
να ξεσκονίσει ξεχασμένα θεωρήματα
στέλνοντας τη μισή Ιστορία στην Προϊστορία·
να εφεύρει ξανά τη φύση
δημιουργώντας μιαν αλλόκοτη πανίδα
από μαγνητικά τέρατα και φωσφορούχα κατοικίδια·
να στήσει έναν καινούργιο Ζωδιακό
με κεραίες, καμπάνες και φτερωτά αστρόπλοια,
προβλέποντας το τέλος του τέλους ή απλούστερα
να βρει το μαθηματικό τύπο της μνήμης και της λήθης,
να μαρμαρώσει τη ροή,
να κάνει ορατή την τέταρτη διάσταση.

Μου φτάνει η παραλία·
το σύννεφο που κόβει τη Σελήνη·
το φόρεμά της πάνω στα νερά·
ο τρούλος τ' ουρανού – κι απόψε γεμάτος
με ασημένια ιδεογράμματα·
ο καταπέλτης των άστρων.

時間盡頭

一百萬噸燃燒的煤
燒盡了所有書、資料和紙莎草，
女王克利歐鬱鬱寡歡。

幾個世紀後銀河將充滿
盲眼的神像和視線之外的鼓聲。
也許有一天時間
將不再是一種假設
有人限定了定義
專注於遺忘的理論
將一半歷史送回史前年代
再次發明自然
創造神秘的動物群
有磁化的怪物也有含磷的家養獸
建立起新的黃道十二宮
用天線、鐘和帶翼的星際飛船
來預測結局的結局或至少
來尋找記憶和遺忘的數學公式
將流淌的時間石化
使第四維度顯現於人前。

海灘已足以滿足
雲朵遮蔽了月亮
水面掀起了波浪
天空的穹頂——今夜將佈滿
銀色的文字
那是恆星的發射軌道。

The End of Time

A billion tons of coal
burned for books, statistics,
and for Clio, unsmiling queen of papyrus.

In a century or two
we'll cram the galaxy
with blind idols, invisible drumbeats.

Someday time may be more
than hypotheses, its sense recast,
the dust of lost theorems
brushed off, consigning half of history
to the prehistoric. Someone
will refashion nature as strange fauna
of magnetic beasts, phosphoric livestock;
a new Zodiac
with antennas, huge bells, winged starships
predicting the end of the end; or simply
contrive a formula to remember
and forget, freezing any drift,
the fourth dimension now in sight.

For me this shoreline is enough,
how that cloud bisects the moon,
its skirt trailing through waves.
Tonight the sky's a cupola
strewn with figured silver,
the far-flung catapult of stars.

揚・瓦格納（德國），生於漢堡，1995 年至今定居柏林。集詩人、散文家與翻譯家於一身，著有七本詩集，詩作被翻譯成超過三十種語言。他亦把查爾斯・西米克、詹姆斯・泰德、西門・阿米塔齊、馬修・斯維尼、羅賓・羅伯遜等英語詩人的作品翻譯成德語。曾獲獎項包括萊比錫書展大獎、安娜・西格斯獎、弗里德里希・霍爾德林獎、畢希納獎等。現為德國語言文學學院院士。

Jan Wagner (Germany) was born in Hamburg and has been living in Berlin since 1995. Poet, essayist, translator of Anglo-American poetry (Charles Simic, James Tate, Simon Armitage, Matthew Sweeney, Robin Robertson and many others), Wagner has published seven collections of poetry and his works have been translated into more than thirty languages. Wagner is the recipient of the Award of the Leipzig Bookfair, the Anna-Seghers-Award, the Friedrich Hölderlin Award, the Georg Büchner Prize, etc. He is a member of the German Academy of Language and Literature.

揚 · 瓦格納

JAN WAGNER

中文翻譯：姚月

English translation by Iain Galbraith and David Keplinger

champignons

wir trafen sie im wald auf einer lichtung:
zwei expeditionen durch die dämmerung,
die sich stumm betrachteten. zwischen uns nervös
das telegraphensummen des stechmückenschwarms.

meine großmutter war berühmt für ihr rezept
der *champignons farcis*. sie schloß es in
ihr grab. alles was gut ist, sagte sie,
füllt man mit wenig mehr als mit sich selbst.

später in der küche hielten wir
die pilze ans ohr und drehten an den stielen –
wartend auf das leise knacken im innern,
suchend nach der richtigen kombination.

In Jan Wagner, *Selbstporträt mit Bienenschwarm. Ausgewählte Gedichte 2001–2015* (Munich: Hanser Berlin, 2016).

蘑菇

我們在林間空地遇見它們：
兩支探險隊透過朦朧暮色，
默默注視對方。我們之間
一群蚊子緊張地發著電報。

我的祖母，因為她的菜譜
「蘑菇釀肉」而遠近聞名。
她把它鎖進了自己的墳墓。
好東西，她說，少許足矣。

後來在廚房，我們將蘑菇
放到耳邊和轉動它的菌柄——
等待內部輕微的噼噼啪啪，
試圖尋找一列正確的組合。

mushrooms

we came across them in a forest glade:
two expeditions in crepuscular light
mutely eying each other. between us
the telegraphic whine of swarming gnats.

my grandmother was famed for her recipe
for *champignons farcis*. she locked it away
in her grave. all that is good, she told us,
should be filled with little more than itself.

later in the kitchen we held
the mushrooms to our ears and turned their stems,
listening for the gentle snap within,
hoping for the right combination.

In Jan Wagner, *Self-Portrait With a Swarm of Bees*, trans. by Iain Galbraith (Todmorden: Arc Publications, 2015).

chamäleon

älter als der bischofsstab,
den es hinter sich herzieht, die krümme
des schwanzes. komm herunter, rufen wir
ihm zu auf seinem ast, während die zunge
als teleskop herausschnellt, es das sternbild
einer libelle frißt: ein astronom
mit einem blick am himmel und dem andern
am boden—so wahrt es den abstand
zu beiden. die augenkuppeln, mit schuppen
gepanzert, eine festung, hinter der
nur die pupille sich bewegt, ein nervöses
flackern hinter der schießscharte (manchmal
findet man seine haut wie einen leeren
stützpunkt, eine längst geräumte these).
komm herunter, rufen wir. doch es regt
sich nicht, verschwindet langsam zwischen
den farben. es versteckt sich in der welt.

In Jan Wagner, *Selbstporträt mit Bienenschwarm. Ausgewählte Gedichte 2001–2015* (Munich: Hanser Berlin, 2016).

變色龍

比主教權杖更加古老，
拖在自己的身後，尾巴的
彎。下來吧，我們呼喚
樹上的牠，當牠迅疾伸出
像望遠鏡的舌頭，吞下
蜻蜓的星圖：一位天體學家
用一隻眼洞天，用另一隻
察地——保持兩者間的距離。
半球形的眼皮，鱗片裝甲，
一座堡壘，後面只有瞳孔轉動，
緊張地閃動在射擊孔之後
（有時，人們找到牠的皮，
如同一個被清空的據點，
一個早已被否定的觀點）。
下來吧，我們呼喚。
而牠似乎不動，緩慢
消失於色彩。隱藏於世界。

chameleon

older than the pastoral staff
it drags along behind it, its crook
of a tail. come down, we call
to it on its branch, while its telescope
tongue snaps out to consume
a dragonfly constellation: an astronomer
gazing simultaneously at the sky
and the ground, keeping his distance
from both. the dome of its eye, armour-
plated with scales, is a fortress. only
a pupil moves within, an edgy
flicker behind the arrow-slit (sometimes
you'll find its skin, like some deserted
outpost or long-discarded theory).
come down, we call. but it doesn't
budge, vanishing slowly among
the colours. hiding itself in the world.

In Jan Wagner, *Self-Portrait With a Swarm of Bees*, trans. by Iain Galbraith (Todmorden: Arc Publications, 2015).

gecko

sitzt plötzlich dort, als das licht angeht, eilt über die wand: ein wandernder riß, der sich hinten schließt, während er in laufrichtung das weiß zerteilt, rot und pulsierend, eine winzige lavaspalte. was man im schatten des ätna erzählt: daß er nur die wohnungen solcher menschen aufsucht, die freundlichen geistes sind. die dächer von syrakus, die wellen vor messina. tage später sein heller bauch auf dem kiesweg—und binnen stunden ein brodeln von ameisen, das seine form perfekt imitiert, eine wimmelnde mimikry. kieloben liegt das sizilianische fischerboot am strand, ein wrack, seine rippen porös und ausgebleicht von der sonne. am morgen darauf nichts als das zierliche rückgrat, ein verschwindend weißes stäbchen, das übrigbleibt; ein bloßer zahnstocher im breiten maul des august.

In Jan Wagner, *Selbstporträt mit Bienenschwarm. Ausgewählte Gedichte 2001–2015* (Munich: Hanser Berlin, 2016).

壁虎

坐在那裡，當燈亮起，出乎意料牠迅疾爬牆：一條遊走的裂縫，在身後自行合攏，當牠撕開前方的白色，有節奏和紅色，一條細小的熔岩縫隙。人們在埃特納火山的陰影下講述：牠只出現在那些人的房間裡，而他們是善良友好的人。敘拉古城市的屋頂，墨西拿海岸的波浪。幾天後牠淺色的肚子出現在石子路上—— 幾個小時之內，一群螞蟻沸騰，將它的身影完美地呈現，一種蜂擁的生物模擬狀態。西西里島的漁船底朝天在海岸，一艘廢船，骨架千瘡百孔被太陽曬得蒼白。第二天清晨，剩下的只是那瘦小的背脊，一根不易察覺的白色竹筷；一根不起眼的牙簽在奧古斯特寬大的嘴中。

gecko

suddenly stands there when the light snaps on, hurrying over the wall: a wandering crack that heals itself from behind, while opening the plaster in front of him, running. a throbbing, reddish, tiny gash of lava. a story told in the shadow of etna: how he visits only the houses of people with a gracious, gentle spirit. the rooftops of syracuse; the waves of messina. days later: his translucent belly on the gravel path—and within an hour, a seething of ants, exactly imitating his form, their teeming mimicry. overturned lies this sicilian skiff on its beach, wrecked, its ribs porous and bleached by sun. the morning after, nothing but the nuance of a spine, a vanishing white wand that remains. a mere toothpick in the broad maw of august.

In Jan Wagner, *The Art of Topiary: Selected Poems*, trans. by David Keplinger (Minneapolis: Milkweed Editions, 2017).

historien: onesilos

„Der Leiche des Onesilos schnitten die Amathusier, weil er ihre Stadt belagert hatte, den Kopf ab und nahmen ihn mit nach Amathus, wo sie ihn über dem Stadttor aufhängten. In dem schon ausgehöhlten Schädel setzte sich später ein Bienenschwarm fest und füllte ihn mit Honigwaben."
(Herodot, *Historien*, V, 114)

da oben, der schädel am stadttor,
der mit dem ersten licht zu summen beginnt,
mit dem noch immer leicht verdatter-
ten ausdruck, wo sich ein gesicht befand.

dahinter arbeitet es: die feine
schwarmmechanik im kranium,
die goldenen zahnräder der bienen,
die ineinandergreifen. geranien

und tulpen, wilder mohn und gladiolen –
stück für stück kehrt alles in den blinden
korb zurück, bis in den höhlen
die bienenaugen zu rollen beginnen.

den jungen ist es egal,
wie man ihn nannte, bettler oder könig,
sobald sie über sonnenwarme ziegel
nach oben klettern, der honig,
den er sich ausdenkt, an den händen klebt.
der bienentanz, ein epitaph.
er hatte fast ein land, als er noch lebte.
nun lebt in seinem kopf ein ganzer staat.

In Jan Wagner, *Selbstporträt mit Bienenschwarm. Ausgewählte Gedichte 2001–2015* (Munich: Hanser Berlin, 2016).

歷史：歐涅西洛

「歐涅西洛[1]的頭被阿馬圖斯人砍下，並被帶回到阿馬圖斯[2]，
因為他曾經包圍過他們的城市。他們把頭掛在城門口。後來，
一蜂群在被挖空的顱骨中築窩，並用蜂房將它填滿。」
—— 希羅多德[3]，《歷史》，卷五，114

高處，城門上的顱骨，
當第一束光出現，開始蜂鳴。
帶著依舊微微吃驚和疑惑的
神情，在曾經有一張臉的地方。

裡面有什麼東西在工作：
頭顱中的一組精密機械，
蜜蜂的金色齒輪，
環環相扣。天竺葵

和鬱金香，野罌粟和劍蘭——
一塊一塊，全部回到
看不見東西的筐，直到
洞中的蜜蜂眼睛開始轉動。

少年並不在乎人們
如何稱呼他，乞丐或國王，
只要沿著太陽曬暖的磚
蜜蜂向上攀爬，

他想像的蜂蜜黏在手指。
蜜蜂的舞蹈，一塊墓誌銘。
活著時他幾乎擁有一片國土。
現在一個國家活在他的頭顱。

---

1 譯註：歐涅西洛是希臘塞拉利昂島薩拉米斯城的國王戈爾果斯的兄弟。戈爾果斯是在伊奧尼亞起義後（前500 / 499–前494）擔任國王的。歐涅西洛通過希羅多德的作品而聞名（《歷史》，卷五，104–115）。薩拉米斯，古希臘城邦，位於塞浦路斯東海岸派迪亞斯河河口處，今法馬古斯塔（阿莫霍斯托斯）以北六公里處。

2 譯註：阿馬圖斯是塞浦路斯最古老的皇家城市之一。

3 譯註：希羅多德，前五世紀（約前484–前425）的古希臘作家，他把旅行中的所聞所見，以及波斯阿契美尼德帝國的歷史記錄下來，著成《歷史》一書，成為西方文學史上第一部完整流傳下來的散文作品。

histories: onesilos

> *"The people of Amathus cut the head from Onesilos' dead body, for he had besieged the city; they took the head with them to Amathus and hung it high above the gates. Later a swarm of bees settled in the hollow skull, filling it with honeycombs."*
> —Herodotus, *Histories V*, 114

up there: the skull at the city gate
that with the first light starts to hum,
still holds to that slightly agape
expression, where the face had been.

something labors behind it: the del-
icate swarm-mechanics in the cranium,
the bees a set of golden cog wheels
that intertwine. geraniums

and tulips, wild poppies, gladiolas—
piecemeal all things return in their ways
to the blind hive, until the bee eyes
in their sockets commence to roll.

for the boys it makes no difference
what name they called him once,
beggar or king, when they scale the
sun-warmed bricks, and the honey

he invents sticks to their fingers.
the bee dance is an epitaph.
he almost had a kingdom while alive.
now, inside his head: this empire.

In Jan Wagner, *The Art of Topiary: Selected Poems*, trans. by David Keplinger (Minneapolis: Milkweed Editions, 2017).

selbstporträt mit bienenschwarm

bis eben nichts als eine feine linie
um kinn und lippen, jetzt ein ganzer bart,
der wächst und wimmelt, bis ich magdalena
zu gleichen scheine, ganz und gar behaart

von bienen bin. wie es von allen seiten
heranstürmt, wie man langsam, gramm um gramm
an dasein zunimmt, an gewicht und weite,
das regungslose zentrum vom gesang...

ich ähnele mit meinen ausgestreck-
ten armen einem ritter, dem die knappen
in seine rüstung helfen, stück um stück,
erst helm, dann harnisch, arme, beine, nacken,

bis er sich kaum noch rühren kann, nicht läuft,
nur schimmernd dasteht, nur mit ein paar winden
hinter dem glanz, ein bißchen alter luft,
und wirklich sichtbar erst mit dem verschwinden.

In Jan Wagner, *Selbstporträt mit Bienenschwarm. Ausgewählte Gedichte 2001–2015* (Munich: Hanser Berlin, 2016).

蜂群自畫像

之前還只是一條細絨毛圍著下巴
和嘴唇，此刻已長出所有的鬍鬚，
它生長和密密麻麻，瑪格達蕾娜
甚至覺得我的臉上長滿了蜜蜂。

如同它們從四周蜂擁而至，
如同人們緩慢地，一克又一克
增加存在，增加重量和寬度，
歌唱的中心紋絲不動……

我伸著自己的手臂，如同
一名騎士，當侍童幫他披上
他的鎧甲，一件又一件，
先頭盔，然後胸甲、手臂、腿、頸，

直至他無法動彈，
閃耀地站著，輝煌背後
有幾道風，一些古代的氣息，
和消失時才真正清晰可見。

self-portrait with a swarm of bees

a moment ago i wore at best a fuzz
around my chin and lips; but now my beard
is growing and seething i might even pass
for magdalena: all my face hirsute

with bees. how they come buzzing from every side,
and, ounce by ounce, how a person's being
slowly but steadily gains in weight and spread
to become the stone-still centre of song...

my arms outstretched i bear a resemblance
to some ancient knight whom bustling varlets help
to fit his suit of armour, piece by piece—
first the helmet, then the harness, arms, legs, nape,

until he can barely move—who does not tread,
just stands there gleaming, with barely a hint
of wind behind the lustre, lingering breath,
and only vanishing becomes distinct.

In Jan Wagner, *Self-Portrait With a Swarm of Bees*, trans. by Iain Galbraith (Todmorden: Arc Publications, 2015).

恩尼斯特・維茨納（德國），1952 年生於羅馬尼亞。曾於蒂米什瓦拉西部大學學習德語文學和羅馬尼亞語文學；1975 年移居西柏林，並於柏林自由大學進修德語文學和政治學。多年來一直在柏林文學館工作，2003 至2017 年間擔任館長。維茨納的文學作品包括詩歌集和散文集，以及眾多羅馬尼亞語的改編與翻譯。2005 年獲頒明斯特國際詩歌獎，譯著*Cătălin Mihuleacs* 獲提名萊比錫書展大獎。

Ernest Wichner (Germany) was born in Romania in 1952. He studied German and Romanian literature at the West University of Timișoara. In 1975, he emigrated to West Berlin, where he continued his studies of German literature and political science at the Freie Universität. After many years of working for the Literaturhaus Berlin, he served as its director from 2003 to 2017. Wichner's literary works include poetry and essay collections as well as numerous adaptations and translations of Romanian. In 2005, Wichner was awarded the city of Münster's International Poetry Prize. His translation of *Cătălin Mihuleacs* has been nominated for the Leipzig Book Fair Prize.

恩尼斯特 · 維茨納

ERNEST WICHNER

中文翻譯：歐建梆

English translation by Laurie Schwartz

Levkojen

du legst den hörer auf und willst jetzt nicht mehr weiterleben,
das maß sei voll und jeder weg dir abgeschritten. wo mal ein
gott war, klafft nun in der wand ein loch, doch deine blumen
stehn im eng von mauern eingefaßten garten und blühen den

abend an, sie werden heute auch zur nacht noch blühen und
ihren schweren duft verströmen als hättest du versucht,
die nacht zurückzuschieben in jenen sommer fünfundsechzig
als meine nackten beine mittels zackenschere im blumenbeet

gelandet waren bei den levkojen. ihr duft lag wie vergossenes
parfüm im garten, spreizte sich den sommer lang durch jede
nacht und schwieg bloß, wenn gewitter tobten, doch wenn die
blitze nur noch ferne glommen, war er als erster wieder wach.

so ging noch ein jahrzehnt dahin, wir zogen westwärts, wo
ich allein das wort noch fand für deine trauer. jetzt willst
du nicht mehr länger leben und legst den hörer auf, läßt mich
zurück, den kleinen garten noch im blick, und in der zimmerecke
dort weiß ich mich angeschaut von deinen leeren schuhen.

紫羅蘭

你放下聽筒，不想活了，
忍無可忍，無路可走。神存在過的
地方，現在卻是牆上一個裂開的洞，而你的花朵
卻密密地矗立於圍牆內的花園中，在黃昏

盛開，今天晚上依舊綻放，
瀰漫著濃郁的芳香，彷彿你曾努力
把晚上拖回從前的六十五個夏天
我赤裸雙腳，如鋸齒的剪刀

落在紫羅蘭附近的花床上。花的芳香就像是
打翻的香水，每天晚上整個夏天遍地
四散，只有在雷暴怒吼時，沉默不語，卻當閃電
在遠處閃爍時，搶先一步再次甦醒。

另一個十年過去，我們移居西部，但我
仍獨自找尋可以形容你悲傷的文字。現在
你不想活了，並放下聽筒，等著我
回來，小小的花園重現眼前，而在房間一角
我意識到，你空著的鞋子在凝視著我。

Matthiola

you hang up the phone and now don't want to live any more,
it's the last straw and every path's been tread. where once was a
god, now a gaping hole in the wall, yet your flowers
stand in the garden closely framed by walls and bloom at the

evening, today they'll still bloom at night and
exude their heavy fragrance as if you had tried
to push back the night into that summer of sixty-five
when my naked legs landed with pinking shears in the flower bed

near the matthiola. their fragrance lay like spilled
perfume in the garden, the whole summer long straddling each
night and only falling silent when storms raged, yet when
lightening glimmered in the distance, it was the first to reawaken.

another decade passed, we moved westward. now
you don't want to live any more and hang up the phone, leave
me behind, the small garden still in view, and from the
corner of the room i know i'm being watched by your empty shoes.

Chrysanthemen

ich habe gelbe chrysanthemen mitgebracht vom markt
für dich, er war schon beinah abgeräumt, und wo der fisch-
händler gestanden hatte, lagen eine lachskarkasse und ein

augenloser heringskopf im sonnenschein, es stank, die
vögel hatten hier schon etwas aufgeräumt, nur die salat-
blätter und einstmals grünes möhrenkraut, platt nun wie

pflastersteine, in deren fugen über die ganze fläche hin
sich reste eingenistet hatten, zertretene champignons und
apfelspalten, die bunten blütenblätter, die der wind verstreut,

dort auch die sandale eines kindes, sie mußte hier schon
länger liegen, nur ein salatblatt beugte sich noch handschalig
nach oben, ein faden möhrenkraut unter den welken stengeln,

etwas pastinakengrün, noch kippten der und jene eimer aus,
während am rand die kehrmaschine losfuhr und rissige bretter
auf die ladeflächen flogen, auch flatterten wie fait divers

in allen farben plastikschwaden, zeitungsreste, mit senf und
blut beschmierte pappen knapp in bodenhöhe durch dieses licht.
nimm mit stand hier zu lesen, die läden ringsum waren dicht,

und wolken schoben ihre dunklen bäuche vom land her
kommend in den frühen abend, nimm etwas mit, dies beinah
noch winkende salatblatt, lies in seinen müde geschwungenen

rippen, daß nur geräusch wie vom maschinenbesen deine rede
sei, geh endlich heim, ein auto fuhr in lichtenberg in die pas-
santen, hier sägten krähenflügel durch die tür zum supermarkt.

菊花

我從市集給你帶來黃色的
菊花，市集已收拾得七七八八，
漁販所站的附近，放著一條三文魚的屍體和

一條沒有眼睛的鯡魚，暴露在陽光下，魚腥熏天，
群鳥已經清理過此處，只有生菜
葉和曾經綠過的蘿蔔葉，現在平坦得像

鋪路的石板，粉身碎骨，撒滿
整個地方，支離破碎的蘑菇以及
一片片蘋果，色彩繽紛的花瓣，隨風飄散

甚至在那裡可以看到小孩的涼鞋，想必是擱置
已久，只有一塊生菜葉像合成杯狀的雙手
往上曲起，一束蘿蔔葉在枯萎的木莖下，

像是防風草般的綠色，等待清理的一個個桶子，
當清潔工人快要沿著路邊出發，把一條條的木板
運到載貨區，就像所有顏色膠條，報紙的殘骸，

沾滿芥末和血的硬紙板中的社會新聞，
低低地在地面上，穿過這道光線飄動著。
帶走我，在此站著閱讀，周圍的店舖已關閉，

雲霧把他們肥厚的肚皮推至初夜，
你帶走一些東西吧，這幾乎仍舊在
晃動的生菜葉，在疲憊的弧形肋骨上

閱讀，只有像掃地機似的聲音才是你的
説話，回家吧，一架車在利希滕貝格開近
路人，在這裡烏鴉的雙翼鋸穿超級市場的大門。

Chrysanthemums

i brought yellow chyrsanthemums from the market
for you, it was almost cleared away, and in place of the fish-
monger's stand, lay a salmon carcass and the

eyeless head of a herring in the sunlight, it stank, the
birds had already cleaned up a bit here only the lettuce
leaves and what were once green carrot tops, now flat as

cobblestones, nestled in their cracks over the whole area,
the remnants of trampled mushrooms and
apple pieces, the colorful flower petals, scattered by the wind,

there too, a child's sandal, it must have lain here
a long time, only one leaf of lettuce curved like a cupped hand
upward, a thread of carrot tops under the wilting stems,

some parsnip greens, one or the other pails still being emptied,
while along the edge the street sweeper powered up as rough planks
flew onto the loading areas, fluttering, too, like fait divers

in all colors swaths of plastic, newspaper remnants, mustard and
blood stained cardboard close to the ground through this light.
take me they read, the surrounding shops were closed,

and coming from the land, clouds pushed their thick bellies
into the early evening, take something with you, this almost
still waving lettuce leaf, read in its wearily curved

ribs that only noise as from the sweeping machine is what you say,
just go home, a car in lichtenberg drove into pedestrians,
here crows' wings sawed through the door of the supermarket.

„Further und die Gegenwart“

Further und die Gegenwart
und sich nicht für maßgeblich halten
aus den Augenwinkeln aber
auf Sichtweite stets die beiden Alten

「再度與現在」

再度與現在
你的眼角不要
自視過高過重
兩個舊的角度要經常放在視線內

“Further and the present”

Further and the present
and don’t consider yourself essential
from the corners of your eyes but
keep the two old ones in sight

„Further und die Seelen“

Further und die Seelen
alter Bügeleisen
die vom Lesen wie
vom Reisen träg gewordnen
Routen fallen in die Zeilen
strecken alle Winde glatt
zum Strich   ich seh dich
beglückt in einen seelenlosen
aber grüngestrichnen
Apfel beißen

「再度與靈魂」

再度與靈魂
舊鐵
讀者的靈魂就像
旅者的靈魂一樣變得懶洋洋
路線排成一行行
沿直線拉緊風的
一舉一動　我看著你
快活地咬著
無靈魂的綠色的
蘋果

"Further and the souls of old irons"

Further and the souls of old irons
whose routes that got lazy
from reading as from traveling fall
into rows, stretch all winds
smooth to the line. I see you
happily biting into a soulless but
green-coated apple.

楊佳嫻（台灣），高雄人。台灣大學中文所博士，台灣清華大學中文系助理教授，台北詩歌節協同策展人。著有詩集《屏息的文明》、《你的聲音充滿時間》、《少女維特》、《金烏》，散文集《海風野火花》、《雲和》、《瑪德蓮》、《小火山群》，以及文學選集、學術著作若干種。

Yang Chia-Hsien (Taiwan) was born in Kaohsiung. She obtained her doctorate from Department of Chinese Literature of National Taiwan University. She is currently Assistant Professor at the Department of Chinese Literature of National Tsing Hua University as well as the Associate Curator of Taipei Poetry Festival. Her oeuvre includes poetry collections *Breathtaking Civilisation*, *Your Voice is Full of Time*, *Werther the Young Lady*, *Golden Crow*; prose collections *Flame Tree in Sea Breeze*, *Yunhe*, *Magdalene*, *Rolling Small Volcanoes*; as well as several literary digests and academic publications.

楊佳嫻

YANG CHIA-HSIEN

English translation by Jennifer Feeley

信物

我給過你的
你不要再給我
歲月停下來又開走
重複的夏季裡變換過
硝煙與螢火
你沒有給我的那些
原來我當初已經
加倍給過你

你喜歡的老歌手
磨得更老，我們一直沒有
一起去過的港灣
被填得更小
重複的八號風球
變幻的地震
深埋過幾顆子彈
浮世裡難免
浮出胸膛

住過的房間
仍能清晰望見天亮
海堤漸次熄滅的
那一排燈嗎
你為我在信裡
重繪過，你把不變的
風景當作信物

你搬離了那房間
信物有信，而寫信那人
已然查無此人

你怕老的
但是你老了
我給過你的
你又轉贈給時間嗎
而時間給了你的
你卻也如此慷慨
提早給了我

Keepsake

Don't give back to me
what I've given you
The years stop and start
summers alternate between
gun smoke and fireflies
What you haven't given me
I've already
given you twofold

Your favorite old singer
has grown older, the harbor
we never visited together
smaller from landfill
Recurring typhoon no. 8 signals
unpredictable earthquakes
In the floating world
bullets buried deep
inevitably float from my chest

In the room where you once lived
by the early light of dawn can you still clearly see
that row of lights
snuffed out one by one along the seawall?
In a letter you repainted it
for me, taking the unchanging
landscape as a keepsake

You've moved out of that room
the keepsake has been kept, but the letter writer
is nowhere to be found

You dread growing old
but now you're old
Have you given time
what I gave you?
And what time has given you
you've also generously
left me, ahead of schedule

暴力華爾滋

用槍托打碎太陽
用頭髮勒死聒噪的夜
我抱住天空搖晃，所有的星星都丟下了面具

大霧裡投下愛人的眼睛作材薪
床單上的經血可以生飲
我越過風雨後凌亂的草原
追趕想要逃走的無數標語

跳舞吧臃腫的冰河
脫掉黑暗脫掉仿冒的智慧
直接以誠實的頭骨向痛苦行禮

Violent Waltz

Shatter the sun with the butt of a gun
Strangle the boisterous night with hair
I clasp the sky and shake, the stars all drop their masks

Throw down a lover's eyes to make kindling in the fog
Menstrual blood on the sheets can be drunk raw
I cross a prairie bedraggled after a storm
Chasing after countless slogans on the run

Dance, puffed-up glacier
Strip off the darkness strip off counterfeit wisdom
Salute the pain head-on with an honest skull

守候一張香港來的明信片

一個回歸與出走
均無法被立即決定的年代
熱帶草木依舊蓬勃
耳語如蚊蚋飛翔於大氣
你說，曾在驀然迸開的
煙花中看見：天使墜毀
而歡愉的喊聲剛好蓋過一切

星座是否依舊
沿太古的軌道繞行
意識微涼，當暴雨毫無預警
擊打著書店的窗玻璃
霓虹管是胭脂慢慢溶解
節慶之後，你也許更蕭索了
像半截吸過的煙頭
擱在夢境邊緣，閃爍

時光持續發酵，從鏡中
辨認髮上微微湧出的星霜
夏天街道浮道著酸意
玻璃的稜線起伏
我們各據海角，僅僅能夠得知
新聞標題上彼此城市的輪廓
風向如此猶疑……

你曾許諾的那張明信片
仍未到達。彷彿傍晚的碼頭
一隻鷗鳥凝視水色
你的字跡將對我說些什麼呢
濃霧掩蓋航線，如抵抗一般地
隱約有船引擎隆隆犁開寂靜

Waiting for a Postcard from Hong Kong

An era in which homecomings and departures
can't be determined right away
Tropical vegetation still thrives
gnat-like whispers fly into the air
You say, amid the fireworks that suddenly
burst open, you saw: angels crashing
joyous shouts drowning everything out

Whether or not constellations still
circle around an ancient orbit
consciousness is a bit cool, when a rainstorm strikes
the bookstore's windowpane without warning
the neon tube is a slowly dissolving rouge
After the festivities, you may feel even more blue
like a half-smoked cigarette butt
placed on the edge of a dreamland, flickering

Time keeps on fermenting, in the mirror
I make out the slight surge of star frost in my hair
Sourness wafts through summer streets
ridges in the glass undulate
We each occupy a corner of the sea, only learning
the outlines of each other's cities from news headlines
the winds so hesitant...

The postcard you promised
has yet to arrive. It's like a seagull contemplating
the color of the water on the pier at dusk
What will your handwriting say to me?
Thick fog obscures the route, as though in resistance
a ship's engine faintly rumbles as it plows through the silence

挪亞的情書

大雨打鐵
房間正在變形
醒來望見露台積水
一隻藍白拖小舟
從此逝——不，它的餘生
寄在薔薇花叢那一邊

你曾為末日做過打算嗎
比如衣櫃底層
裝箱的翅膀（不是蠟做的）
比如門邊一只皮箱
床頭的寶篋
（鑰匙哪裡去了）
縮小燈，橡膠靴，
一打飛鴿
還有我（是呀還有我）

當然我們不怕
你的書堆得那麼高
必要的時候
沿天梯逃生
星星是暫存的航燈
雲是帳篷
夜虛無地湧動
一如你牧過的雲
洗濯過的風景

下一次旱季時
我們將退回地面嗎
天梯變成了鹽柱
醃漬著不同年代的海浪
而忘了帶走的房間
風化到最少最少
只剩下你用來凝視我
看得見薔薇花叢的
那個窗口

Noah's Love Letter

Heavy rain pelts iron
the room contorting
I wake up and find the terrace pooled with water
From now until it disappears—no, for the rest of its life
a blue-and-white slipper-boat
is lodged beside the rose bush

Have you ever planned for doomsday?
For example, at the bottom of the wardrobe
the wings of crates (not made of wax)
For example, the leather trunk by the door
the bedside treasure chest
(Where is the key?)
Small lamps, rubber boots,
a dozen flying pigeons
and me (oh yes, and me)

Of course we're not afraid
Your books stacked so high
if need be
we could escape along the ladder to the sky
Stars are temporary navigation lights
clouds are tents
Night surges in nothingness
like the clouds you've herded
the landscape you have cleansed

During the next dry season
will we return to ground?
The ladder to the sky turns into a pillar of salt
pickling waves of different decades
forgetting the room that's been taken away
weathered into nearly nothing
The only thing that remains is the window
through which you gazed at me
through which the rose bush can be seen

四元康祐（日本），詩人、隨筆作家、文學批評家和翻譯家，現居德國慕尼黑。首部詩集《大笑的臭蟲》出版於1991年，其後八本詩集相繼出版。其中《午後禁語》（2003）獲荻原朔太郎獎，《日本囚徒》獲鮎川信夫獎。四元康祐的作品曾被翻譯成多種語言。他是「Poetry International Web」的日語編輯，也是詩歌雜誌《びーぐる》的編輯。

Yotsumoto Yasuhiro (Japan) is a poet, essayist, literary critic and translator, living in Munich, Germany. His debut *A Laughing Bug* was published in 1991, followed by eight collections of poetry. His *Afternoon of Forbidden Words* (2003) won the Hagiwara Sakutarō Award and *Prisoner of Japanese* the Ayukawa Nobuo Award. His works have been translated into various languages. He is the Japanese editor of Poetry International Web and is on the editorial board of the poetry magazine *Beagle* in Japan.

四元康祐

YOTSUMOTO YASUHIRO

中文翻譯：田原、劉沐暘

English translation by Jordan Smith, Akiko & Yasuhiro Yotsumoto and Leith Morton

父鉱石

父が石になった
朝、ふとんの上でごろりと
サッカーボールほどの大きさだがめちゃくちゃに重くて
家族総がかりでもびくとも動かなかった
石の表面は滑らかに黒光りしていて
よく見ると金属の粒々みたいなものが混じっていた

気丈な母は翌週から仕事を探しはじめたが
四十九日を迎える前の晩、風呂場で
マリアナ海溝になってしまった

そして今日フォークリフトが父を母に投げ込む

父親礦石

父親變成了石頭
滾落在早晨的被子上
雖只有足球那麼大，分量卻很重
全家人都推不動
石頭表面光滑，散發黑光
仔細一看，還混雜著一些金屬顆粒

剛強的母親從第二週開始找工作
但在迎來七七四十九天的前一晚，她在浴室
變成了馬里亞納海溝

然後今天一輛鏟車把父親扔給了母親

Mineral Dad

One morning, Dad turned to stone.
He just lay there on the bed,
no larger than a soccer ball, but so damn heavy,
even with the whole family pushing, we couldn't budge him.
The stone's surface with its smooth, black radiance,
looking closer: we found all these metallic flecks mixed in.

The next week, my stalwart Mom began to look for a job,
and on the eve of the forty-ninth day, in the bath,
she turned into Mariana Trench.

And today, today a forklift is tossing Dad into Mom.

(Translated by Jordan Smith)

影のなかの邂逅

夜眠る前だったか
朝目を覚ました直後だったか
あなたのお母さんに会ってきたわよ
と妻が云った
その時はただ、うん、と応えただけだったが

ぼくは知っていた二十五年も前に死んだ母が
あっちからやってきた訳じゃないと
妻の方から出向いたのだ
夢の野を横切り　死の谷をくだって

臆病なくせに向こう見ずなのは
二十五年前に初めて会ったときのまま
バタンと閉じる扉の音に飛び上がり
太陽の誘いにやすやすと弄ばれ
たったひとりでも踊ることのできるひと

だが風が止むと死んだように静かだ
閉じた瞼の丘の向こうから
妻が歩いてくる
泥だらけで　頬に血を滲ませて
胸の中に珍しい獣のような沈黙を抱えて

影中邂逅

是在夜晚睡覺前
還是在早晨醒來時
妻子説
「我去見了你母親」
那時我只是簡單應了聲「嗯」

我清楚，二十五年前死去的母親
不可能從那裡趕來見她
一定是妻子去了那裡
橫穿過夢的原野，再走下死亡的山谷

明明膽小卻又莽撞
跟二十五年前第一次見她時一樣
被關門的聲音嚇得跳起來
輕易被太陽的邀請耍弄
獨自一人也能跳舞的她

可是，風停後是死一般的寂靜
閉上眼，從山丘對面
妻子向我走來
她渾身泥濘，臉頰滲血
懷抱著珍奇野獸的沉默

An Encounter in Shadows

Was it before we fell asleep at night
or just after we woke up?
My wife said,
"I saw your mother."
I just answered then, "Oh."

I knew that my mother, dead these twenty-five years,
couldn't have come to see my wife.
My wife must have gone to see her
crossing a dream-field and descending into the valley of death.

She is timid but bold,
the same as when I first met her twenty-five years ago.
The door slams and she jumps.
Easily tempted by sunlight, and tossed about,
she is a woman able to dance even just by herself.

But when the wind dies down, everything is as still as death.
In my dream
my wife comes walking from over the hill,
covered with mud, her cheeks bloodied up,
the silence, as of a rare beast, in her breast.

(Translated by Akiko & Yasuhiro Yotsumoto)

父の肖像

消防服を着た男たちが
だらしなく地べたに座りこんでいる

顔じゅう煤だらけで
なおも燻りつづける焼け跡に背中を向けて

男たちはなにを見ているのだろう
だれひとり口を利かない

女がよそってくれる温かい食事や
窓辺の貝殻から遠く離れて

彼らは寛いでみえる
まるで暗闇と疲労困憊と敗北こそが

本当の故郷だというように
右から三番目で膝の上にヘルメットを載せている

まばらな無精ひげを生やしたあの若者が
無言の裡にもう君を預言している

父親的肖像

穿著消防服的男人們
懶散地坐在地上

滿臉煙灰
背對著仍冒煙的火場

男人們在看什麼呢
沒人開口詢問

遠離女人為我們準備的熱食物
和窗邊的貝殼

他們看起來很放鬆
彷彿在說：黑暗、疲憊與敗北

才是他們真正的故鄉
右數第三位把頭盔戴在膝蓋上

長著稀疏又邋遢的鬍子的年輕人
已經在無言中預言了你

Portrait of a Father

Men in fire fighter suits
are slouched on the ground,

their faces covered with soot,
their backs towards the debris still smoldering.

What are they watching?
None of them utters a single word.

Far away from the warm meals served by women,
far away from the seashells placed by the window,

they look relaxed
as if to say in the very darkness, exhaustion and defeat

they had found their true home.
A young man with a patchily shaven face,

the third from the right with a helmet on his lap
is prophesying you within his silence.

(Translated by Akiko & Yasuhiro Yotsumoto)

オ・モ・テ・ナ・シ

私はモノクロームな入国管理局員です。
海の果てから来るものは
みんな鬼だと心得て島の操を守ります。

私は国際派の神主です。
英仏独語で祝詞を唱え賽銭は外貨で運用
夢は世界各地の原理主義者と泥んこ相撲とることです。

私はグローバリズムにひとり敢然と立ち向かう盗撮者です。
今やスカートの奥の暗がりだけが
この惑星に残された最後のフロンティア。

私は新米の自殺者です。娑婆のしがらみ振りほどき
山の手ラインに身を翻せば
輪廻の輪のなか未生の自分がワルツを踊る。

私は夢見がちな地震予報士です。
それはきっと来るでしょう。来れば沢山死ぬるでしょう。
さあ吉野家へ行きましょう。

私は多情な検事です。
ガイシャの無念に号泣し、ホシの身の上思いやり
判事の法衣に横恋慕。

私は刹那に潜む放火魔です。
寒空を舐める炎が紙と木で出来たこの国にはよく似合う。
半鐘と野次馬の歓声が生きとし生ける証です。

私はナノミクロンのゴジラです。
口から可愛い放射能吐き散らし分子に蹴躓きながら
あなたの細胞のなかで暴れています。

私は大腸過敏な国家主義者です。
ここは美しい、ここは美しい、ひたすらそう唱えていれば
厠の臭さもバラの香り。

私はもう一人の天皇です。
象徴なんかじゃありません。確たる実体持てばこそ
こうしてパチンコ玉も弾けるのです。

私は悩める言語聴覚士です。
論より情のこの国で言葉って一体なんなんでしょうか。
本当はただ歌ってるだけでいいんじゃないか。

私は僻みっぽい憲法第九条です。
結局私って、あなたの気まぐれな呟き(ツイート)に過ぎなかったのね。
クリックひとつで上書きなさるおつもりなのね。

私は猫背で近視の易者です。
だから自分で自分の手相を読んでいます。
でも案外そこにこそ時代の縮図が丸ごと全部入ってたりして。

私は幻滅について考えている小学生です。
先生は夢の地図を描けと言います
曳かれてゆく牛の眼で。

私は切断された猫の首です。
お辞儀と敬語の裏に隠された憎悪の光を瞳に灯し
文科省の正面玄関前に置かれています。

私はよろめくミセス・ワタナベです。
日銀総裁の迂闊な一言で株価反転自己破産。
個人資産1400兆円はハゲタカどもの腹の中。

私はナニゲなホームレスです。
スマホ片手によさげな人の絶えるざる流れを
まばたきごとに断層撮影しています。

私は耽美的な寿司職人です。
獲れたての命を捌いて、食べる宝石作ります。
夢は店に本物のルノワールを飾ること。

私は集合的無意識の徘徊老人です。
GPSで私の足跡を辿ってごらんなさい。
魂の輪郭が浮かび上がるよ。

私は真夜中のコンビニ店長です。
地球の上にはもう誰ひとり残っていません。
グラドル達に見守られながら私はおでんのツユを足します。

私は真理を追うストーカーです。
もうすぐあの女が改札から出てくるでしょう。
自分が何を隠し持っているのかまるっきり無自覚な足取りで。

私は9784014400107です。前世は9784014400106でした。
次に生まれ変わったら、匿名的なシフォナプテラ、通称ノミになりたいけれど、
やっぱり9784014400108の定めでしょうか。

私は拒食症の歌人です。飽食の世に生まれ
食べる端から吐き出してしまうのは
言葉だかヘドだか。

私は左右対称な理髪師です。
鏡の前で剃刀片手に
正午の時報を待っています。

私は千差万別多彩な顔を持っていますが
本当はただ一人
鏡張りのカラオケルームの真ん中に立ち尽くし

あなたのお越しを待っています。

為・您・服・務

我是單色的入國管理局職員。
深知從海那邊來的全是妖魔鬼怪
以此守衛島國的貞潔。

我是國際派神主。
用英法德語祭文禱告，香火錢當外幣投資
夢想和世界各地的原教旨主義者在泥地裡比賽相撲。

我是獨自勇敢迎戰全球主義的偷拍者。
現在只有裙底深處的那片黑
才是這顆行星上最後殘留的邊境。

我是新手自殺者。拋棄人世糾葛
如果縱身躍進山手線
輪迴圓環中尚未出生的自己會跳起華爾茲。

我是愛做夢的地震預報員。
地震將會發生吧。將會出現大量傷亡吧。
讓我們去吉野家吃一頓吧。

我是多情的檢察官。
因被害人的不甘痛哭，又擔心嫌疑人的處境
還和法官的法袍發生婚外情。

我是潛藏於剎那的縱火犯。
舔舐寒冷天空的火苗與這個用紙和木頭建起來的國家十分相稱。
報火警的鐘聲和瞎起哄的人的歡呼是生存的證明。

我是微米級別的哥斯拉。
一邊噴出可愛的放射性物質，被分子絆得踉踉蹌蹌
一邊在你的細胞裡大鬧一場。

我是大腸過敏的國家主義者。
這裡如此美麗，這裡如此美麗，只要悶頭多歌頌幾遍
連廁所的臭味都散發玫瑰香。

我是另一個天皇。
我不是什麼象徵。正因為擁有實體
才能像這樣玩彈子球遊戲。

我是苦惱的語言治療師。
比起論理更重感情的這個國家的語言到底是什麼。
其實只要唱著歌兒就行了吧？

我是生僻的憲法第九條。
説到底，我不過是你隨意發佈的一條推特吧？
只要點擊一下就能輕鬆重寫是吧？

我是駝背又近視的占卜師。
所以自己給自己看手相。
説不定掌紋中正好收進了時代的縮影。

我是思考何為幻滅的小學生。
老師讓我們描繪夢想的地圖
用拽著走的牛之眼。

我是被斬首的貓頭。
眼裡閃著藏在鞠躬和敬語背後的憎惡的光
被放置在文部科學省的大門前。

我是迷迷糊糊的「渡邊太太」
因為日本銀行總裁粗心大意的一句話導致股價暴跌自己破產。
個人資產1400兆日元全進了禿鷹的肚子。

我是故意的流浪者。
單手拿著智能手機對著看起來不錯的不絕人潮
每眨一次眼便進行一次斷層拍攝。

我是唯美的壽司工匠。
剖開剛捕上來的新鮮生命，製作可以吃的寶石。
夢想店裡能掛上一幅雷諾瓦的真跡。

我是集合性無意識的徘徊老人。
請用GPS追蹤我的足跡。
會浮現出靈魂的輪廓喲。

我是深夜的便利店店長。
地球上已經一個人都不剩。
在雜誌封面女郎的注視下我添上關東煮的湯。

我是追逐真理的跟蹤狂。
很快那個女人就要從檢票口出來了。
邁著對自己隱藏什麼毫無知覺的步伐。

我是9784014400107。前世曾是9784014400106。
下次轉生想成為匿名的蚤目完全變態類昆蟲通稱跳蚤，
但命運還是要讓我成為9784014400108吧。

我是得厭食症的歌人。生在這個飽食的世上
剛吃進去就吐出來的
是語言還是嘔吐物呢。

我是左右對稱的理髮師。
對著鏡子單手拿著剃刀
等待正午報時。

雖然我擁有千差萬別的多彩面孔
但實際上我只是獨自
站在有鏡子的卡拉OK房間正中央

等待您的惠顧。

Ho-Spit-Al-Ity

I am a monochrome immigration officer.
People coming from the far end of the Earth
I know all are demons: I protect the honor of this island.

I am an internationalist Shinto priest.
Intoning Shinto prayers in English, French and German and managing
offerings in foreign currencies
My dream is to engage in a mud-wrestling match with fundamentalists
from all over the world.

Alone, snapping voyeuristic pictures with a hidden camera,
I stand against globalism.
At this point in time only the darkness under the skirt
Remains the last frontier left on this planet.

I am a novice at suicide. When I free myself from the burdens of this
mundane world
And leap onto Yamanote-line tracks
My unborn self will dance a waltz on the loop of reincarnation.

I am a dreamer, an earthquake predictor.
It will come for sure. And when it does many will die.
Let's go and have a beef bowl at Yoshinoya.

I am a sentimental prosecutor.
I weep copiously in sympathy with the chagrin of the victims, and empathize with
the future travails of the offenders
And secretly lust for the judge's robes.

I am a spur of the moment arsonist.
The flames lickering at the cold sky suit this country made with paper and sticks.
The cries of admiration from the watchtowers and onlookers is proof of all that lives.

I am a nano-micron Godzilla.
Spitting out tiny bursts of radiation tripping over molecules
I run amuck inside your cells.

I am a nationalist suffering from colitis.
While constantly chanting how beautiful Japan is, how beautiful Japan is,
The stink from the jakes is the fragrance of a rose.

I am another Emperor.
Not a symbol. Because I have real substance
I can play the slot machines like this.

I am a troubled speech therapist.
In this country of emotion rather than reason what on earth do words mean?
Shouldn't we just sing?

I am Article 9 of the Japanese Constitution, I am paranoid. In the end I am nothing more than your fickle tweet.
With one click you intend to overwrite me, don't you?

I am a short-sighted, hunchback palm reader.
So I read my own palm.
But oddly enough a miniature map of the world is wholly contained on it.

I am a primary school student who thinks about disillusionment.
The teacher told me to draw a map of my dream.
With the eyes of a cow dragged to the abattoir.

I am the decapitated head of a cat.
Reflected in my eyes hatred glints hidden behind the bows and polite words
Am I am placed right in the hallway entrance of the Ministry of Science and Education.

I am the unfaithful Mrs. Watanabe.
With the careless words of the head of the Bank of Japan, shares collapse people go into voluntary bankruptcy.
Individual capital to the values of 1400 trillion yen ends up in the gullets of the vultures.

I am a common garden variety of homeless person.
Every time I blink I take a photograph of
The unending flow of the fine people, smart phones in hand.

I am an artistic Sushi chef.
I cut up the life of freshly caught fish and create jewels for consumption.
My dream is to have a genuine Renoir on the walls of my shop.

I am the demented old man of the collective unconscious.
Try and find my footsteps with GPS.
My soul will appear in outline.

I am the night manager of a convenience store.
Nobody is left on the Earth.
I add sauce to my stew watched over by posters of pin-up girls.

I am a stalker in pursuit of the truth.
Any moment now the girl will emerge from the train exit gates.
Walking completely unaware of what she is hiding.

I am 9784014400107. In my previous life I was 9784014400106.
In my next incarnation I would like to be an anonymous Siphonaptera, a common flea.
I guess my destiny is 9784014400108.

I am an anorexic poet. Born into this world of gullony
As soon as I eat I spew out
Words or vomit?

I am a symmetrical barber.
In front of the mirror with razor in hand
I await the alarm signaling noon.

I have an infinite variety of faces But in reality they are all just me
Standing motionless in the middle of a Karaoke room covered with mirrors

I am waiting for your arrival.

(Translated by Leith Morton)

余幼幼（中國大陸），1990 年生於中國四川，2004 年開始寫詩，現出版詩集《7 年》、《我為誘餌》。曾獲《詩選刊》年度先鋒詩人獎、星星詩歌獎 2012 年度大學生詩人。作品曾發表於《詩刊》、《星星》、《今天》、《天南》等刊物。

Yu Youyou (Mainland China) was born in Sichuan in 1990. She started writing poetry in 2004. She has published poetry collections *7 Years* and *Me As Bait*. She was awarded Pioneer Poet of the Year by *Poem Selection Magazine* and University Student Poet of the Year by Stars Poetry Awards 2012. Her poems are published in *Poetry Magazine*, *Stars*, *Jintian* and *Chutzpah!*.

余幼幼

YU YOUYOU

English translation by A. K. Blakemore and Dave Haysom

不能的風

我聽到灰塵
在返回的空氣裡
我又聽到
一些人在談論骯髒
在返回的話中
風不能把
連接灰塵的語氣
和想跟它一起
懸浮的衝動帶回
只有灰塵本身
在它應該在的位置
不能喊它
它不會答應
不能拉開距離
它就在聲音的隔壁

wind can't

i hear dust
in the returning air
and i hear
some discussion of dirt
in the returning words
wind can't bring back
the voice that joins dust
or the urge to float
together
only dust itself
where dust belongs
can't call to it
it can't reply
can't leave
a wall away from sound

磨刀

磨好刀，去戀愛吧
找一個人從背面刺入
向他打招呼説明你的來意
在身體裡磨刀
越磨越鈍的
刀刃會向他證明
時間已經不多
不戀愛的人不配流血
不配和刀融為一體

戀愛吧，攜手去磨刀
你和我一人捅對方一刀
沒有人死亡
也沒有人生還
磨好刀，把愛情都
留在刀刃上

sharpening the knife

once it's keen
go out and fall in love
find a man and slide it in his back
say hello and tell him
why you're here
sharpen the knife inside him
the sharper it gets
the blunter it is—
time running out
anyone who refuses love
doesn't deserve to bleed
doesn't deserve to melt into the blade

go out and fall in love—
hand in hand to sharpen the knife
in each other
no-one dies
no-one's left alive and
love's left
on the sharpened edge

自由

半斤白酒
我的身體自由了
這自由
東倒西歪，失去了平衡
我被它撂倒在床上
起先我吞下了一個酒瓶
我想到飛的感覺
可我被自由撂倒在床上
浪費了享樂的時機
床上只有我一個人
房間更是悄無聲息
於是我又浪費了全部的自由

freedom

five shots of baijiu
my body free and
freedom,
thrashing everyway,
loses footing
knocks me down onto the bed
first i swallowed a whole bottle
i want the sensation of flight but i am
knocked down on the bed by freedom
wasting another opportunity to enjoy life
i'm the only person in the bed
the room gets quieter
and all freedom's wasted
again

無骨

她飛翔的動作
像蜕掉翅膀的羽毛
每個姿勢都很輕
與海岸線重合

延伸到飄渺之中
海水浸泡著
她的每一寸挪動
吞沒著另一個國度的慌張

除非有更沉痛
的東西甦醒
她的生命
就是迫不得已地打撈

未經同意而落入水中
疲憊上岸
無骨、逆風
沒有希望

boneless

the way she soars
molt of wing
every gesture light
tesselate
with coastline

an extension
into haze—
salt water drenches
her every incremental movement
swallowing a foreign panic

unless a bitter thing
awakes
her life is nothing
but dredging

the unwilling fall to water
the exhausted climb ashore
hopeless, boneless thing
against the wind

遠岸（中國大陸），中國作家協會會員，中國詩歌學會理事，《國際漢語詩歌》執行主編，紅帆詩社創始社長，曾任海南省青年詩人協會主席、海南省青年作家協會名譽主席，出版過詩集《無岸的遠航》、《帶上我的詩歌去遠行》，在《人民文學》、《詩刊》等發表作品數百篇。

Yuan An (Mainland China) has published two collections of poetry. His poems have been widely published in China. He is a member of the Chinese Writers Association, councilor of the Poetry Institute of China, managing editor of *International Chinese Poetry*, and founding president of the Red Sail Poetry Society. He has been the president of the Association of Young Poets in Hainan Province, honorary president of the Young Writers Association of Hainan Province.

遠岸

YUAN AN

English translation by Lucas Klein and Chris Song

鷹的呼嘯

每一次相遇
都在高處
注定與星光一起漂泊

紅椰仙子
可可精靈
奮不顧身潛伏其中

像戀愛時的天使
最愛的一種深呼吸

體香極致溫軟
舌尖極致誘惑

所有鬼魅的芬芳
赤裸飛蕩

慾望之泉噴湧
太陽在杯底豔舞

鷹的呼嘯
萬里搖撼

寒風中全是翅膀
黑暗裡焰火狂笑

一百年
一百五十年……

納帕谷紫色發鬢的高度
海口灣摩天祥雲的高度

極致的高度
剛剛開始

a hawk whistles

every encounter
is up high
a destiny of drifting with starlight

lipstick palm fairies
and cocoa elves
recklessly sneaking in

like the kind of deep breath
that angels in love have loved the best

a physical fragrance extremely tender
the extreme allure of the tip of the tongue

all ghostly scents
nakedly floating

the spring of desire surges
sunlight dancing at the bottom of a glass

a hawk whistles
ten thousand miles

all wings in the cold wind
all flames guffaw in the dark

one hundred years
one hundred and fifty years…

the height of Napa Valley's purple sideburns
the height of Haikou Bay's sky-high clouds

this extremity of height
has just begun

黑暗中，聽萊昂納德・科恩

沒有比科恩更加男性的聲音了
沒有比科恩更加傷感的歌吟了

一些音符從深海升起
一些節拍在雲端夢遊

剛剛還在細語纏綿
馬上又要離別無期

關了燈
閉上眼睛
端杯紅酒輕輕説聲
「晚上好，科恩」

神秘的深喉佇立空中
靈魂的交歡發出尖叫

你把日子過成詩
在空無一人的地方
充滿勇氣大聲宣佈
「我愛你」

你的屋子你的世界
像一隻地球之外的大船
既使在漆黑的夜裡
也那麼閃亮的
自由晃蕩

in the dark, listening to Leonard Cohen

no voice is more manly than Cohen's
no singing sadder

some notes rise from the bottom of the sea
some beats sleepwalk on the edge of a cloud

just now we were chatting and lingering
and are now about to part without knowing when we might meet again

turn of the light
close your eyes
glass of wine in hand, softly say,
"Good evening, Leonard"

a mysterious deep throat in mid-air
the scream of mating souls

you turned your days into poems
in an empty place
full of courage, you called out,
"I love you"

your house, your world
like an extraterrestrial ship
even in the dark of night
it shines so brightly
it drifts so free

鄭小瓊（中國大陸），四川南充人，2001 年南下廣東打工，迄今出版詩集《女工記》、《玫瑰莊園》、《黃麻嶺》、《鄭小瓊詩選》、《純種植物》、《人行天橋》等十二部，其中《女工記》被喻為「中國詩歌史上第一部關於女性、勞動與資本的交響詩」，有作品譯成印尼語、英語、法語、德語、日語、韓語、土耳其語及越南語等語種。曾獲莊重文文學獎、十月文學獎、人民文學獎等。曾應第二十屆法國「詩人之春」邀請往法國多個城市朗誦，應維也納大學、維也納藝術大學邀請，在維也納及格拉茨等城市舉辦其個人朗誦會，其詩歌在被多次被國外藝術家譜成不同形式的音樂、戲劇在美國、德國等國家上演。

Zheng Xiaoqiong (Mainland China) was born in Nanchong, Sichuan. She went south to Guangdong for work in the year 2001. To date, she has published twelve books, including *Notes of a Woman Worker*, *Rose Manor*, *Huang Maling*, *Poetry Collection by Zheng Xiaoqiong*, *Pure-Species Plant*, and *Footbridge*. *Notes of a Woman Worker* was hailed as "the first symphony-poem about the female gender, work, and capitalism in the history of Chinese poetry." Her works have been translated into various languages, such as Bahasa Indonesia, English, French, German, Japanese, Korean, Turkish, and Vietnamese. Her numerous accolades include Chuang Chong Wen Literature Awards, October Literature Awards and People's Literature Awards. She was invited to recite poems in various cities in France at the 20th Le Printemps des Poetes, and to hold solo poetry recitals in Vienna and Graz upon the invitation of the University of Vienna and University of Applied Arts Vienna. Her poems have been adapted into songs and stage plays and performed in Germany and the United States.

鄭小瓊

ZHENG XIAOQIONG

English translation by Eleanor Goodman

黃麻嶺

我把自己的肉體與靈魂安頓在這個小鎮上
它的荔枝林，它的街道，它的流水線一個小小的卡座
它的雨水淋濕的念頭，一趟趟，一次次
我在它的上面安置我的理想，愛情，美夢，青春
我的情人，聲音，氣味，生命
在異鄉，在它的黯淡的街燈下
我奔波，我淋著雨水和汗水，喘著氣
—— 我把生活擺在塑膠
產品，螺絲，釘子
在一張小小的工卡上……我的生活全部
啊，我把自己交給它，一個小小的村莊
風吹走我的一切
我剩下蒼老，回家

（選自詩集《黃麻嶺》，長征出版社，2006）

Huangmaling Mountains

I settle my body and soul in this small town
its lychee trees, lanes, assembly lines and one tiny station
its ideas drenched in rain, trip after trip, time after time,
I find places for my thoughts, my love, my dreams, my youth on its surfaces
my lover, voice, smell, life
are here away from home, beneath its dim streetlamps
I dash around, I'm soaked in rain and sweat, panting—
I arrange my life on plastic products, screws, nails
on a tiny employee ID… my entire life
oh, I give myself to it, this tiny village
the wind blows away everything I have
all I have left is old age, and returning home

涼山童工

生活只會茫然　時代逐漸成為
盲人　十四歲小女孩要跟我們
在流水線上領引時代帶來的疲憊
有時　她更想讓自己返回四川鄉下
砍柴　割草　摘野果子與野花
她瘦小的眼神浮出荒涼　我不知道
該用怎樣的句子來表達　只知道
童工　或者像薄紙樣的嘆息
她的眼神總能將柔軟的心擊碎
為什麼僅有的點點同情
也被流水線的機器輾碎
她慢半拍的動作常常換來
組長的咒罵　她的淚沒有流下
在眼眶裡轉動　「我是大人了
不能流淚」　她一本正經地說
多麼茫然啊　童年只剩下
追憶　她說起山中事物比如山坡
比如蔚藍的海子　比如蛇　牛
也許生活就是要從茫然間找出一條路
返回到它的本身　有時她黝黑的臉
會對她的同伴露出鄙視的神色
她指著另一個比她更瘦弱的女孩說
「她比我還小　夜裡要陪男人睡覺」

（選自詩集《女工記》，花城出版社，2012）

A Child Laborer on Mt. Liang

Life is nothing but confusion　this era gradually turns
blind　a fourteen-year-old girl wants to come with us
pulling the exhaustion of the era toward her on the assembly line
sometimes　she wants to let herself return to her Sichuan village
chop firewood　cut grass　pick wild fruits and flowers
her small weak gaze reveals desolation　I don't know
how to describe it　I only know
child workers　and sighs thin as paper
her gaze can always smash a soft heart
why is it that what little sympathy exists
always gets crushed by the assembly line machines
her slow tempo movements are frequently answered
by the supervisor's abusive curses　she does not cry
her tears swim in her eyes　"I'm an adult
I don't cry"　she says somberly
it's bewildering　what is left of youth is only
memory　she speaks of mountain things like hillsides
like bright blue ponds　like snakes　and cows
perhaps life is finding a path out of bewilderment
and back to itself　sometimes her dark face
reveals a hint of hatred
and she'll point at another weaker girl and say
"She's younger than I am but she's sleeping around"

中年妓女

城中村低矮的瓦房　陰暗而潮濕的光線
骯髒而黴味的下水道　她們坐在門口
織毛衣　聊天　打量來去匆匆的男人
她們的眼影　胭脂掩飾不了她們的年齡
三十多歲或者更大　在混雜的城中村
她們談論她們的皮肉生意與客人
三十塊　二十塊　偶爾會有一個客人
給五十塊　她們談論手中毛衣的
花紋與顏色　她們幫遠在四川的
父母織幾件　或者將織好的寄往
遙遠的兒子　她們動作麻利
有時她們會談論鄰近被抓的同行
罰款四千　她們説每個月交了三百塊
給知情人士　雖然這些所謂的保護費
是她們十椿普通生意　她們認為
算被鬼壓了十次　雖然這鬼
龐大而虛無　她們有些失落
我想像她們現在的生活　過去的生活
以及未來的生活　就像她們手中的毛衣下
潛藏著一顆母親的心　妻子的心以及
女兒的心　她們在黑暗中的嘆息以及
掩上門後無奈的呻吟　在背後她們是
一群母親　在門口織著毛衣　這些
中年妓女的眼神有如這個國家的面孔
如此模糊　令人集體費解

（選自詩集《女工記》，花城出版社，2012）

Middle-Aged Prostitutes

Low tiled houses of the urban village　gloomy humid light
filthy mildewed sewers　they sit in the doorways
knitting sweaters　chatting　sizing up the men coming and going
their eye-shadow　and rouge can't hide their age
thirty or older　in the chaotic urban village
they talk about their business of the flesh and their customers
thirty kuai　twenty kuai　occasionally a customer
who pays fifty　they discuss the clothes they're holding
their patterns and colors　how they'll knit something for their distant
parents in Sichuan　or send the finished pieces
to a distant son　their movements are agile
sometimes they'll discuss another girl working nearby who's been arrested
and fined four thousand kuai　they say each month they give three hundred kuai
to an insider　although this so-called protection fee
is ten times their normal income　they say
it's like being crushed ten times by a ghost　although this ghost
is enormous but empty　they lose out
I imagine their current lives　and their former lives
and their future lives　as though under the sweaters they're knitting
is a mother's heart　a wife's heart and
a daughter's heart　they breathe in the dark and
moan helplessly after shutting the door　seen from behind they are
a bunch of mothers　sitting in a doorway knitting sweaters　these
middle-aged prostitutes　with eyes like this country's face
just as uncertain　turning everyone obscure together

穿越星宿的針孔

穿越星宿的針孔，警示器像黃昏中的
烏鴉停在鋼針機上嘶叫，煤氣燈分割的
月亮，它四分之一的光與陰影，被酸液
灼傷的皮膚，除鏽劑在太陽的深處清洗
晝與夜。鐵，一根工業的肋骨，撫摸
飽受傷害的城市。生存在切割機下
斷裂，消逝，絕不妥協。

下午沿著螺絲的紋路徐徐而行
楔入黑夜的沼澤，佝僂的月亮像
職業病患者，在霧霾下咳喘。超聲波
起伏、降落，像不知疲倦的饒舌歌手
它不知風趣，睡意從機台爬出來
落在我的睫毛，綠色的指示燈閃爍
機械手從電鍍水池取出一捆捆亮晶晶的
黎明。生活從移動滑輪上經過，流逝
沉入工業廢水池。

啟動器迅速沉入酸液，黑夜脫去
它的黑衣裳。月亮，夜的警報器，
它亮著，雪終於沒落下。電鍍液冒出的
濃烟與泡沫，一塊鐵片在死去或誕生
疼，變得遲疑與疲倦，它們被塞入
熱處理悶罐，月亮，從天空巨大容器裡
逃逸。生命囚於天地間，像鐵
在熱處理後變得堅硬

A Needle Hole through the Constellations

A needle hole through the constellations, a safety alarm like a crow at dusk
cawing from atop a steel-needled sewing machine, moonlight partitioned
by gaslight, the skin of a quarter of its light and shadow
burned by the acid bath, a rust cleanser purging day and night
from the deep recesses of the sun. Iron, rib of industry, fondles
the injured city. Under the cutting machine, existence
cracks, fades, refuses to compromise.

Afternoon follows the screw-threads' steady motion
wedging into the marsh of evening, and the rickety moon
is a patient with an occupational disease, gasping in the haze. An ultrasonic wave
undulates and descends, like a tireless loquacious singer
knowing nothing of humor, drowsiness crawling up from the machine
to fall on my eyelashes, the green indicator flashing
the mechanical arm pulls from the electroplated sink bundles of bright shiny
dawns. Life passes on a pulley, elapsing,
sinking into an industrial cesspool.

The machine starter sinks rapidly into the acid bath, the night throws off
its dark clothing. Moonlight, night's safety alarm,
begins to shine, the snow finally stops falling. Electroplating solution seeps out
in thick smoke and foam, each iron sheet between death and birth
hurts, becomes hesitant and weary, they're stuffed into
the heat treatment tank, the moon absconds from the enormous container
of the sky. Life imprisoned between sky and earth, like iron
in the heat treatment tank, hardening.

跪著的討薪者

她們如同幽靈閃過　在車站
在機台　在工業區　在骯髒的出租房
她們薄薄的身體　像刀片　像白紙
像髮絲　像空氣　她們用手指切過
鐵　膠片　塑膠……她們疲倦而麻木
幽靈一樣的神色　她們被裝進機台
工衣　流水線　她們鮮亮的眼神
青春的年齡　她們閃進由自己構成的
幽暗的潮流中　我無法再分辨她們
就像我站在她們之中無法分辨　剩下皮囊
肢體　動作　面目模糊　一張張
無辜的臉孔　她們被不停地組合　排列
構成電子廠的蟻穴　玩具廠的蜂窩　她們
笑著　站著　跑著　彎曲著　蜷縮著
她們被簡化成為一雙手指　大腿
她們成為被擰緊的螺絲　被切割的鐵片
被壓縮的塑料　被彎曲的鋁線　被剪裁的布匹
她們失意的　得意的　疲憊的　幸福的
散亂的　無助的　孤獨的……表情
她們來自村　屯　坳　組　她們聰明的
笨拙的　她們膽怯的　懦弱的……
如今　她們跪著　對面是高大明亮的玻璃門窗
黑色制服的保安　鋥亮的車輛　綠色的年桔
金燦燦的廠名招牌在陽光下散發著光亮
她們跪在廠門口　舉著一塊硬紙牌
上面笨拙地寫著「給我血汗錢」
她們四個毫無懼色地跪在工廠門口
她們周圍是一群觀眾　數天前　她們是老鄉
工友　朋友　或者上下工位的同事
她們面無表情地看著四個跪下的女工
她們目睹四個工友被保安拖走　她們目睹
一個女工的鞋子掉了　她們目睹另一個女工
掙扎時褲子破了　她們沉默地看著
下跪的四個女工被拖到遠方　她們眼神裡
沒有悲傷　沒有喜悅……她們目無表情地走進廠房
她們深深的不幸讓我悲傷或者沮喪

（選自詩集《女工記》，花城出版社，2012）

Kneeling Workers Demanding Their Pay

The women flash by like ghosts   at bus stops
machine stations   industrial zones   filthy rented rooms
their thin bodies   like razor blades   like white paper
like strands of hair   like the air   they use their fingers to slice
iron   film   plastics... their exhausted numb
faces are like ghosts   they're stuffed into machine stations
work uniforms   assembly lines   their bright gazes
young ages   they hide in their self-constructed
dark tidal currents   I can't tell them apart anymore
just like no one can tell me apart from them   leftover leathery
bodies   motion   blurred faces   one after another
innocent faces   they're constantly put together   arranged
into an electronics factory ants nest   a toy factory hive   they
laugh   stand   kneel   bend   huddle
they've been simplified down to fingers   and legs
they've become tightened screws   sliced iron sheets
compressed plastic   bent aluminum wire   cut cloth
their expressions of disappointment   pride   exhaustion happiness
chaos   helplessness   loneliness...
they come from villages   hamlets   valleys   neighbor-hoods   they're smart
clumsy   timid   weak...
today they kneel   facing the big bright window
the black-uniformed guards   the shiny cars   the green bushes
the dazzling factory sign shines in the sun
they kneel at the factory entrance   holding a cardboard sign
with the scrawled words   *Give us our hard-earned money*
the four women kneel in the factory entrance without fear
a group of onlookers has surrounded them   for several days
    people from the same village
coworkers   friends   or those who work the same workstations
they watch the kneeling women impassively
they witness their four coworkers dragged off by the guards   they witness
one of the worker's shoes falling off   they witness another worker's
pants ripped in the struggle   they watch silently
as the four workers are dragged somewhere far away   their eyes
hold no sorrow   and no pleasure   they impassively enter the factory
it depresses me no end

周雲蓬（中國大陸），出生於中國遼寧瀋陽，中國獨立民謠歌手、詩人。幼年因患眼疾而導致九歲時失明。後入盲人學校學習，個人努力至1994年長春大學中文專業畢業。大學畢業後分配至一家工廠領取保障金，1995年到北京圓明園開始了賣唱生涯，其後四處遊蕩並進行創作。2007年自費錄製唱片《中國孩子》，音樂風格優美傷感而反映社會現實，一舉拿下第八屆華語音樂傳媒大獎最佳民謠藝人和最佳作詞人兩項大獎。2011年詩集《不會説話的愛情》獲人民文學獎詩歌獎。

Zhou Yunpeng (Mainland China), born in the city of Shenyang in Liaoning Province, is an independent folk singer and poet. At the age of nine, he has lost his eyesight to an eye disease and then studied at the school for the visually impaired. With perseverance, he graduated as a Chinese major from Changchun University in 1994. Afterwards, he was assigned to work at a factory and received social security payments. In 1995, he started busking in the Old Summer Palace in Beijing and then continued to write as he wandered the country. In 2007, he produced the album *Children of China* at his own expense, the music of which is beautifully melancholic and reminiscent of social reality. The album earned him the Best Folk Artist and the Best Lyricist at the 8th Chinese Music Media Awards. In 2011, his poetry collection *The Love That Cannot Speak* won the Poetry Prize at the People's Literature Awards.

周雲蓬

ZHOU YUNPENG

English translation by Canaan Morse

不會說話的愛情

繡花繡得累了吧牛羊也下山嘍
我們燒自己的房子和身體生起火來
解開你的紅肚帶灑一床雪花白
普天下所有的水都在你眼中蕩開

沒有窗亮著燈沒有人在途中
我們的木床唱起歌兒說幸福它走了
我最親愛的妹呀我最親愛的姐呀
我最可憐的皇后我屋旁的小白菜

日子快到頭了果子也熟透了
我們最後一次收割對方從此仇深似海
你去你的未來我去我的未來
我們只能在彼此的夢境裡虛幻地徘徊
徘徊在你的未來徘徊在我的未來
徘徊在水裡火裡湯裡冒著熱氣期待
期待更美的人到來期待更好的人到來
期待我們的靈魂附體重新回來
重新回來重新回來

2002 年 1 月寫於北京

Mute Love

You must be tired from embroidering the goats and cows have come off the mountain
We burn our own houses and bodies start a fire
Undo your red cummerbund spew snowflake-white all over the bed
All the water in the wide world ripples outward in your eyes

No windows are lamp-lit no travelers on the road
Our wooden bed sings Happiness has gone
My beloved little sister oh beloved big sister
My pitiable empress the baby bok choy beside my home

Time is running out fruit is overripe
Our last harvest, bottomless hatred for each other from now on
You go to your future I go to mine
We merely wander like ghosts through each other's dreams
Wander in your future wander in my future
Wander through water fire boiling broth waiting amid steam
Wait for a prettier person a better person to come
Wait for our dispossessed souls to return again
Return again return again

January 2002, Beijing

如果你突然瞎了該怎麼辦

我要去跳樓
我要立即向我的女友提出分手，並祝她幸福
我要去殺人殺死我一生中最仇恨的人
我給父母打電話，告訴他們以後多保重
我要想辦法毀掉一個純潔無辜的姑娘
我立刻加入基督教
我必須立刻離開這個城市永遠不回來
我一直喝酒喝死拉倒
我要把所有的錢散給乞丐，然後自己去沿街乞討
我無所畏懼去吃泥土喝陰溝裡的水
我得去買個盲杖練習著上廁所
我吃飯睡覺一如既往地生活
我要託人到鄉下買個善良的媳婦
我天天睡覺夢著過去的日子
我白天微笑，夜晚咬牙切齒詛咒全世界
我弄一本《易經》學算命
我幻想能有一個心靈美的姑娘愛上我，感動得自己熱淚盈眶
我像一隻食草動物，陰鬱多疑，不發出一點聲響
我下午抱著收音機在門口曬太陽
我學習張海迪整天聽《命運交響曲》做全人類的榜樣
我發呆，像一根陽光下的爛木頭，什麼也不想
我學會吹口琴去地鐵賣唱
我不要孩子也不結婚，一個人在黑暗中默默了此一生
我吃肉罵人單相思出賣朋友
我走遍八千里水路永遠在路上不斷離開
我去神農架的深處去梅里雪山
進入天坑，去藏北無人區，以凋零殘破的人生來一次輝煌的豪賭
我在一個陌生的城市凍餓死去安靜得沒有人哭泣

2003年2月寫於北京

What Would You Do If You Suddenly Went Blind?

I'm going to jump off a building
I'm going to break up with my girlfriend at once, and wish her the best
I'll kill someone, kill people I've always hated most
I'll call my parents, tell them to take care of themselves
I'll find a way to destroy a pure and innocent girl
I'm converting to Christianity right now
I have to leave this city at once and never return
I'll keep drinking and if I die fuck it
I'm going to give all my money to beggars then go beg on the streets
I'm going to eat mud and drink ditchwater without hesitation
I need to buy a blind cane and practice going to the toilet
I eat and sleep and live as I always have
I'm going to hire someone to buy me a good-natured wife
I dream of how life used to be every day
I smile in the daytime, curse the whole world at night
I find an *I Ching* and learn to tell fortunes
I fantasize about a good-hearted girl until I'm moved to tears
I'm like an herbivore, self-contained and cagey, making no noise
I sun myself on the doorstep, holding my radio
I imitate Zhang Haidi and listen to Beethoven's Fifth all day to be a model for mankind
I zone out like a rotting log in the sun and think of nothing
I learn the harmonica and play for change in the subway
I want no kids and won't marry, but live a silent, unobtrusive life in the shadows
I eat meat spew profanity love unrequitedly betray my friends
I travel thousands of miles of river, always on my way, constantly leaving
I penetrate the deepest forests, climb snow-capped mountains
Enter the heavenly gorge and the Tibetan wilderness
I freeze to death in a strange city so quietly no one weeps

February 2003, Beijing

水的一生

旋渦瘋狂的沙漏暴風雨臨盆
冷卻成鵝卵石的皺紋動就是生
一圈圈漾著焦慮八千英尺深處幽暗的苦悶
美人魚月光中的鮫人泡沫沉船破碎的漁網岸
燈塔海鳥冰山白鯨噴射的水柱荒島上的篝火珊瑚礁精衛的怨恨洛神
鐘乳石井中的哭喊一九三八年的洪水烏鴉銜起石頭奧德賽開始漂泊西
　　湖裡的白蛇
塞壬歌唱溺死者尋找替身衰老的龍王大西洋底的古國蒸騰的沼澤瀑布
　　滂沱窮人多餘的精液
湘夫人的婚床元稹的滄海巫峽的神女死魚眼中的黎明始皇帝期盼永生
　　的眼沉沒的仙山
老子的善被分開的紅海亞拉臘山上的方舟伯牙折斷流水瞿塘賈的輕薄
李白撈月赫拉克利特渡河婚禮上的水變成酒絞刑架上憤懣的血恆河沙
　　般多的佛
瘋子身後的忘川初夜女子的淚羊皮紙上流過約旦河中國人的腎許由濕
　　潤的耳朵
約拿在魚腹中遇見上帝滄浪之水濁兮屈原洗腳莊周知道魚的快樂
西施在越國曬衣服紂王在北方支起油鍋雪萊的靈魂盈滿海水吊瓶裡殘
　　留著不新鮮的歲月

2002年1月寫於北京

The Life of Water

Fierce whirlpool in an hourglass tempest crowning
Chills into cobblestone wrinkles moving is living
In rings of ripples spectral frustration beneath eight thousand yards of
　　worry
Mermaid half dragon in moonlight bubbles sinking ships broken bank of
　　fishing nets
Lighthouse seabirds iceberg white whale spouts a column of water
　　campfires on a deserted island coral reef the bird-maiden Jingwei's
　　resentment Luo River goddess
Wailings out of a stalactite cavern the floods of 1938 crow picks up a stone
　　Odyssey begins white snake floating on West Lake
Sirens sing of drowned men looking for a substitute aging Dragon King
　　ancient kingdom beneath the Atlantic boiling marsh waterfall's deluge
　　useless semen of the poor
Xiang River goddess's marriage bed Yuan Zhen's green sea Wu Gorge
　　maiden dawn in a dead fish's eye First Emperor's immortality-hungry
　　eye sinking mountain of immortals
Lao Tzu's goodness parted Red Sea Ark on Mount Ararat Bo Ya stopping a
　　current Qutang Gu leaving lover for money
Li Bai scooping the moon's reflection Heraclitus crossing the river wedding
　　water turned to wine blood spattered over the gallows as many
　　Buddhas as grains of sand in the Ganges
Styx behind the madman a girl's tears on her first night Jordan River
　　flowing over lambskin kidneys of Chinese people Xu You's moist ears

Jonah meets God in the belly of a whale Oh the ocean's waves are turgid
Qu Yuan washes his feet Zhuang Zhou knows the happiness of fish
Xi Shi hangs up laundry in the south King Zhou sets up a cauldron of oil
in the north Shelley's soul overfills with seawater an IV bag holds the
dregs of an unfresh age

January 2002, Beijing

遠望北京

北方很熱，南方很涼
北方有人繼續喝醉，北方有風雲和政治
南方我早早上床睡覺
北方有徹夜的酒局
南方我裝滿一茶缸黃酒
自己往自己的深處頹
北方有北京
南方有緩慢的時間
爬滿青苔的廟宇
死去的古人
北方有青春野心
南方有關於這一切的回憶
北方有暴雨
南方有綿長的梅雨季節
細小的不舒服
均勻的不高興
蛀空你
你成了重新變空的容器
等待著再裝點什麼
還有些殘年和留白
可以小心地早起
兑換
交易

2009年10月寫於紹興

Looking out Towards Beijing

The North is hot, the South is cool
Up north people keep getting drunk; up north there are crises and politics
Down south I went to bed long ago
Up north they have all-night drinking parties
Down south, I fill a teapot with yellow wine
And wilt into my own darkest corners
The North has Beijing
The South has languid time
And moss-covered temples
Dead ancients
The North has the hunger of youth
The South has memories of all this
The North has rainstorms
The South has a season of fine Plum Rain
Delicate discomforts
Uniform frustrations
That hollow you out until
You become an empty vessel once more
Waiting to receive something else
Left with some last years and blank spaces
Which you may rise early
To exchange
Or trade on

October 2009, Shaoxing

民謠是什麼

民謠是你騎自行車遠行
後面帶著女友
路旁有大片的麥田
半路上，你的女友要「唱歌」，她躲進麥地噓噓地方便，你靠在單車上點了一支煙
她出來了，被蚊子咬了七八個包，你把風油精塗在她手上
晚上，你們在一家鄉村客棧過夜
就著一台黑白電視
你們想做，但沒有安全套
一直到天亮
你們又想做又恐懼懷孕
早上，你的女友啐了一口黑白電視
然後，繼續上路

民謠是你騎著自行車給人送信一家挨一家
你把單車支在電線桿旁敲門
按門鈴大喊大叫
有一些信你真想拆開看看那些散發著淡淡體香的精巧的信封，裡面的信紙疊成一朵花或者是隻燕子，啥時候決心不幹這行了，就拆它幾封，但怕的是那時候你已經老了

民謠是你騎自行車尋找你的兒子，他被人販子拐走了你辭了工作，身上帶著所有的銀行卡一個城市一個城市地找呀找，見了牆就貼尋人啟事吃飯的時候問飯店老闆，睡覺的時候問旅店服務生。你對兒童小孩幼兒牧童放牛娃童工等詞格外敏感，彷彿每個詞後面都隱藏著通往你兒子的道路，等你走到了陸地的盡頭前面是大海

你在海邊的小鎮上，貼了最後一張尋人啟事就坐在路旁喝啤酒
一瓶一瓶又一瓶，空啤酒瓶跟你走過的城市一樣的多，最後喝得大海都立起來了，這時有個小姐走過來問：先生需要嗎？你說：多少錢？她說：屋裡哇啦。好
這一夜你又成了一個男人，像你未婚的少年時代忘了尋找期盼未來，忘了自己一本正經當過父親

民謠是你騎自行車，不知道要去哪裡不知道這自行車是誰的，不知道自己多大了女朋友是誰還有沒有親人在人世上，春花秋月啥個時候完到底愛小紅還是小蘭。騎著騎著你睡著了連同自行車摔在路邊，這時一個趕路的賊經過他掏了你的錢包手機糧票鑰匙身份證，朝著你的屁股踢了一腳罵一聲這個傻逼，然後騎上你的自行車走了
民謠是你騎自行車，在夢裡你唱老百姓今兒真高興，蹬呀蹬左手扶著車把，右手拄了一根盲杖，實際上，你根本沒看過自行車，你走路還得人領著呢，你也沒坐過飛機
在夢裡，飛機上有個售票員在座位間走來走去，她讓大家買票你也沒親近過女人。在夢裡，她是早上剛出鍋的煮雞蛋你吹著氣，小心地一片一片剝開先是指甲蓋大的熾熱軟潤，然後逐漸擴大越來越燙手越來越不敢剝

2004年4月寫於北京

What Is a Folk Song?

A folk song is taking a long-distance bike ride
Your girlfriend behind you
Vast wheat fields by the road
On the way, your girlfriend wants to "sing a song." She sneaks into a wheat field to pee; you lean on the bike and light a cigarette
She comes out with mosquito bites; you rub oil on her hands
You spend the night at a village guest house
Next to a black-and-white TV
You want to do it, but didn't bring any condoms
All night long
You really want to do it, but fear getting pregnant
The next morning, your girlfriend spits on the TV
And you continue on your way

A folk song is you delivering mail house-to-house on your bike
You lean the bike on a telephone pole to knock on doors
Push doorbells, call out loudly
Some letters you really want to open, the sweet-smelling neatly-written ones with the page inside folded into a flower or a swallow, one day you'll quit, and you'll open a few, by then maybe you'll be too old

A folk song is you riding your bike looking for your son, who was kidnapped, so you quit your job and collected all your money and went city to city to find him, posting missing notices on every wall asking restaurant owners over every meal and bellhops at every hotel. Words like child kid toddler herd boy herding baby child labor sting your ear,

as if every one of them held a hidden path to your son, and when you
get to land's end the ocean's before you
You post your last missing sign in a coastal town and sit by the roadside
drinking beer
Bottle after bottle, as many empty bottles as cities you visited, you drink
until the sea stands up. A prostitute walks over, asks: Do you need
anything, sir? You ask: How much? She says: Walla walla walla. Okay
That night you become a man again. Like when you were young and
single, you forget your search and look forward to the future, you
forget you once were an honest-to-goodness father

A folk song is riding your bicycle, not knowing where you're going or whose
bike this is, not knowing how old you are who your girlfriend is or if you
even have family left on earth, when your days of fancy and romance
will ever be done or if you love Xiao Hong or Xiao Lan. You ride and ride
till you fall asleep and you and the bike fall off the road; a thief comes by
and takes your wallet phone meal tickets keys ID card, kicks your ass a
few times and calls you an idiot, then gets on your bike and takes off

A folk song is riding your bike, dreaming of yourself singing All the people
are so happy these days, as you pedal and pedal your left hand holds
the handlebar, your right hand grips a blind man's cane, and the fact is
that you've never seen a bicycle, you can't even walk without someone
leading you, you've never ridden on a plane
In your dream, a ticket agent on the plane paces between the seats,
making people buy tickets you've never actually been with a girl
before. In your dream, she's a boiled egg fresh from the pot you
blow on it and carefully pick off pieces of shell at first the size of your
fingernail, smooth, soft, and hot, then gradually larger and hotter and
you're afraid to peel off any more

April 2004, Beijing